1/8

JUDGMENTAL
MAPS

JUDGMENTAL MAPS

TRENT GILLASPIE

FLATIRON
BOOKS
NEW YORK

JUDGMENTAL MAPS © 2016 by Trent Gillaspie.
All rights reserved. Printed in China.
For information, address Flatiron Books,
175 Fifth Avenue, New York, N.Y. 10010.

www.flatironbooks.com

The Library of Congress Cataloging-in-Publication Data is available upon request.

ISBN 978-1-250-06854-5 (hardcover)
ISBN 978-1-250-06855-2 (e-book)

Our books may be purchased in bulk for promotional, educational,
or business use. Please contact your local bookseller or the Macmillan
Corporate and Premium Sales Department at (800) 221-7945,
extension 5442, or by e-mail at MacmillanSpecialMarkets@macmillan.com.

First Edition: October 2016

10 9 8 7 6 5 4 3 2 1

Judgmental Maps is a registered trademark of Judgmental Maps LLC.

Dedicated to your mom.

*And to all the moms out there for raising the judgmental
assholes who contributed to this book.*

*To my mom, dad, brother, and my beautiful wife, Anne,
for encouraging my bad jokes. And to my daughter,
Emeryn, for laughing at them.*

*To my English teachers who said I would never write a book.
Even though it is mostly pictures.*

CONTENTS

JUDGMENTAL
MAPS

INTRODUCTION

The idea of a judgmental map is nothing new. Terms like "wrong side of the tracks," "backwoods," "boondocks," and myriad other judgmental geographic phrases are embedded in our everyday speech. To describe and name is, in a way, to judge, and it's what the "snarktographers"—the brave, sharp-tongued, and brilliant men and women who have contributed to these maps—relish and delight in.

One of the first great examples of a snarktographer in action is Saul Steinberg's now classic "View of the World from 9th Avenue," which served as the cover of the March 29, 1976, edition of *The New Yorker*. The map presents a perspective of the United States as seen by a New Yorker from 9th Avenue looking west, where Manhattan is the center of the world and the rest of the country is a barren rectangle with city and state names absentmindedly scrawled in, an afterthought to the Big Apple's all-consuming self-importance.

Just imagine how outraged Middle Americans were when they saw that map—everyone was throwing corn at each other; there were ride-by shootings on horseback and tornadoes running rampant across the prairie. I'm kidding. I know people in Wichita switched from throwing corn to throwing cow pies immediately following the Dust Bowl.

So, maybe there weren't riots in the streets, but the map tapped into a lot of stereotypes, attitudes, and identities we all have bouncing around in our minds. It captures the perspective of geography through the eyes of a specific person—the New Yorker—whose existence starts at the East River and stops at the Hudson, and isn't it charming that *The New Yorker* calls them out for thinking they're better than everyone? And to the rest of the country, it reinforces the shortsighted arrogance of a city they probably think is too dirty anyway. It's a smart, funny cartoon. Just a shame it had to run in *The New Yorker*.

The very concept of a map, one (well, I) could argue, is inherently judgmental. Google a world map right now. Do it. See, right there in the middle left is the good old US of A, looking big and powerful. There's Europe to its right also looking pretty strong, and then the southern hemisphere below: South America scrunched up to roughly the size of Canada, Africa about the size of Greenland. This is the Mercator projection (Google that, too—let's make this feel educational), and we've been staring at it every day since preschool. And it's wrong! It is a western European judgmental

reflection of what they deemed important—themselves and the trade routes they needed to use to take over the world.

Now, with the advent of the Internet and social media, maps like Steinberg's and Mercator's have found a digital home. These maps can be created by a single snarktographer or quickly and accurately crowd-sourced by a number of authors, and shared with hundreds of thousands of people through chain e-mails that your grandmother forwards to everyone she has never met. These maps become a sort of skewed reality of the cities we know and love—biased and shockingly incorrect, but in the same way that Steinberg showed the ego of Gotham, there is a truth in these perspectives that resonates deeply not only with a city or state's inhabitants, but also with those of us who live elsewhere.

Seeing a map of the world with labels on each country is fun, but people can look at the "Freedom and Jesus" label of the United States or Mexico's "Siestas and Donkey Shows" for only so long before getting bored. The devil is in the details (as are the laughs). Drilling down to cities and neighborhoods allows the true culture and flavor of the place to come alive. Boston's downtown area may offer a plethora of delectable restaurants scattered between Boston Harbor and Boston Common—the park that hosted British troops during the American Revolution—but to most locals of Beantown, the labels "Historic Shit" and "Wants to Be NYC" are pretty spot-on. To many, the contagious energy

of downtown San Francisco has created a technology hotbed, anxiously awaiting the discovery of the next life-changing app. Even so, the labels "Twitterland, Minefield of Human Feces" and "The Face of Addiction" are hard for even those in the "Late-Stage Start-up Wasteland" to argue with.

I will always consider Denver my hometown, and so the Judgmental Map of my Mile-High City was created as an amalgamation of bits I used in my comedy routine and the labels I would give to the neighborhoods surrounding Denver when I talked with people about where something was located. People would refer to Little Raven or Colfax Avenue, but how they really felt was "Douchey Rich" and "Drunk/Homeless/Weed/ Drunk/Homeless/Weed." Looking at boring, practical maps of Denver one day in January 2013 sparked the idea to smother it with

the labels our city had been using in daily conversations for years. The unexpected viral success of the map led to the creation of JudgmentalMaps.com—a Tumblr blog intended to serve as a place where people from other cities could share Judgmental Maps of their hometowns, while maintaining their anonymity, just in case they did not want to get fired from their day job. To start getting these maps created for additional cities, I reached out to the network I knew best—other comedians. After receiving a few submissions from friends for cities like Manhattan, Albuquerque, and Chicago, I suddenly started to see maps being submitted organically from people to whom I had absolutely no connection. That is when the community of snark-tographers really started to take shape. Maps started pouring in from all over the world. And the communities responded. Local real-estate agents began to feature the maps as a tool on their websites, and people started to share them with friends to help in their move to a new city. The maps, although blunt and crude, were hilarious. And apparently useful. They each reflect a certain love and affection for the city itself in all its flawed, weird glory.

The maps you will find in this book are a collection from people who live (or have lived) in the towns they judge. The accuracy and local flavor each map has to offer come from people who know the city best. This book **was** created not by one single person, but with the help of an entire community. Are these maps offensive? Yes. Are these maps meant to hurt anyone intentionally? No. Did we try to offend everyone equally? Yes. To whom should you complain if you are offended by the content of this book? Go fuck yourself. Life is too short. Relax, laugh a little, and just enjoy it. If you feel bad for laughing at these maps, please don't. I'm sure you were a bad person before you picked up this book. Think of it as your uncensored truth atlas of cities across the United States.

This book is divided into five regions of the United States, so you can explore your hometown, find your favorite cities, or try somewhere new in a part of the country you think you might love. Just don't be offended when you find your neighborhood labeled "Downtown for Basic Bitches Who Literally Can't Even" because, well, that would be a pretty basic bitch thing to do.

The northeastern United States is where the United States became the United States. Its history is as thick as the accents of the people who live there, and as whitewashed as Bruce Springsteen's jeans. The region is ethnically diverse, and is home to the richest, most highly educated people in our country—and they will make sure you know it. The primary forms of communication in the Northeast are middle fingers and car horns. People here are serious about their sports and are most competitive when it comes to drinking lager and being mean to outsiders. An easy way to tell if someone was not born in the Northeast is if you hear them say "thank you."

The crown jewel is, of course, New York City. (Unless you're reading this in Boston. Then please, those guys are wicked pissas. Mark Wahlberg is the real crown jewel.) The Big Apple! The Capital of the World! The City That Never Sleeps because it has a slight coke problem.

It forces you to walk 90 miles per hour, slaloming through millions of tourists, getting bagels schlepped at you on every corner, only to return home to your 25-square-foot apartment that you spent every last penny on and never sleep in because of that slight coke problem.

But there's so much more to love than the concrete jungle. Vermont attracts thousands each year for the best skiing east of the real mountains, and the Oompa Loompa tans on the Jersey Shore attract lucrative television deals. Philadelphia has the cracked Liberty Bell, and a fair amount of crack to spare. Pittsburgh's "Stench of Death" and the "Free Wi-Fi" part of the Bronx are only a few of the enticing characteristics you will find in the Northeast. And it is hard not to love the changing colors of the fall leaves in the Northeast, just before every living thing dies in the blistering cold winters.

BOSTON
MASSACHSETTS

Boston is considered by many as the birthplace of the American Revolution, and considered by all to be the capital of horrible accents. Most people in Boston are of Irish descent, whether they are illegitimate Kennedy offspring or not. And, they love booing the Yankees more than they enjoy cheering for a losing baseball team. What's more, any city that calls itself home to such famous American visionaries as Paul Revere, Ralph Waldo Emerson, and Marky Mark and the Funky Bunch is a city that has already made its "mark" on the map.

HISTORIC SHIT

"I wonder if all of the historic shit around Boston was a clusterfuck of tourists back in the 1700s when it wasn't all that historic. I'm sure Samuel Adams didn't put up with all these iPads and selfie sticks and shit."
HEATHER W.

WANTS TO BE NYC

"America runs on Dunkin'. Obviously, so does Boston. One time, I even saw a Dunkin' Donuts inside a Dunkin' Donuts. The problem is, Boston doesn't have any public restrooms. That's probably why this city smells so bad. Dunkin' runs through Boston."

EVAN T.

IMMIGRANTS

CENTRAL AMERICAN HIPSTERS

SANTAHPIO'S

OTHER BENCH SCENE FROM GOOD WILL HUNTING

NEW

SINGLE FINANCE JERKOFFS

DRUNK 20 SOMETHINGS

THE DUMBEST COLLEGE KIDS

IRISH TRASH

GAY YUPPIES NEXT TO OLD IRISH BIGOTS

NO MAN'S LAND

YOUNG, RICH DOUCHES AND SEAFOOD

TOWNIES

WHITE PEOPLE ON PERMANENT DISABILITY

SOMEHOW BOTH HISTORIC AND POOR

OUT OF PLACE NAVY YARD

YUPPIE FAMILIES

HISTORIC SHIT

HISTORIC SHIT

I-TALIANS & PARALEGALS

"IA'S"

HISTORIC SHIT

"ILLUMINATI"

WANTS TO BE NYC

PARKING LOT

GINGER HIPSTERS

STREET FIGHTING

COMMUTERS

RANDOM CHICKENS

HEROIN

MORE HOMELESS & A HOSPITAL

HOMELESS

"CRIME"

LAW SCHOOL FROM THE DEPAHTED

GOLD DOME BENCH SCENE FROM GOOD WILL HUNTING

COULDN'T AFFORD THE SOUTH END

YUPPIE COUPLES

OLD MONEY

GOOD RESTAURANTS

TOM BRADY IS KING

DOCTORS AND BOATS

HOSPITALS

SALT 'N' PEPPAH

OLDEST MONEY

TOM + GISELE

OLDER MONEY

S'TRIPPERS AND WANNABE HOLLYWOOD TOURISTS

EVERYWHERE

GCWOKS

RAINBOWS

LINE OF DEMARCATION

BORDERLINE

TECH MONEY

DIRTY WATER

WINDOW SHOPPING

GRIDLOCK

JOGGAHS AND GEESE

LATE 20'S SINGLES

ANONYMOUS GAY SEX

WHERE YOU DUMP BODIES

TOTALLY AVERAGE COLLEGE KIDS

NOPE!

NOT BOSTON

SCISSORING HIPSTERS

COVER BAND WANT AD CENTRAL

THE NEXT GATES OR ZUCK

SMART LEGACIES

TOO RICH TO BE HIPSTERS

INSUFFERABLE GRAD STUDENTS

BEARDED LIBERAL ARTS DROPOUTS

NON-TENURED PROFESSORS

SMART ASIANS/NON-LEGACIES AND 2-3 FEMALES

INTERNATIONAL STUDENTS WITH MASERATIS

DUMB COLLEGE KIDS

MORE HOSPITALS

MUSEUMS

DISGRUNTLED YOUTH

HIT OR MISS (BUT MOSTLY MISS)

SLUMAHVILLE

WHITE GANGSTERS

KITSCHY SHOPS

FREE MARKET REPUBLICANS

A COUPLE OF GENIUSES

ROWAHS

COLLEGE HIPSTAHS

LESS POOR STUDENTS

POOR-ISH HIPPIES

WHY DO THEY KEEP MAKING MOB MOVIES ABOUT THIS TOWN?

HORNY GIRLS

CROSSFITTAHS

JEW-ISH

STRUGGLING ARTISTS/HUNGRY KIDS

PUNK AND LESBIAN HIPSTERS

FREE BEER & DOYLE'S

HIPSTERS IN DENIAL

IVY LEAGUE REJECTS

TENURED PROFESSORS

FAMOUS & DEAD

BICYCLES

THE WORST

FREE BEER & DOYLE'S

9

NEW YORK

NEW YORK

New York City. The Big Asshole. The City that Never Sleeps With the Same Person Twice. The Ball-Dropping Capital of the World. Whatever you call it, there is no denying that New York City is one of the greatest cities in the world. From rich culture, fame and fortune, to a suffocating housing market, pizza rat, and the American Dream, New York City has it all.

GAYS

"It hasn't been gay here in over twenty years. This area should be relabeled 'Entitled White People That Inherited Their Dead Gay Uncle's Place.'"

GINO S.

CANADA

JAZZ

GREAT SOUTHERN FOOD

SMART KIDS

NEW KICKS

LOW RIDERS

LITTLE MEXICO

MARIACHI BANDS

STILL FAR-FROM-POOR PEOPLE

PREP SCHOOL KIDS

CASUALLY RICH PEOPLE

NANNIES

JOGGERS

INCREDIBLY RICH PEOPLE

VERY RICH PEOPLE

WASPS

OVERPRICED CLOSETS

SMALL REPUBLICAN HAMLET

MEGA-RICH PEOPLE

FILTHY RICH PEOPLE

CAVEMEN AND DINOSAURS

QUITE RICH PEOPLE

FRISBEE

CULTURED PEOPLE DUCKS

DEAD BODIES

IBIZA RAVERS/ LOST TOURISTS

GREATEST FRANCHISE EVER

MORE GUNS

PROBABLY WON'T GENTRIFY FOR A WHILE

BIRDS

PRISONERS

LIL WEEZY

MORE POOP

ELECTRICITY FOR IPADS

TUMBLEWEEDS

POOP

LOW FLYING PLANES

HOOKAH BARS

LITTLE EGYPT

YE OLDE DRINKING TAVERN

GREAT GREEK FOOD

BRUCE FANS

NEW YORK SPORTS TEAMS?!

CHEAP CIGARETTES

CHEAP THRILLS

CHEAP GAS

SOPRANOS

NYC'S TRASH

STRANGE SMELLS

BRIDGE-AND-TUNNEL CROWD

Credit: RBD Enterprises

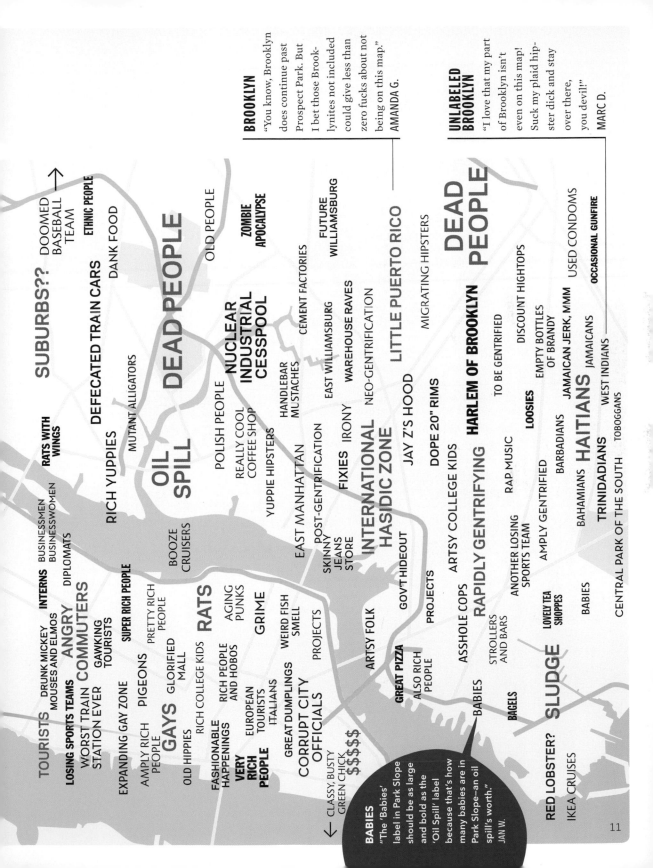

BROOKLYN
"You know, Brooklyn does continue past Prospect Park. But I bet those Brooklynites not included could give less than zero fucks about not being on this map." AMANDA G.

UNLABELED BROOKLYN
"I love that my part of Brooklyn isn't even on this map! Suck my plaid hipster dick and stay over there, you devil!" MARC D.

SUBURBS??

DOOMED BASEBALL TEAM

ETHNIC PEOPLE

DEFECATED TRAIN CARS

DANK FOOD

RATS WITH WINGS

RICH YUPPIES

MUTANT ALLIGATORS

DEAD PEOPLE

OLD PEOPLE

OIL SPILL

POLISH PEOPLE

REALLY COOL COFFEE SHOP

ZOMBIE APOCALYPSE

NUCLEAR INDUSTRIAL CESSPOOL

HANDLEBAR MUSTACHES

CEMENT FACTORIES

YUPPIE HIPSTERS

EAST WILLIAMSBURG

FUTURE WILLIAMSBURG

EAST MANHATTAN

POST-GENTRIFICATION

FIXIES   IRONY

WAREHOUSE RAVES

SKINNY JEANS STORE

NEO-GENTRIFICATION

LITTLE PUERTO RICO

INTERNATIONAL HASIDIC ZONE

GOV'T HIDEOUT

JAY Z'S HOOD

MIGRATING HIPSTERS

DOPE 20" RIMS

PROJECTS

ARTSY COLLEGE KIDS

RAPIDLY GENTRIFYING

HARLEM OF BROOKLYN

TO BE GENTRIFIED

DEAD PEOPLE

DISCOUNT HIGHTOPS

RAP MUSIC

ANOTHER LOSING SPORTS TEAM

LOOSIES

EMPTY BOTTLES OF BRANDY

AMPLY GENTRIFIED

BARBADIANS

JAMAICAN JERK, MMM   JAMAICANS

USED CONDOMS

BAHAMIANS   **HAITIANS**

TRINIDADIANS

WEST INDIANS

OCCASIONAL GUNFIRE

BABIES

CENTRAL PARK OF THE SOUTH   TOBOGGANS

TOURISTS

DRUNK MICKEY MOUSES AND ELMOS

INTERNS   BUSINESSMEN
BUSINESSWOMEN

LOSING SPORTS TEAMS   **ANGRY**

WORST TRAIN COMMUTERS

STATION EVER

DIPLOMATS

GAWKING TOURISTS

EXPANDING GAY ZONE

SUPER RICH PEOPLE

AMPLY RICH PEOPLE

PIGEONS

PRETTY RICH PEOPLE

GAYS   GLORIFIED MALL

OLD HIPPIES

RICH COLLEGE KIDS

RATS

FASHIONABLE HAPPENINGS

RICH PEOPLE AND HOBOS

AGING PUNKS

EUROPEAN TOURISTS

GRIME

VERY RICH PEOPLE

ITALIANS

WEIRD FISH SMELL

GREAT DUMPLINGS

CORRUPT CITY OFFICIALS

PROJECTS

$$$$$

ARTSY FOLK

BOOZE CRUISERS

GREAT PIZZA

ALSO RICH PEOPLE

ASSHOLE COPS

STROLLERS AND BARS

BABIES

BAGELS

AMPLY GENTRIFIED

LOVELY TEA SHOPPES

SLUDGE

BABIES

RED LOBSTER?

IKEA CRUISES

↓ CLASSY, BUSTY GREEN CHICK

BABIES
"The 'Babies' label in Park Slope should be as large and bold as the 'Oil Spill' label because that's how many babies are in Park Slope—an oil spill's worth." JAN W.

11

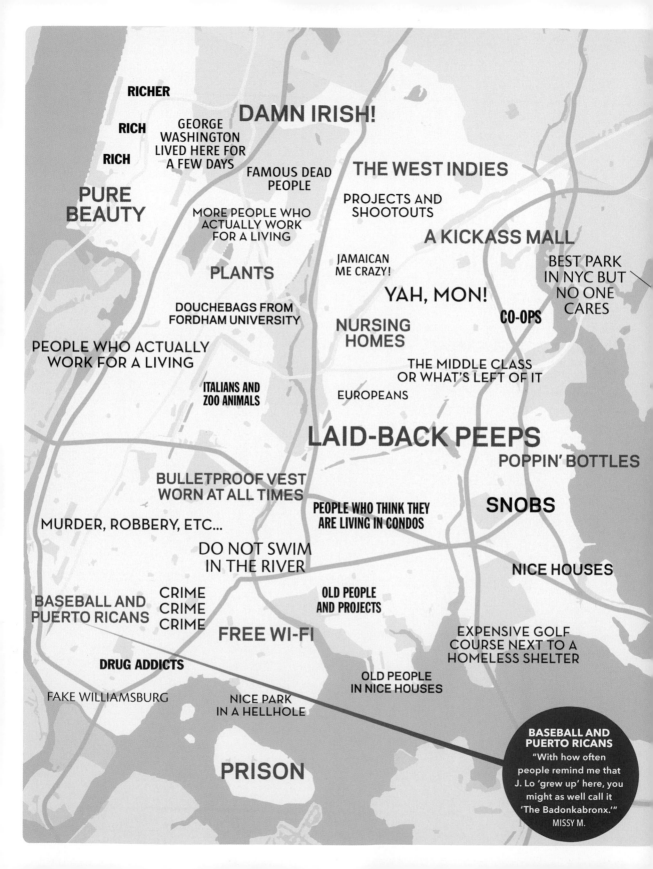

BRONX
NEW YORK

The Bronx is the official origin of hip-hop music and culture, giving birth to such rappers and DJs as Afrika Bambaataa, Kurtis Blow, Grandmaster Flash, and Edgar Allan Poe. But, there is more to the burning borough than "heys" and "hos." It is also home to the Bronx Zoo, streets covered in graffiti, and the most hated team in all of baseball.

WASTELAND, I MEAN ORCHARD BEACH

J. CREW POPPED COLLARS WITH BOATS

A COLLEGE FOR BOATS?

EUROPEANS

"The Bronx, named after farmer Jonas Bronck, is actually the only NYC borough named after a commoner instead of royalty. The fact that the eighteenth-century Bronck's River's name was misspelled 'Bronx,' and that was the name that eventually stuck, is a good representation of our education system hard at work."

TY L.

WILLIAMSBURG
NEW YORK

Beards and flannel! Warby Parker glasses and used bookstores! Pretentious liberal arts majors quickly pricing out a rich and colorful culture. Williamsburg is the birthplace of east-coast hipsters. This Brooklyn 'hood features four-hour waits for restaurants that charge for a glass of tap water, higher rents than Manhattan, and record stores booming with business. Don't let the 2025 price of goods fool you though—this neighborhood is happily stuck in the 1960s.

YOU CAN'T AFFORD THIS
"You might be intrigued, but you actually can't afford this."
WILL M.

STUPID HAIRCUTS
"Most of Brooklyn has stupid haircuts. I guess somewhere around here must be where they get them?"
DIANE J.

LI'L ISRAEL
"The OGs of the neighborhood, these bearded men and long-dressed women, are fighting the good fight against gentrification and Hipsterdom. Also, fun fact, I don't think they pay taxes!"
GEORGE T.

ODD SMELL

"I live here. My god, I hope the odd smell is not coming from me."

GRAHAM A.

BROKE ASS BROS

COOL FAMILIES

POLISH HIPSTERS

PIEROGIES

DIE

LAME CONCERTS

BROS

BROS

BEER

LOOK AT ME! LOOK AT ME!

KICKBALL

WE TAKE A BUS

CHOLESTEROL

VICE

TATTOOED MOMS

POOP POOL

DON'T SWIM HERE EVER

ASSHOLES

BROS

FULLY GENTRIFIED

$$$$$$$$

ODD CONDOS

HIPSTER OR HOMELESS?

WALL STREET $$$$

$3500 STUDIOS

"ARTISTS"

PRETTY FUCKIN' NICE

DOMINO

TRUST FUND HIPSTERS

THE MOB

MOUSTACHES

YOU CAN'T AFFORD THIS

FIESTA DEL GIGLI

MORE ITALIANS

ODD SMELL

STUPID HAIRCUTS

ITALIANS

PIZZA

MUSIC

HIPSTER MARIO BROS.

WHITE CASTLE

FIXIE BIKES

HIPSTERS WITH REALLY RICH PARENTS

GAY BAR

EM CE UNSH

FRIENDS YOU DON'T TRUST

ADIOS AMIGOS

AVERAGE DINER

HIPSTERS

MOB BAKERY

DEAD BANDS

LATINOS MOVING OUT

DIRTY

WORKER BEES

HEROIN

BOURDAIN

TRAFFIC TRAFFIC TRAFFIC

TRYING SO HARD TO BE COOL

BETTER, FOR NOW

NO LADIES ON BIKES

LOWER CLASS HIPSTERS

SECOND WORST BODEGA

STEAK

HASIDIC JEWS

5 LATINOS

VORTEX

ALL LESBIANS

CRAIGSLIST BEDFORD APARTMENTS

CAR PARTS

SUNDOWN SIREN

NON L TRAIN HIPSTERS

POOR HIPSTERS

SHADY

ENDED UP AT A PARTY HERE ONCE

NOTHING OF INTEREST

WORST BODEGA

C'MON NOW...

LI'L ISRAEL

WILLIAMSBURG, ONLY BY ZIP CODE

"NO, NO, SERIOUSLY, I LIVE IN BILLYBURG."

BUS TAKERS

SCARY HOSPITAL

LONG ISLAND CITY
NEW YORK

Long Island City is considered by many to be the fastest growing (and gentrifying) neighborhood in New York City, and many believe it to be a rival to Williamsburg in Brooklyn. However, that rivalry is like pitting a hipster beard against a hipster man bun in a battle of which is more overrated. Do you enjoy urban blight and piss-filled streets masked by million-dollar condos? Does stepping in dog shit on the way to the newest over-priced restaurant in town appeal to you? Then don't miss out on Long Island City in Queens.

TOTAL FUCKING MYSTERY
"It's either used for top secret government testing, or where we used to dump our garbage before we started sending it to New Jersey."
JAMES M.

FAMOUS SODA AD
"Long Island City is the Pepsi to Manhattan's Coke. Great in small sips, but it will never be the same thing."
COLIN D.

BARS, BURGERS
"I burger and bar hop every Sunday. We got artisanal burgers, artisanal beers, vegan burgers, vegan juice bars. Basically a burger for every drink, as long as both are organic."
TIMOTHY W.

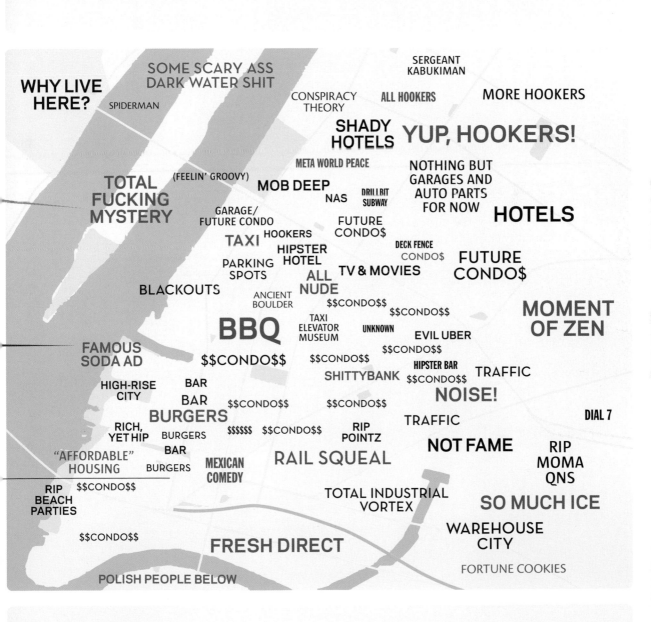

WHY LIVE HERE?

SPIDERMAN

SOME SCARY ASS DARK WATER SHIT

SERGEANT KABUKIMAN

CONSPIRACY THEORY

ALL HOOKERS

MORE HOOKERS

SHADY HOTELS

YUP, HOOKERS!

META WORLD PEACE

NOTHING BUT GARAGES AND AUTO PARTS FOR NOW

TOTAL FUCKING MYSTERY

(FEELIN' GROOVY)

MOB DEEP

NAS

DRILL BIT SUBWAY

HOTELS

GARAGE/ FUTURE CONDO

FUTURE CONDO$

TAXI

HOOKERS

HIPSTER HOTEL

DECK FENCE CONDO$

FUTURE CONDO$

PARKING SPOTS

ALL NUDE

TV & MOVIES

BLACKOUTS

ANCIENT BOULDER

$$CONDO$$

$$CONDO$$

MOMENT OF ZEN

BBQ

TAXI ELEVATOR MUSEUM

UNKNOWN

EVIL UBER

$$CONDO$$

FAMOUS SODA AD

$$CONDO$$

$$CONDO$$

HIPSTER BAR

TRAFFIC

SHITTYBANK

$$CONDO$$

HIGH-RISE CITY

BAR

NOISE!

BAR

$$CONDO$$

$$CONDO$$

TRAFFIC

DIAL 7

BURGERS

RICH, YET HIP

BURGERS

$$$$$$

$$CONDO$$

RIP POINTZ

NOT FAME

RIP MOMA QNS

BAR

BURGERS

MEXICAN COMEDY

RAIL SQUEAL

"AFFORDABLE" HOUSING

RIP BEACH PARTIES

$$CONDO$$

TOTAL INDUSTRIAL VORTEX

SO MUCH ICE

$$CONDO$$

WAREHOUSE CITY

FRESH DIRECT

FORTUNE COOKIES

POLISH PEOPLE BELOW

LONG ISLAND
NEW YORK

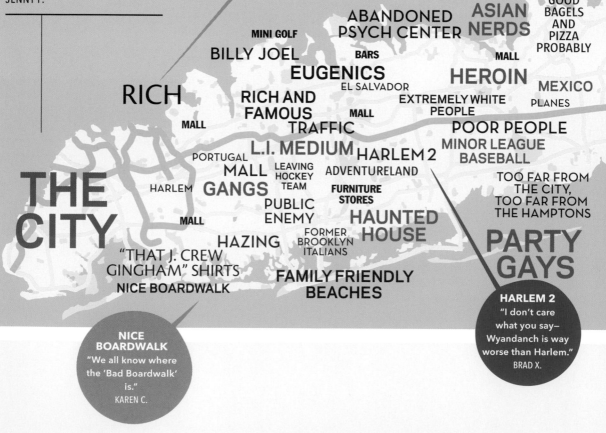

THE CITY

"Queens and Brooklyn actually are 'the city.' Only tourists think Manhattan is just NYC. Like, OMG, make sure you go to Serendipity to get their awesome frozen hot chocolate! Why don't you go tell Jay Z and the Ramones they aren't actually from NYC? Mmmkay?"

JENNY P.

RICH
"You could just label all of Long Island 'Rich' and this map may even be more accurate. Well, I guess you'd still have to account for all the heroin."
NATE S.

MINI GOLF

ABANDONED PSYCH CENTER

ASIAN NERDS

REALLY GOOD BAGELS AND PIZZA PROBABLY

BILLY JOEL

BARS

MALL

EUGENICS

HEROIN

EL SALVADOR

MEXICO

RICH

RICH AND FAMOUS

EXTREMELY WHITE PEOPLE

PLANES

MALL

MALL

TRAFFIC

POOR PEOPLE

L.I. MEDIUM

HARLEM 2

MINOR LEAGUE BASEBALL

PORTUGAL

MALL

LEAVING HOCKEY TEAM

ADVENTURELAND

TOO FAR FROM THE CITY, TOO FAR FROM THE HAMPTONS

HARLEM

GANGS

FURNITURE STORES

THE CITY

PUBLIC ENEMY

HAUNTED HOUSE

PARTY GAYS

MALL

HAZING

FORMER BROOKLYN ITALIANS

"THAT J. CREW GINGHAM" SHIRTS

FAMILY FRIENDLY BEACHES

NICE BOARDWALK

HARLEM 2
"I don't care what you say— Wyandanch is way worse than Harlem."
BRAD X.

NICE BOARDWALK
"We all know where the 'Bad Boardwalk' is."
KAREN C.

If you love rich people, then you will love Long Island. Just kidding—don't get your $250 diamond-bedazzled panties in a bunch. There are plenty of poor people in Long Island too. Long Islanders consider themselves New Yorkers because New York is a state, not just a city, you guys. But, much like the iced tea named after the region, the island is stronger than you think and can mess you up pretty badly if you wander into the wrong rich neighborhood.

LESS IMPRESSIVE LIGHTHOUSE

"I've never been less impressed by a lighthouse in all my life."
CANDACE O.

LESS IMPRESSIVE LIGHTHOUSE

CAROUSEL

PRIVATE PROPERTY

WINE   ALTERNATIVE HAMPTONS

LIGHTHOUSE

MORE BEACHES

RICH PEOPLE

SURFING

RICH BEACHES

SPLISH SPLASH MALL

BIG DUCK

COUNTRY FOLK

INDIAN RESERVATION

POOR PEOPLE NEAR HAMPTONS

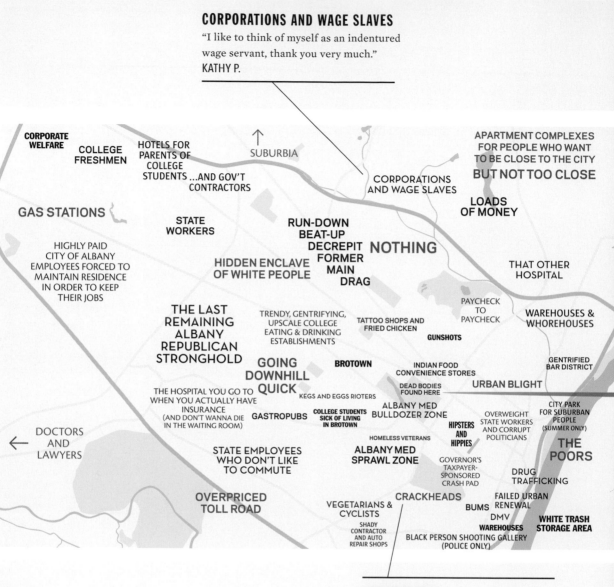

CORPORATIONS AND WAGE SLAVES

"I like to think of myself as an indentured wage servant, thank you very much."
KATHY P.

CORPORATE WELFARE

COLLEGE FRESHMEN

HOTELS FOR PARENTS OF COLLEGE STUDENTS ...AND GOV'T CONTRACTORS

↑ SUBURBIA

CORPORATIONS AND WAGE SLAVES

APARTMENT COMPLEXES FOR PEOPLE WHO WANT TO BE CLOSE TO THE CITY **BUT NOT TOO CLOSE**

GAS STATIONS

STATE WORKERS

RUN-DOWN BEAT-UP DECREPIT FORMER MAIN DRAG

NOTHING

LOADS OF MONEY

THAT OTHER HOSPITAL

HIGHLY PAID CITY OF ALBANY EMPLOYEES FORCED TO MAINTAIN RESIDENCE IN ORDER TO KEEP THEIR JOBS

HIDDEN ENCLAVE OF WHITE PEOPLE

THE LAST REMAINING ALBANY REPUBLICAN STRONGHOLD

TRENDY, GENTRIFYING, UPSCALE COLLEGE EATING & DRINKING ESTABLISHMENTS

TATTOO SHOPS AND FRIED CHICKEN

GUNSHOTS

PAYCHECK TO PAYCHECK

WAREHOUSES & WHOREHOUSES

GENTRIFIED BAR DISTRICT

GOING DOWNHILL QUICK

BROTOWN

INDIAN FOOD CONVENIENCE STORES

DEAD BODIES FOUND HERE

URBAN BLIGHT

THE HOSPITAL YOU GO TO WHEN YOU ACTUALLY HAVE INSURANCE (AND DON'T WANNA DIE IN THE WAITING ROOM)

GASTROPUBS

KEGS AND EGGS RIOTERS

COLLEGE STUDENTS SICK OF LIVING IN BROTOWN

ALBANY MED BULLDOZER ZONE

OVERWEIGHT STATE WORKERS AND CORRUPT POLITICIANS

CITY PARK FOR SUBURBAN PEOPLE (SUMMER ONLY)

← DOCTORS AND LAWYERS

STATE EMPLOYEES WHO DON'T LIKE TO COMMUTE

HOMELESS VETERANS

ALBANY MED SPRAWL ZONE

HIPSTERS AND HIPPIES

GOVERNOR'S TAXPAYER-SPONSORED CRASH PAD

THE POORS

DRUG TRAFFICKING

OVERPRICED TOLL ROAD

VEGETARIANS & CYCLISTS

CRACKHEADS

BUMS

FAILED URBAN RENEWAL

DMV

SHADY CONTRACTOR AND AUTO REPAIR SHOPS

BLACK PERSON SHOOTING GALLERY (POLICE ONLY)

WAREHOUSES

WHITE TRASH STORAGE AREA

CRACKHEADS

"There's a very good reason 'Crackheads' are across the park from the Governor's crash pad. A very good reason."
MATTHEW S.

ALBANY

NEW YORK

THAT OTHER CITY ACROSS THE RIVER

"I used to live in 'That Other City Across the River.' We don't even have a name."

JIM K.

↑
THAT OTHER CITY ACROSS THE RIVER

SMELLY RIVERSIDE BIKE TRAIL

SLIGHTLY LESS POORS

DEAD BODIES FOUND HERE

"The dead bodies in Washington Park are in the wrong spot. They actually should be throughout the entire city. When the zombie apocalypse comes, we're screwed."

CHER I.

REDNECKS
↓

While Albany is the capital of the Empire State, it is also a college town at heart. Its skyline plays host to the Empire State Plaza that destroyed over 300 businesses and evicted 9,000 people in the 1970s, with exterior walls that represent the Black Gate of Mordor. But, if you love vibrant fall colors, and don't mind freezing your balls off while you try to keep from drinking yourself to death when everything around you dies, then Albany might just be the city for you.

Credit: VGR & NDRU

STAMFORD
CONNECTICUT

Stamford has one of the largest concentrations of corporations in the United States—*The Office* could have taken place here. If you enjoy being surrounded by wealthy jerks and the soul-sucking banality of Corporate America, you've come to the right place. Fun fact, you could actually have your soul sucked out in Stamford. The city has a rich history rooted in witchcraft and the witch trials of 1692. Which probably IS why the city motto is: "If you live in Stamford, you'll probably die here." Sleep well tonight!

SUBURBAN WHITE MOMS
"Pinot in the fall, rosé in the summer and Xanax all year round."
SUSAN O.

SUBSTITUTE TEACHER JERKED OFF HERE
"The pay is low, but it comes with great benefits!"
JOSHUA P.

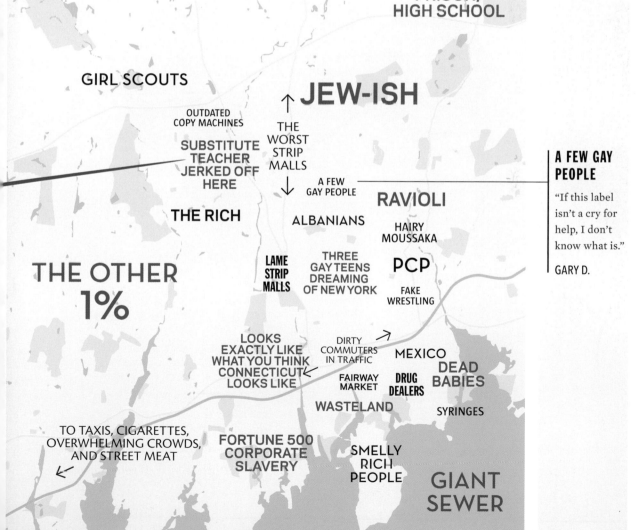

CELEBRITIES

OLD PEOPLE

THE 1%

SUMMER CAMPS

SUBURBAN WHITE MOMS

PRISON/ HIGH SCHOOL

GIRL SCOUTS

JEW-ISH

OUTDATED COPY MACHINES

THE WORST STRIP MALLS

SUBSTITUTE TEACHER JERKED OFF HERE

A FEW GAY PEOPLE

RAVIOLI

A FEW GAY PEOPLE

"If this label isn't a cry for help, I don't know what is."

GARY D.

THE RICH

ALBANIANS

HAIRY MOUSSAKA

LAME STRIP MALLS

THREE GAY TEENS DREAMING OF NEW YORK

PCP

THE OTHER 1%

FAKE WRESTLING

LOOKS EXACTLY LIKE WHAT YOU THINK CONNECTICUT LOOKS LIKE

DIRTY COMMUTERS IN TRAFFIC

MEXICO

DEAD BABIES

FAIRWAY MARKET

DRUG DEALERS

WASTELAND

SYRINGES

TO TAXIS, CIGARETTES, OVERWHELMING CROWDS, AND STREET MEAT

FORTUNE 500 CORPORATE SLAVERY

SMELLY RICH PEOPLE

GIANT SEWER

23

PITTSBURGH
PENNSYLVANIA

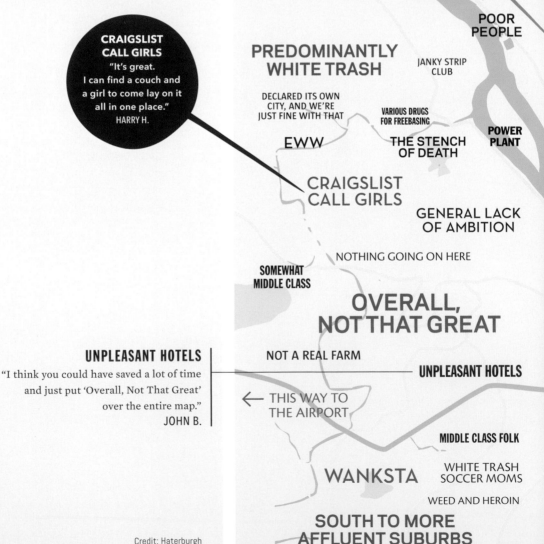

SNOBS, HIPSTERS, AND HEROIN
"Funny, this is also the title of the next Noah Baumbach film."
JERRY S.

POOR PEOPLE

CRAIGSLIST CALL GIRLS
"It's great. I can find a couch and a girl to come lay on it all in one place."
HARRY H.

PREDOMINANTLY WHITE TRASH

JANKY STRIP CLUB

DECLARED ITS OWN CITY, AND WE'RE JUST FINE WITH THAT

VARIOUS DRUGS FOR FREEBASING

POWER PLANT

EWW

THE STENCH OF DEATH

CRAIGSLIST CALL GIRLS

GENERAL LACK OF AMBITION

NOTHING GOING ON HERE

SOMEWHAT MIDDLE CLASS

OVERALL, NOT THAT GREAT

UNPLEASANT HOTELS
"I think you could have saved a lot of time and just put 'Overall, Not That Great' over the entire map."
JOHN B.

NOT A REAL FARM

UNPLEASANT HOTELS

← THIS WAY TO THE AIRPORT

MIDDLE CLASS FOLK

WANKSTA

WHITE TRASH SOCCER MOMS

WEED AND HEROIN

SOUTH TO MORE AFFLUENT SUBURBS

Credit: Haterburgh

It is easy to find someone from Pittsburgh wherever you go in the United States. That's because everyone leaves Pittsburgh. The city is best personified as an old fat guy who loves to drink PBR, watch football, and avoid sexual assault allegations. If you hate Cleveland, but still love ice-cold winters and laughable accents, Pittsburgh may just steel your heart.

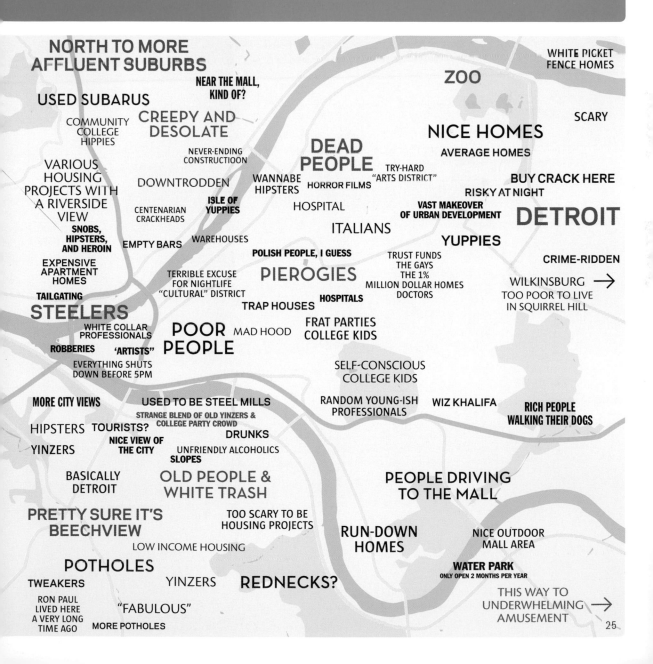

NORTH TO MORE AFFLUENT SUBURBS

WHITE PICKET FENCE HOMES

USED SUBARUS

NEAR THE MALL, KIND OF?

ZOO

COMMUNITY COLLEGE HIPPIES

CREEPY AND DESOLATE

NICE HOMES

SCARY

NEVER-ENDING CONSTRUCTIOON

DEAD PEOPLE

AVERAGE HOMES

VARIOUS HOUSING PROJECTS WITH A RIVERSIDE VIEW

DOWNTRODDEN

WANNABE HIPSTERS

HORROR FILMS

TRY-HARD "ARTS DISTRICT"

BUY CRACK HERE

RISKY AT NIGHT

CENTENARIAN CRACKHEADS

ISLE OF YUPPIES

HOSPITAL

VAST MAKEOVER OF URBAN DEVELOPMENT

DETROIT

ITALIANS

YUPPIES

SNOBS, HIPSTERS, AND HEROIN

EMPTY BARS

WAREHOUSES

POLISH PEOPLE, I GUESS

TRUST FUNDS THE GAYS THE 1% MILLION DOLLAR HOMES DOCTORS

CRIME-RIDDEN

EXPENSIVE APARTMENT HOMES

PIEROGIES

WILKINSBURG →

TOO POOR TO LIVE IN SQUIRREL HILL

TAILGATING

TERRIBLE EXCUSE FOR NIGHTLIFE "CULTURAL" DISTRICT

HOSPITALS

STEELERS

TRAP HOUSES

POOR PEOPLE

MAD HOOD

FRAT PARTIES COLLEGE KIDS

WHITE COLLAR PROFESSIONALS

ROBBERIES

'ARTISTS'

EVERYTHING SHUTS DOWN BEFORE 5PM

SELF-CONSCIOUS COLLEGE KIDS

MORE CITY VIEWS

USED TO BE STEEL MILLS

RANDOM YOUNG-ISH PROFESSIONALS

WIZ KHALIFA

RICH PEOPLE WALKING THEIR DOGS

STRANGE BLEND OF OLD YINZERS & COLLEGE PARTY CROWD

HIPSTERS

TOURISTS?

DRUNKS

YINZERS

NICE VIEW OF THE CITY

UNFRIENDLY ALCOHOLICS

SLOPES

BASICALLY DETROIT

OLD PEOPLE & WHITE TRASH

PEOPLE DRIVING TO THE MALL

PRETTY SURE IT'S BEECHVIEW

TOO SCARY TO BE HOUSING PROJECTS

RUN-DOWN HOMES

NICE OUTDOOR MALL AREA

LOW INCOME HOUSING

POTHOLES

YINZERS

REDNECKS?

WATER PARK ONLY OPEN 2 MONTHS PER YEAR

TWEAKERS

RON PAUL LIVED HERE A VERY LONG TIME AGO

"FABULOUS"

MORE POTHOLES

THIS WAY TO UNDERWHELMING AMUSEMENT →

PHILADELPHIA
PENNSYLVANIA

STRATEGICALLY PLACED SPORTS BARS OWNED BY RETIRED COPS

"Philly is known as the City of Brotherly Love. Why can't we all just get along better? Maybe if the Eagles were better."

JAN P.

BILL COSBY'S OLD HAUNTS
"People used to be so proud to say Bill Cosby grew up here. Don't hear that too much these days."
RAY N.

BROS IN BIRKENSTOCKS
"I moved here for college, and stayed here for the cheesesteaks and Tastykakes."
GEOFF L.

ARSON

KOREANS

FUCK NO

HISPANICS ON THE COME-UP

POST-SECONDARY PREP SCHOOLS

YUPPIES TRYING TO FISTICUFF AT FOUR IN THE MORNING

HELL NO

CRACK DENS

QUAKERS ROLLING IN THEIR GRAVES

BROS IN BIRKENSTOCKS

BASIC BITCHES
AUDREY HEPBURN WANNABES

CHICKEN SHOPS SELLING WEED

BELEAGUERED PUERTO RICAN HOUSEHOLDS

WHAT OPEN CONTAINER LAWS?

BEAN PIES AND FORTIES

MAIN LINE GERIATRICS

YUPPIE JESUIT UNIVERSITY

WARY ELDERLY

BILL COSBY'S OLD HAUNTS

STUDENTS DODGING BUCKSHOT

RACIAL TENSIONS AT A BOILING POINT

THE FRESH PRINCE

RELENTLESS GENTRIFICATION

TRYING TOO HARD

SUBURBAN DYSFUNCTION

UNFAZED ETHIOPIANS

BARISTAS AND HAUNTED PRISONS

CORPORATE CASINOS

ROCKY REENACTORS

TRIAD OWNED RESTAURANTS

HOME INVASIONS

CRUNCHY PARENTS AND CRACKHEADS

MISERABLE DOCTORATE STUDENTS

PEOPLE SHITTING IN PUBLIC

FIREBOMBED BY POLICE IN THE EIGHTIES

COMCAST EXECUTIVES

OLD DICKBAGS AND UKRAINIAN MAIL ORDER BRIDES

LOW END STATE UNIVERSITIES

QUASI-BOHEMIANS

OUTLOOK NOT SO GOOD

ANARCHISTS WITH DAY JOBS

EVERY DAY IS ST. PATRICK'S DAY

TRYHARDS

DYSFUNCTION

QUESTLOVE

WALT WHITMAN'S HOOD

FREQUENT SHOOTINGS

MEEK HILL

ENCROACHING LAMES

PEOPLE WHO STILL SAY "JAWN"

CHEESESTEAK TOURIST TRAPS

OPEN AIR DRUG MARKETS

ITALIANS TRYING TO RETIRE

TO HELLAWARE ↓

WHITE GIRLS GONE WILD

A PROUD LEGACY OF VOMITING ON CHILDREN AT BASEBALL GAMES

Philadelphia was the first capital of the United States. So, we can blame them for starting the mess that is the U.S. government. The city's famous brotherly love shines through the passionate sports fans commiserating with each other for having the worst teams in the U.S. However, sorrows are quickly drowned through Tastykakes and the city's infamous greasy cheesesteaks. And, any city that can drive Will Smith to move to Bel-Air is worth at least seven pounds of heroin, Philly's drug of choice.

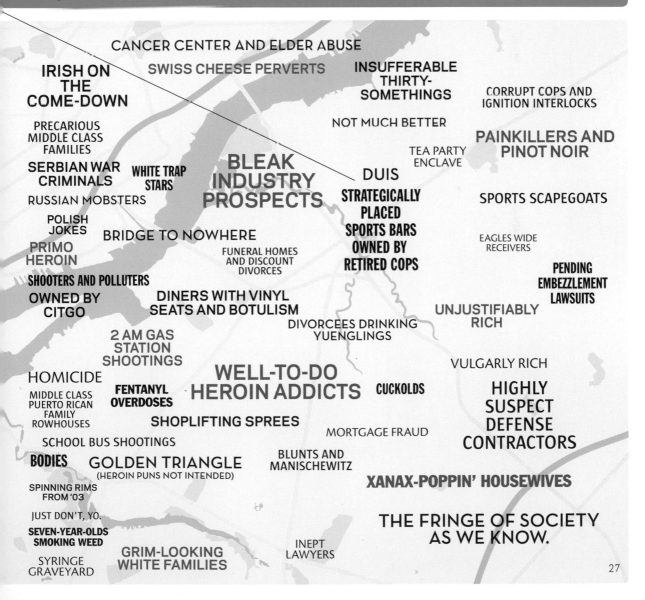

CANCER CENTER AND ELDER ABUSE

SWISS CHEESE PERVERTS

IRISH ON THE COME-DOWN

INSUFFERABLE THIRTY-SOMETHINGS

CORRUPT COPS AND IGNITION INTERLOCKS

NOT MUCH BETTER

PRECARIOUS MIDDLE CLASS FAMILIES

PAINKILLERS AND PINOT NOIR

TEA PARTY ENCLAVE

SERBIAN WAR CRIMINALS

WHITE TRAP STARS

BLEAK INDUSTRY PROSPECTS

DUIS

RUSSIAN MOBSTERS

STRATEGICALLY PLACED SPORTS BARS OWNED BY RETIRED COPS

SPORTS SCAPEGOATS

POLISH JOKES

BRIDGE TO NOWHERE

EAGLES WIDE RECEIVERS

PRIMO HEROIN

FUNERAL HOMES AND DISCOUNT DIVORCES

PENDING EMBEZZLEMENT LAWSUITS

SHOOTERS AND POLLUTERS

OWNED BY CITGO

DINERS WITH VINYL SEATS AND BOTULISM

UNJUSTIFIABLY RICH

DIVORCEES DRINKING YUENGLINGS

2 AM GAS STATION SHOOTINGS

VULGARLY RICH

HOMICIDE

WELL-TO-DO HEROIN ADDICTS

CUCKOLDS

HIGHLY SUSPECT DEFENSE CONTRACTORS

MIDDLE CLASS PUERTO RICAN FAMILY ROWHOUSES

FENTANYL OVERDOSES

SHOPLIFTING SPREES

SCHOOL BUS SHOOTINGS

MORTGAGE FRAUD

BODIES

GOLDEN TRIANGLE
(HEROIN PUNS NOT INTENDED)

BLUNTS AND MANISCHEWITZ

SPINNING RIMS FROM '03

XANAX-POPPIN' HOUSEWIVES

JUST DON'T, YO.

SEVEN-YEAR-OLDS SMOKING WEED

THE FRINGE OF SOCIETY AS WE KNOW.

SYRINGE GRAVEYARD

GRIM-LOOKING WHITE FAMILIES

INEPT LAWYERS

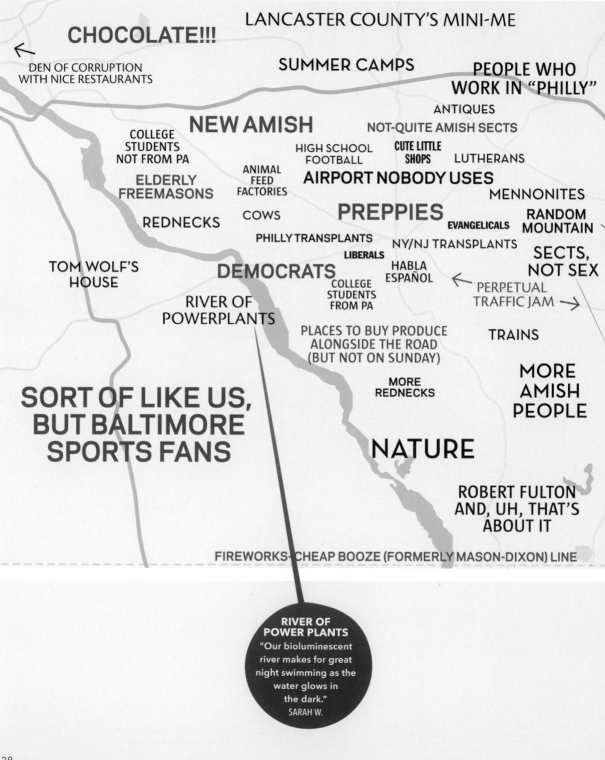

CHOCOLATE!!!

LANCASTER COUNTY'S MINI-ME

DEN OF CORRUPTION
WITH NICE RESTAURANTS

SUMMER CAMPS

PEOPLE WHO
WORK IN "PHILLY"

ANTIQUES

NOT-QUITE AMISH SECTS

NEW AMISH

COLLEGE
STUDENTS
NOT FROM PA

HIGH SCHOOL
FOOTBALL

CUTE LITTLE
SHOPS

LUTHERANS

ANIMAL
FEED
FACTORIES

AIRPORT NOBODY USES

ELDERLY
FREEMASONS

MENNONITES

REDNECKS

COWS

PREPPIES

RANDOM
MOUNTAIN

EVANGELICALS

PHILLY TRANSPLANTS

NY/NJ TRANSPLANTS

LIBERALS

SECTS,
NOT SEX

TOM WOLF'S
HOUSE

DEMOCRATS

HABLA
ESPAÑOL

PERPETUAL
TRAFFIC JAM

RIVER OF
POWERPLANTS

COLLEGE
STUDENTS
FROM PA

TRAINS

PLACES TO BUY PRODUCE
ALONGSIDE THE ROAD
(BUT NOT ON SUNDAY)

SORT OF LIKE US,
BUT BALTIMORE
SPORTS FANS

MORE
REDNECKS

MORE
AMISH
PEOPLE

NATURE

ROBERT FULTON
AND, UH, THAT'S
ABOUT IT

FIREWORKS-CHEAP BOOZE (FORMERLY MASON-DIXON) LINE

**RIVER OF
POWER PLANTS**
"Our bioluminescent
river makes for great
night swimming as the
water glows in
the dark."
SARAH W.

LANCASTER CO.
PENNSYLVANIA

September 27, 1777, marked a special day for Lancaster, PA. The city was the capital of the United States for one day, which was the peak of the city's relevance. While Lancaster County has the second-largest Amish population in the country, it is only a 90-hour buggy ride to the largest: Holmes County, OH. Ironically, while much of the region's population does not believe in using electricity, the city boasts more electronic public security cameras per capita than most cities in the United States. However, most of the activity worth filming can be found in the nearby town of Intercourse.

PENNSYLTUCKY/
PHILLY BUFFER
ZONE

RANDOM MOUNTAIN
"Luckily, there is some separation between the Amish and the Mennonites in our community. I can only imagine what would happen if they ended up in a turf war. Hay dealers communicating about deals and planning attacks through postal mail. Cart wheels sawed in half. Horses covered in graffiti. Ride-by shootings. It would be madness in the dirt roads."
JOHN U.

THE
SHORE
↘

JOE
PITTS

MUSHROOMS
(NO, NOT
THAT KIND)

**SECTS,
NOT SEX**
"Intercourse, PA,
is a great fucking
town."
TOM G.

Credit: Jeff D.

29

BURLINGTON
VERMONT

Burlington is a city filled with Chunky Monkey ice cream, exhausting drawn-out psychedelic jam sessions, coat factories, and the progressive belief that, if you own two cows, the government should take one and give it to your neighbor. And the government should probably take your other cow, just to be safe. The city's cost of living is high, but its inhabitants are really high. When Burlington isn't busy shoveling snow, its streets are filled with young hipster families purchasing forty-five-dollar pints of maple syrup at pretentious farmers' markets.

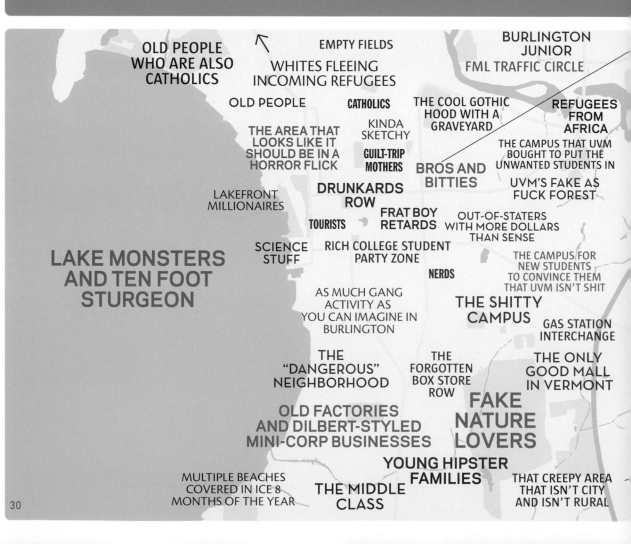

OLD PEOPLE WHO ARE ALSO CATHOLICS

EMPTY FIELDS

WHITES FLEEING INCOMING REFUGEES

BURLINGTON JUNIOR
FML TRAFFIC CIRCLE

OLD PEOPLE

CATHOLICS

THE COOL GOTHIC HOOD WITH A GRAVEYARD

REFUGEES FROM AFRICA

THE AREA THAT LOOKS LIKE IT SHOULD BE IN A HORROR FLICK

KINDA SKETCHY

GUILT-TRIP MOTHERS

BROS AND BITTIES

THE CAMPUS THAT UVM BOUGHT TO PUT THE UNWANTED STUDENTS IN

UVM'S FAKE AS FUCK FOREST

LAKEFRONT MILLIONAIRES

DRUNKARDS ROW

FRAT BOY RETARDS

OUT-OF-STATERS WITH MORE DOLLARS THAN SENSE

TOURISTS

LAKE MONSTERS AND TEN FOOT STURGEON

SCIENCE STUFF

RICH COLLEGE STUDENT PARTY ZONE

NERDS

THE CAMPUS FOR NEW STUDENTS TO CONVINCE THEM THAT UVM ISN'T SHIT

AS MUCH GANG ACTIVITY AS YOU CAN IMAGINE IN BURLINGTON

THE SHITTY CAMPUS

GAS STATION INTERCHANGE

THE "DANGEROUS" NEIGHBORHOOD

THE FORGOTTEN BOX STORE ROW

THE ONLY GOOD MALL IN VERMONT

OLD FACTORIES AND DILBERT-STYLED MINI-CORP BUSINESSES

FAKE NATURE LOVERS

YOUNG HIPSTER FAMILIES

MULTIPLE BEACHES COVERED IN ICE 8 MONTHS OF THE YEAR

THE MIDDLE CLASS

THAT CREEPY AREA THAT ISN'T CITY AND ISN'T RURAL

BROS AND BITTIES

"Everyone here is your friend. Come for the beer pong, but stay for the peer bong."
JOEY Z.

FAKE HICKS WITH QUARTER MILLION DOLLAR CABINS AND FAKE FARMS

"City slickers trying to be country folk. I usually knock out their teeth when I see them, just to accelerate the process."
WALLY R.

DUBIOUSLY LEGAL MASSAGE PARLORS

FAKE HICKS WITH QUARTER-MILLION DOLLAR CABINS AND FAKE FARMS

SWAMPY AREA

THE KIND-OF POOR

THE NOW UNBEARABLY LOUD AIRPORT

THE UPPER-LOWER MIDDLE CLASS

FLY-BY-NIGHT OFFICE ROWS AND TAX FILING BUSINESSES

THAT CREEPY AREA THAT ISN'T CITY AND ISN'T RURAL

"City or rural, I prefer to think of it as home. Does that make me creepy?"
WHITNEY F.

REAL HICKS

THE POOR

Credit: Styx

31

FREDERICK
MARYLAND

Although you haven't heard of Frederick, it is actually the second most populous city in Maryland after Baltimore. The city falls just south of the Mason-Dixon line, which helped lead it to become a country-western music and redneck destination for the northeast in the mid-twentieth century. But, even with the growth of Frederick due to the northwest expansion of Washington, DC, it's hard to take out all of the yokel. You can still find enough crack to help intensify your experience looking at the town's mural bridge—an average bridge painted to look like a better than average bridge.

NOBAMA

"NObama, no way! Except when I had to go to the ER last month when I mowed over my own toe. Then, he was okay."
CHESTER P.

A TERRIBLE UNIVERSITY NOBODY KNOWS OR CARES ABOUT

"I honestly have no idea what university this is referring to. Unless the arrow is pointing to distant University of Pittsburgh, of which the description is accurate."
DOUGLAS W.

FAST FOOD AND FAT PEOPLE

A TERRIBLE UNIVERSITY NOBODY KNOWS OR CARES ABOUT

NICE WHITE PEOPLE

OLD MONEY

LONELY FOLKS

NOBAMA

FARMS

REDNECKS

FARMS

TRAINS

TRAINS

FARMS

FARMS

FARMS

Credit: Anonymous

REDNECKS

"Redneck is a derogatory term for farmers and those who labor, dating back to 1893, where it was incorporated into political campaigns trying to appeal to rural farmers. We actually grow organic alfalfa and have contracts with farm to table restaurants in DC. So, go fuck yourself, Mr. Mapmaker."
STEPHEN M.

NOTHING

MOUNTAIN LIONS
FAKE REDNECKS
ROLLING COAL
LIBERTY-SOMETHING KKK
LOW INCOME
NOTHING FOX NEWS

CANCER
"OH, THERE'S A WEGMANS"
COWS
ROLLING COAL FAKE REDNECKS

ANTHRAX
WHITE AS SNOW

CARS EVERYWHERE
CRACK

PIÑATA PARTY
FOODIES $$$
SPEEDING TICKETS
WHITE CHRISTIANS

PARADISE
COSTCO
NICE WHITE PEOPLE
CHURCH CHURCH CHURCH
CHURCH CHURCH CHURCH

SPEEDING TICKETS
SOON TO BE URBAN SPRAWL
CHURCH

IS URBAN SPRAWL
THE DUMP
SNOBBY BITCHES

WHITE PEOPLE
BLINDLY IGNORANT &UNHAPPY MIDDLE CLASS
CHURCH

WHITE KIDS SELLING SHIT WEED
DUMB WHITES
CHURCH

SPEEDING TICKETS
$$$
SOON TO BE MORE DUMB WHITES
WHITE TRASH
CHURCH

FARMS
ENCROACHING MEXICANS
CHURCH

SOCCER MOMS
BASKETBALL ALL-STARS
CHURCH
MORE BLINDLY IGNORANT & UNHAPPY MIDDLE CLASS

FAKE REDNECKS, PROBABLY...
CHURCH

FARMS
THEY'RE HOLDIN' ON!
$$$
CHURCH
NO LIQUOR $$$

KEEP THIS A SECRET, PLS
KEEP THIS A SECRET, PLS
COPS
SPEEDING TICKETS

WINE
SPEEDING TICKETS

TRAINS
WEDDING RECEPTIONS
POORLY EXECUTED DEVELOPMENT
MEXICANS ↓

TRAINS
NOTHING
TAILGATERS

33

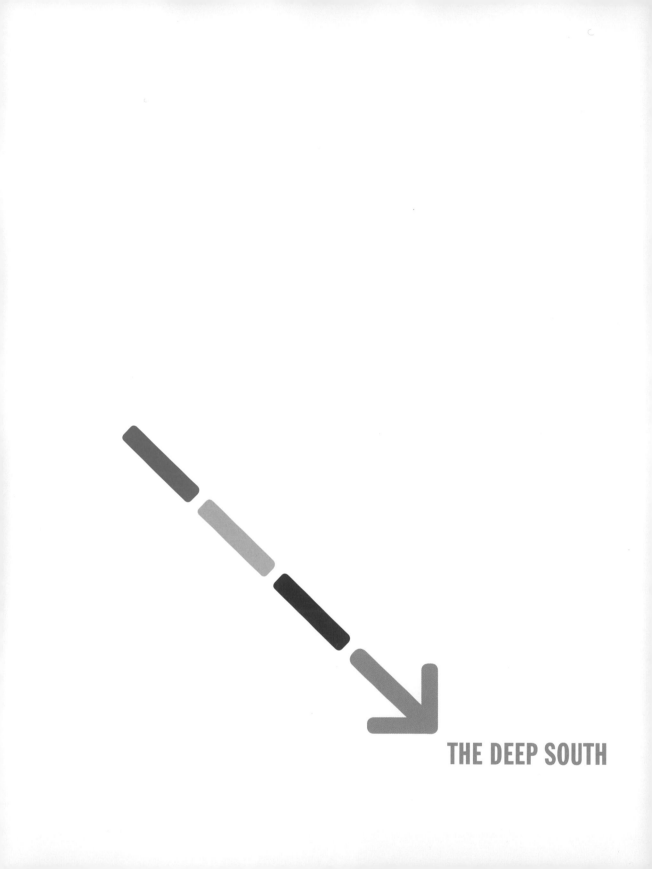

THE DEEP SOUTH

The southeastern United States is best described by its most well-known regionalism: "y'all." It perfectly captures the region's focus on family and community, the inclusive, friendly spirit of its people, and their dedication to laziness—saying one word instead of two. This warm, humidity-filled pocket of the country is known for remarkable hospitality, cute accents, and mistaking a pride in heritage with racism. When people in the Southeast treat you like family, that is because you probably are—the branches of the family tree here do not fork. And the outstanding southern home-style cooking will keep you close to your kinfolk (and immobile). Go ahead and put some south in your mouth—the barbecue in the region is as diverse as the names of the hurricanes that have made landfall there.

But the Deep South is so much more than backwoods towns and shacks. The region is home to some of America's most treasured cities. Atlanta is known as the birthplace of the civil rights movement and famous hip-hop stars such as Kanye West, Kanye West, and Kanye West.

Chapel Hill, North Carolina, is home to a basketball team that knows how to dress up for the court and for the courtroom. And then there's Florida—the state that proves birds are not the only things that move south due to the cold. As Americans get fatter and older, progressing toward their own eternal winter, they can be found playing bingo and sharing a surprising number of venereal diseases in the Sunshine State.

But even if you're not into sack tanning on a nude beach while gracefully aging into the grave, or a big fan of Kanye West (but who isn't? I know he is), you can still find plenty of reasons to visit. Don't let Chattanooga's "Gangs That Kill Cats" or Washington, DC's "Guns & AIDS" scare you, but if your name is Chad and you have dimples, Floridians (read: Cubans) may beat the shit out of you, then hide you in one of Miami's "Boats Carrying Anything Illegal."

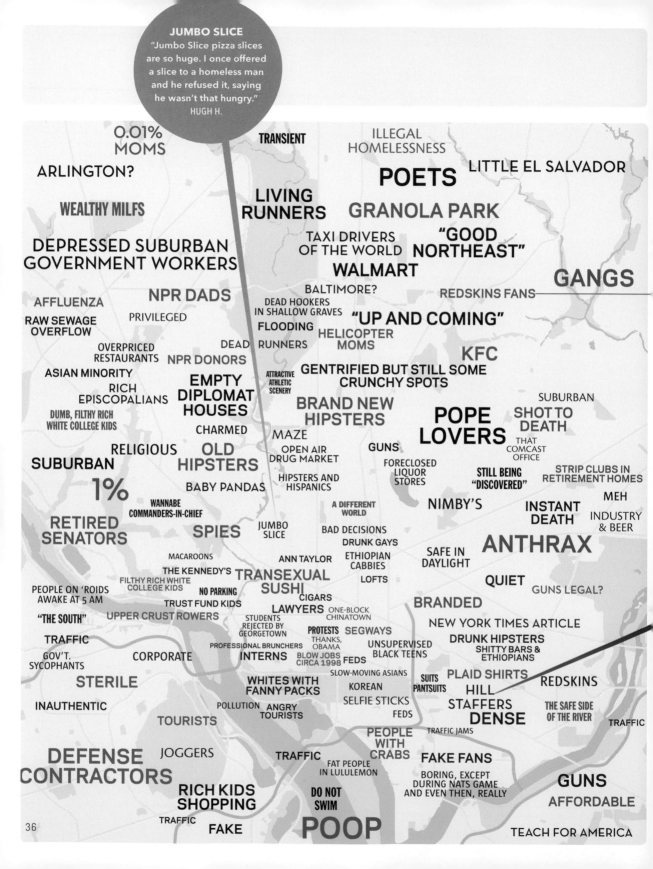

JUMBO SLICE
"Jumbo Slice pizza slices are so huge. I once offered a slice to a homeless man and he refused it, saying he wasn't that hungry."
HUGH H.

0.01% MOMS

TRANSIENT

ILLEGAL HOMELESSNESS

LITTLE EL SALVADOR

ARLINGTON?

POETS

WEALTHY MILFS

LIVING RUNNERS

GRANOLA PARK

TAXI DRIVERS OF THE WORLD

"GOOD NORTHEAST"

DEPRESSED SUBURBAN GOVERNMENT WORKERS

WALMART

GANGS

BALTIMORE?

REDSKINS FANS

NPR DADS

DEAD HOOKERS IN SHALLOW GRAVES

"UP AND COMING"

AFFLUENZA

PRIVILEGED

RAW SEWAGE OVERFLOW

FLOODING

HELICOPTER MOMS

OVERPRICED RESTAURANTS

DEAD RUNNERS

KFC

ASIAN MINORITY

NPR DONORS

GENTRIFIED BUT STILL SOME CRUNCHY SPOTS

RICH EPISCOPALIANS

EMPTY DIPLOMAT HOUSES

ATTRACTIVE ATHLETIC SCENERY

DUMB, FILTHY RICH WHITE COLLEGE KIDS

BRAND NEW HIPSTERS

POPE LOVERS

SUBURBAN SHOT TO DEATH

CHARMED

MAZE

THAT COMCAST OFFICE

RELIGIOUS

OLD HIPSTERS

OPEN AIR DRUG MARKET

GUNS

FORECLOSED LIQUOR STORES

STRIP CLUBS IN RETIREMENT HOMES

SUBURBAN

BABY PANDAS

HIPSTERS AND HISPANICS

STILL BEING "DISCOVERED"

1%

WANNABE COMMANDERS-IN-CHIEF

A DIFFERENT WORLD

NIMBY'S

INSTANT DEATH

MEH

RETIRED SENATORS

SPIES

JUMBO SLICE

BAD DECISIONS

INDUSTRY & BEER

MACAROONS

DRUNK GAYS

SAFE IN DAYLIGHT

ANTHRAX

THE KENNEDY'S

ANN TAYLOR

ETHIOPIAN CABBIES

PEOPLE ON 'ROIDS AWAKE AT 5 AM

FILTHY RICH WHITE COLLEGE KIDS

TRANSEXUAL SUSHI

LOFTS

QUIET

GUNS LEGAL?

NO PARKING

"THE SOUTH"

TRUST FUND KIDS

CIGARS

BRANDED

UPPER CRUST ROWERS

LAWYERS

ONE-BLOCK CHINATOWN

NEW YORK TIMES ARTICLE

TRAFFIC

STUDENTS REJECTED BY GEORGETOWN

PROTESTS

SEGWAYS

DRUNK HIPSTERS

GOV'T. SYCOPHANTS

CORPORATE

PROFESSIONAL BRUNCHERS

THANKS, OBAMA

INTERNS

BLOW JOBS CIRCA 1998

UNSUPERVISED BLACK TEENS

FEDS

SHITTY BARS & ETHIOPIANS

SLOW-MOVING ASIANS

PLAID SHIRTS

STERILE

WHITES WITH FANNY PACKS

KOREAN

SUITS PANTSUITS

HILL STAFFERS

REDSKINS

INAUTHENTIC

POLLUTION

ANGRY TOURISTS

SELFIE STICKS

FEDS

DENSE

THE SAFE SIDE OF THE RIVER

TRAFFIC

TOURISTS

TRAFFIC JAMS

DEFENSE CONTRACTORS

JOGGERS

TRAFFIC

PEOPLE WITH CRABS

FAKE FANS

FAT PEOPLE IN LULULEMON

BORING, EXCEPT DURING NATS GAME AND EVEN THEN, REALLY

GUNS

RICH KIDS SHOPPING

DO NOT SWIM

AFFORDABLE

TRAFFIC

FAKE

POOP

TEACH FOR AMERICA

WASHINGTON, DC

Washington, DC is filled with politicians, criminals, big pharma lobbyists, fat cats, and the finest schmoozers and boozers since the Roman Empire. Founded in 1791, Washington, DC is actually the ninth city to serve as our nation's capital (We're number nine! We're number nine!). Even though DC is the capital of the United States, it still has a lot of crime problems (just look at Frank Underwood). But, if you love the government (and who doesn't?), then DC is the place to be.

REDSKINS FANS

"There's nothing wrong with our team name or logo. Do you realize how much merchandise we already have made?"
JUSTIN R.

HILL STAFFERS

"One time, I overheard a hill staffer complaining about government-run health care. Umm. Don't they have government-run health care? Sounds like you might be able to solve your own problem."
MANNY T.

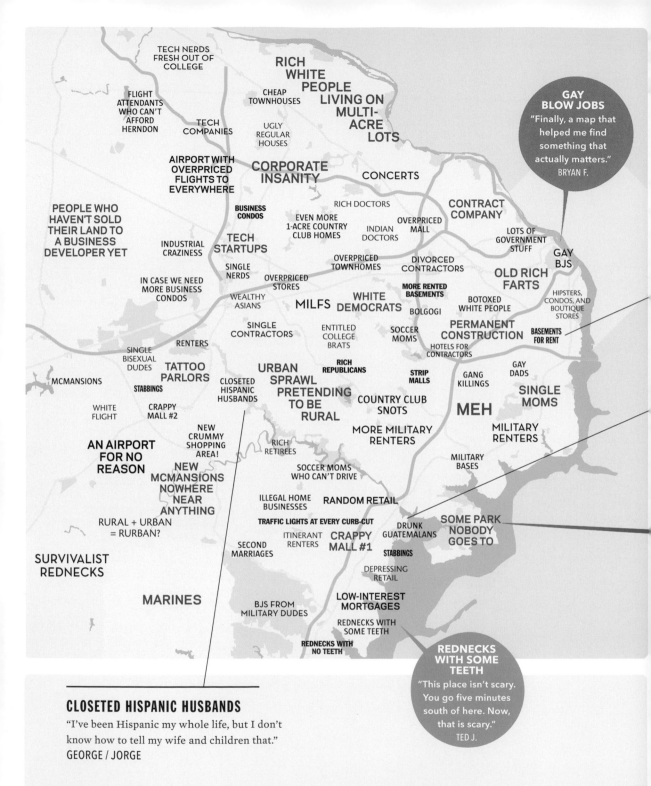

TECH NERDS
FRESH OUT OF
COLLEGE

RICH
WHITE
PEOPLE
LIVING ON
MULTI-
ACRE
LOTS

FLIGHT
ATTENDANTS
WHO CAN'T
AFFORD
HERNDON

TECH
COMPANIES

CHEAP
TOWNHOUSES

UGLY
REGULAR
HOUSES

AIRPORT WITH
OVERPRICED
FLIGHTS TO
EVERYWHERE

CORPORATE
INSANITY

CONCERTS

**GAY
BLOW JOBS**
"Finally, a map that
helped me find
something that
actually matters."
BRYAN F.

PEOPLE WHO
HAVEN'T SOLD
THEIR LAND TO
A BUSINESS
DEVELOPER YET

INDUSTRIAL
CRAZINESS

BUSINESS
CONDOS

RICH DOCTORS

EVEN MORE
1-ACRE COUNTRY
CLUB HOMES

INDIAN
DOCTORS

OVERPRICED
MALL

CONTRACT
COMPANY

LOTS OF
GOVERNMENT
STUFF

GAY
BJS

TECH
STARTUPS

OVERPRICED
TOWNHOMES

DIVORCED
CONTRACTORS

OLD RICH
FARTS

IN CASE WE NEED
MORE BUSINESS
CONDOS

SINGLE
NERDS

OVERPRICED
STORES

HIPSTERS,
CONDOS, AND
BOUTIQUE
STORES

WEALTHY
ASIANS

MILFS

WHITE
DEMOCRATS

MORE RENTED
BASEMENTS

BOLGOGI

BOTOXED
WHITE PEOPLE

BASEMENTS
FOR RENT

SINGLE
CONTRACTORS

ENTITLED
COLLEGE
BRATS

SOCCER
MOMS

PERMANENT
CONSTRUCTION

RENTERS

RICH
REPUBLICANS

HOTELS FOR
CONTRACTORS

GAY
DADS

SINGLE
BISEXUAL
DUDES

TATTOO
PARLORS

CLOSETED
HISPANIC
HUSBANDS

URBAN
SPRAWL
PRETENDING
TO BE
RURAL

STRIP
MALLS

GANG
KILLINGS

SINGLE
MOMS

MCMANSIONS

STABBINGS

COUNTRY CLUB
SNOTS

MEH

WHITE
FLIGHT

CRAPPY
MALL #2

MORE MILITARY
RENTERS

MILITARY
RENTERS

AN AIRPORT
FOR NO
REASON

NEW
CRUMMY
SHOPPING
AREA!

RICH
RETIREES

MILITARY
BASES

NEW
MCMANSIONS
NOWHERE
NEAR
ANYTHING

SOCCER MOMS
WHO CAN'T DRIVE

RURAL + URBAN
= RURBAN?

ILLEGAL HOME
BUSINESSES

RANDOM RETAIL

TRAFFIC LIGHTS AT EVERY CURB-CUT

DRUNK
GUATEMALANS

SOME PARK
NOBODY
GOES TO

SURVIVALIST
REDNECKS

SECOND
MARRIAGES

ITINERANT
RENTERS

CRAPPY
MALL #1

STABBINGS

MARINES

DEPRESSING
RETAIL

BJS FROM
MILITARY DUDES

LOW-INTEREST
MORTGAGES

REDNECKS WITH
SOME TEETH

**REDNECKS
WITH SOME
TEETH**
"This place isn't scary.
You go five minutes
south of here. Now,
that is scary."
TED J.

REDNECKS WITH
NO TEETH

CLOSETED HISPANIC HUSBANDS

"I've been Hispanic my whole life, but I don't
know how to tell my wife and children that."
GEORGE / JORGE

NORTHERN VIRGINIA
VIRGINIA

If you think Washington, DC is bland, just imagine what its suburbs are like. Northern Virginia's traffic is just as miserable as DC, but the area has all the upsides of suburbia: HOAs, soccer moms, botox, and drinking alone at home. The area is commonly referred to as NoVA, which is Spanish for "not going." Yet, some hispanic people end up here, settled in seven of the twenty counties with the highest income in the nation.

BASEMENTS FOR RENT
"I'm currently renting an over-priced basement, but my landlord/dad is a total jerk. 2 stars. Would not rent again."
JOSEPH M.

DRUNK GUATEMALANS
"This map is full of lies. I am Guatemalan, but I'm not drunk right now."
JOSÉ MIGUEL E.

SOME PARK NOBODY GOES TO
"I love this park! I go there all the time!"
NOBODY

RICHMOND
VIRGINIA

For some reason, people really like to judge Richmond. So much in fact that two maps are necessary. Well, as necessary as any of these maps are, which falls in the "not at all" to "slightly" range.

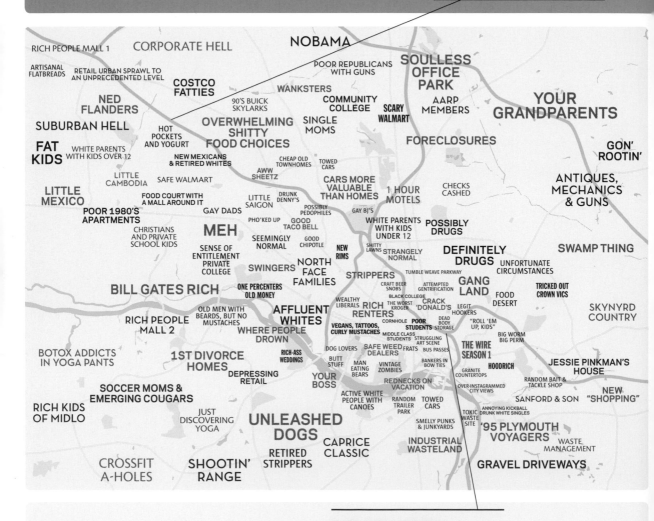

RICH PEOPLE MALL 1   CORPORATE HELL   NOBAMA

ARTISANAL FLATBREADS   RETAIL URBAN SPRAWL TO AN UNPRECEDENTED LEVEL   POOR REPUBLICANS WITH GUNS   SOULLESS OFFICE PARK

COSTCO FATTIES   WANKSTERS   AARP MEMBERS   YOUR GRANDPARENTS

NED FLANDERS   90'S BUICK SKYLARKS   COMMUNITY COLLEGE   SCARY WALMART

SUBURBAN HELL   HOT POCKETS AND YOGURT   OVERWHELMING SHITTY FOOD CHOICES   SINGLE MOMS   FORECLOSURES   GON' ROOTIN'

FAT KIDS   WHITE PARENTS WITH KIDS OVER 12   NEW MEXICANS & RETIRED WHITES   CHEAP OLD TOWNHOMES   TOWED CARS   ANTIQUES, MECHANICS & GUNS

LITTLE CAMBODIA   SAFE WALMART   AWW SHEETZ   CARS MORE VALUABLE THAN HOMES   1 HOUR MOTELS   CHECKS CASHED

LITTLE MEXICO   FOOD COURT WITH A MALL AROUND IT   LITTLE SAIGON   DRUNK DENNY'S   GAY BJ'S

POOR 1980'S APARTMENTS   GAY DADS   POSSIBLY PEDOPHILES   WHITE PARENTS WITH KIDS UNDER 12   POSSIBLY DRUGS   SWAMP THING

CHRISTIANS AND PRIVATE SCHOOL KIDS   PHO'KED UP   GOOD TACO BELL   MEH   SEEMINGLY NORMAL   GOOD CHIPOTLE   NEW RIMS   SHITTY LAWNS   STRANGELY NORMAL   DEFINITELY DRUGS   UNFORTUNATE CIRCUMSTANCES

SENSE OF ENTITLEMENT PRIVATE COLLEGE   SWINGERS   NORTH FACE FAMILIES   STRIPPERS   TUMBLE WEAVE PARKWAY   GANG LAND

BILL GATES RICH   ONE PERCENTERS OLD MONEY   CRAFT BEER SNOBS   ATTEMPTED GENTRIFICATION   FOOD DESERT   TRICKED OUT CROWN VICS

WEALTHY LIBERALS   RICH RENTERS   BLACK COLLEGE   THE WORST KROGER   CRACK 'DONALD'S   LEGIT HOOKERS   SKYNYRD COUNTRY

RICH PEOPLE MALL 2   OLD MEN WITH BEARDS, BUT NO MUSTACHES   AFFLUENT WHITES   WHERE PEOPLE DROWN   VEGANS, TATTOOS, CURLY MUSTACHES   CORNHOLE   POOR STUDENTS   DEAD BODY STORAGE   "ROLL 'EM UP, KIDS"   BIG WORM BIG PERM

MIDDLE CLASS STUDENTS   STRUGGLING ART SCENE   FRATS   BUS PASSES   THE WIRE SEASON 1

BOTOX ADDICTS IN YOGA PANTS   1ST DIVORCE HOMES   RICH-ASS WEDDINGS   DOG LOVERS   SAFE WEED DEALERS   BANKERS IN BOW TIES   GRANITE COUNTERTOPS   HOODRICH   JESSIE PINKMAN'S HOUSE

DEPRESSING RETAIL   BUTT STUFF   MAN EATING BEARS   VINTAGE ZOMBIES   OVER-INSTAGRAMMED CITY VIEWS   RANDOM BAIT & TACKLE SHOP

SOCCER MOMS & EMERGING COUGARS   YOUR BOSS   REDNECKS ON VACATION   SANFORD & SON   NEW "SHOPPING"

RICH KIDS OF MIDLO   JUST DISCOVERING YOGA   ACTIVE WHITE PEOPLE WITH CANOES   RANDOM TRAILER PARK   TOWED CARS   TOXIC WASTE SITE   ANNOYING KICKBALL DRUNK WHITE SINGLES

UNLEASHED DOGS   SMELLY PUNKS & JUNKYARDS   '95 PLYMOUTH VOYAGERS   WASTE MANAGEMENT

CROSSFIT A-HOLES   SHOOTIN' RANGE   RETIRED STRIPPERS   CAPRICE CLASSIC   INDUSTRIAL WASTELAND   GRAVEL DRIVEWAYS

Credit: Benhaus Design

RICHMOND
VIRGINIA

Richmond served as the capital of the Confederate States of America during the Civil War, but who even remembers what all the fuss was about? Today, Richmond has become increasingly diverse and, with the significant decline in crime rates over the last decade, it has become just as boring as most other cities in south.

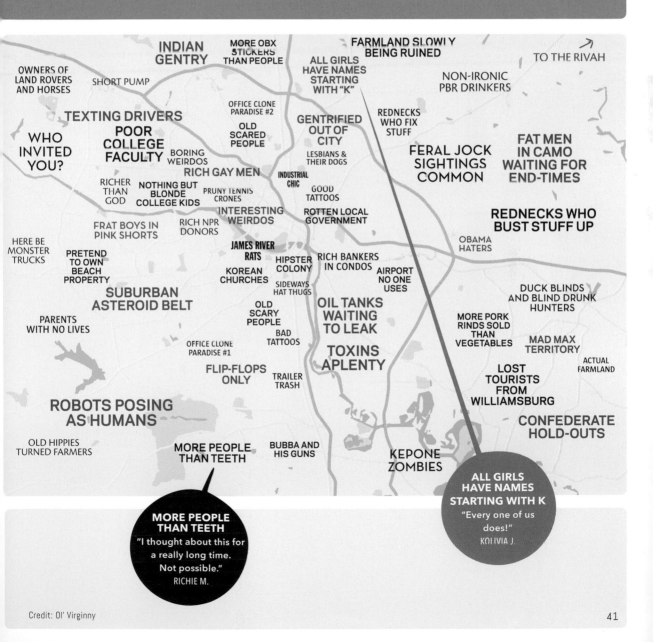

INDIAN GENTRY

MORE OBX STICKERS THAN PEOPLE

FARMLAND SLOWLY BEING RUINED

TO THE RIVAH

OWNERS OF LAND ROVERS AND HORSES

SHORT PUMP

ALL GIRLS HAVE NAMES STARTING WITH "K"

NON-IRONIC PBR DRINKERS

TEXTING DRIVERS

OFFICE CLONE PARADISE #2

OLD SCARED PEOPLE

GENTRIFIED OUT OF CITY

REDNECKS WHO FIX STUFF

FERAL JOCK SIGHTINGS COMMON

FAT MEN IN CAMO WAITING FOR END-TIMES

WHO INVITED YOU?

POOR COLLEGE FACULTY

BORING WEIRDOS

LESBIANS & THEIR DOGS

RICH GAY MEN

INDUSTRIAL CHIC

RICHER THAN GOD

NOTHING BUT BLONDE COLLEGE KIDS

PRUNY TENNIS CRONES

GOOD TATTOOS

REDNECKS WHO BUST STUFF UP

INTERESTING WEIRDOS

ROTTEN LOCAL GOVERNMENT

FRAT BOYS IN PINK SHORTS

RICH NPR DONORS

OBAMA HATERS

HERE BE MONSTER TRUCKS

PRETEND TO OWN BEACH PROPERTY

JAMES RIVER RATS

HIPSTER COLONY

RICH BANKERS IN CONDOS

AIRPORT NO ONE USES

KOREAN CHURCHES

SIDEWAYS HAT THUGS

DUCK BLINDS AND BLIND DRUNK HUNTERS

SUBURBAN ASTEROID BELT

OLD SCARY PEOPLE

OIL TANKS WAITING TO LEAK

MORE PORK RINDS SOLD THAN VEGETABLES

MAD MAX TERRITORY

PARENTS WITH NO LIVES

BAD TATTOOS

TOXINS APLENTY

ACTUAL FARMLAND

OFFICE CLONE PARADISE #1

FLIP-FLOPS ONLY

TRAILER TRASH

LOST TOURISTS FROM WILLIAMSBURG

ROBOTS POSING AS HUMANS

CONFEDERATE HOLD-OUTS

OLD HIPPIES TURNED FARMERS

MORE PEOPLE THAN TEETH

BUBBA AND HIS GUNS

KEPONE ZOMBIES

MORE PEOPLE THAN TEETH
"I thought about this for a really long time. Not possible."
RICHIE M.

ALL GIRLS HAVE NAMES STARTING WITH K
"Every one of us does!"
KOLIVIA J.

HAMPTON ROADS

VIRGINIA

Hampton Roads region consists of seven cities spread across two states. While the cities of Virginia Beach, Norfolk, Chesapeake, and Williamsburg may ring a bell for many, most Americans haven't heard of the area as a whole. This area of the United States is so thick in history, you could drown yourself in it. In fact, Hampton Roads is one of the world's largest natural harbors. So, there are plenty of ways to drown yourself. If you are into shitty drivers, 7-Elevens, and chain restaurants, you may love this region.

ASSHOLES WITH MONEY

"We live out along Broad Bay, and while it is nice, and far away from some of the unpleasantries of the bigger city, it is hardly far enough away to avoid running into some poor people from time to time."
ALAN V.

THE GOOD WAL-MART

"This is probably the best Wal-Mart in Hampton Roads, but that is like saying, 'that alley is the best one to get shot in.'"

PROSTITUTES

"People with money are right next door, and there is a sketchy beach just up the street. Maybe the solution to the problem is where you've already been looking."
ALLEN B.

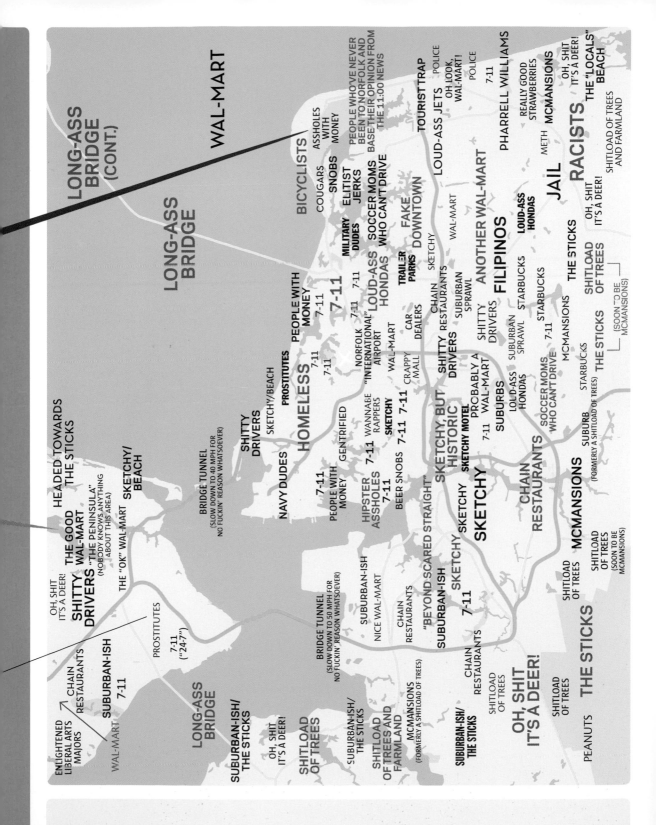

ATLANTA
GEORGIA

The Big Peach. Hotlanta. Black Mecca. The nicknames for Atlanta are as numerous as the overrated rappers that come out of the city. But, the people in A-Town are hot . . . and humid. What's not to love about 5.5 million sweaty people stuck in traffic all the time? And the city is home to the busiest airport in the world, because most Atlantans grew up elsewhere and have migrated to the New York of the south for the fried chicken and segregation.

RICH WHITE PEOPLE AND RICH BLACK PEOPLE LIVING TOGETHER IN RICH UNITY

"Kids who grow up here have absolutely no concept of reality. It's like they live in *The Truman Show* bubble, while the rest of us are out here hustling."
TERENCE P.

3-STAR HOTELS

"I usually only need two stars to have a nooner affair. What a luxury!"
KATHERINE R.

Credit: An Honest Atlantan

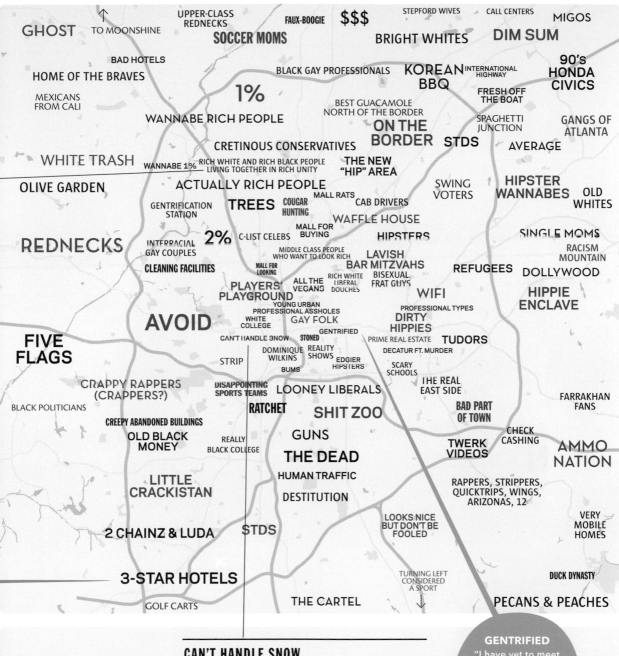

GHOST

↑ TO MOONSHINE

UPPER-CLASS REDNECKS

FAUX-BOOGIE

$$$

STEPFORD WIVES

CALL CENTERS

MIGOS

SOCCER MOMS

BRIGHT WHITES

DIM SUM

BAD HOTELS

BLACK GAY PROFESSIONALS

KOREAN BBQ

INTERNATIONAL HIGHWAY

90's HONDA CIVICS

HOME OF THE BRAVES

MEXICANS FROM CALI

1%

FRESH OFF THE BOAT

WANNABE RICH PEOPLE

BEST GUACAMOLE NORTH OF THE BORDER

ON THE BORDER

SPAGHETTI JUNCTION

GANGS OF ATLANTA

CRETINOUS CONSERVATIVES

STDS

AVERAGE

WHITE TRASH

WANNABE 1%

RICH WHITE AND RICH BLACK PEOPLE LIVING TOGETHER IN RICH UNITY

THE NEW "HIP" AREA

SWING VOTERS

HIPSTER WANNABES

OLD WHITES

OLIVE GARDEN

ACTUALLY RICH PEOPLE

MALL RATS

CAB DRIVERS

GENTRIFICATION STATION

TREES

COUGAR HUNTING

WAFFLE HOUSE

SINGLE MOMS

RACISM MOUNTAIN

REDNECKS

2%

C-LIST CELEBS

MALL FOR BUYING

HIPSTERS

INTERRACIAL GAY COUPLES

MIDDLE CLASS PEOPLE WHO WANT TO LOOK RICH

LAVISH BAR MITZVAHS

REFUGEES

DOLLYWOOD

CLEANING FACILITIES

MALL FOR LOOKING

RICH WHITE LIBERAL DOUCHES

BISEXUAL FRAT GUYS

PLAYERS' PLAYGROUND

ALL THE VEGANS

WIFI

HIPPIE ENCLAVE

AVOID

YOUNG URBAN PROFESSIONAL ASSHOLES

WHITE COLLEGE

GAY FOLK

PROFESSIONAL TYPES

DIRTY HIPPIES

CAN'T HANDLE SNOW

STONED

GENTRIFIED

PRIME REAL ESTATE

TUDORS

FIVE FLAGS

STRIP

DOMINIQUE WILKINS

REALITY SHOWS

EDGIER HIPSTERS

DECATUR FT. MURDER

BUMS

SCARY SCHOOLS

THE REAL EAST SIDE

CRAPPY RAPPERS (CRAPPERS?)

DISAPPOINTING SPORTS TEAMS

LOONEY LIBERALS

BAD PART OF TOWN

FARRAKHAN FANS

BLACK POLITICIANS

RATCHET

SHIT ZOO

CREEPY ABANDONED BUILDINGS

GUNS

CHECK CASHING

OLD BLACK MONEY

REALLY BLACK COLLEGE

THE DEAD

TWERK VIDEOS

AMMO NATION

LITTLE CRACKISTAN

HUMAN TRAFFIC

DESTITUTION

RAPPERS, STRIPPERS, QUICKTRIPS, WINGS, ARIZONAS, 12

VERY MOBILE HOMES

2 CHAINZ & LUDA

STDS

LOOKS NICE BUT DON'T BE FOOLED

3-STAR HOTELS

TURNING LEFT CONSIDERED A SPORT

↓

DUCK DYNASTY

GOLF CARTS

THE CARTEL

PECANS & PEACHES

CAN'T HANDLE SNOW

"We have arguably the world's busiest airport and are in the top five cities with the most Fortune 500 companies in America, but three inches of snow brought our entire city to a grinding halt and caused a state of emergency closing all of Georgia. We almost died."
ROD M.

GENTRIFIED
"I have yet to meet someone who was born in Atlanta and still lives here."
LIZ K.

TRUCKERS AND STRIPPERS

HIDDEN TENT CITY

TOURISTS

BIG-ASS BOATS

YANKEES ↑

SOOT AND CHEMICALS

PAULA DEEN CULT HEADQUARTERS

SALT & BUTTER

AUTOMOBILE MUSICAL CHAIRS

DRUNK CONVENTIONEERS

YOUNG ART STUDENTS

MOLD GROWTH FOSTERING CENTER

FAKE TROLLEYS

BUILDING CODE NAZIS

MARGINALIZED

WAFTING ROTTEN EGGS

HORSE URINE

DAMN YANKEES

NOXIOUS FUMES

TOURISM INDUSTRY WORKERS

PARKING SPOT FUNDRAISING

TALL TALE TOURS

IMAGINARY ECONOMIC DIVIDING LINE

ART STUDENTS BITCHING ABOUT CRIME

LUNCH LINE

AIMLESS PHOTOGRAPHERS

BADLANDS

BLUEBLOODS

← EXPLOSIVE INDUSTRIAL PLANTS

PANHANDLERS

BICYCLE HEIST PRACTICE AREA

POLICE SQUAD CAR RACES

MENTAL ASYLUM DISPLACEMENT EXPERIMENT

FUNERAL PARKING ONLY

JOGGERS

ROCK-THROWING YOUTH PROGRAM

ABOVE AVERAGE LOOKING DEAD PEOPLE

GANG MEMBER TRAINING GROUNDS

REGULAR LOOKING DEAD PEOPLE

STREET LITTER GALLERY

VEGANS

PRAYER THROUGH ROCK CONCERTS HALL

IMBECILE GRAFFITI

STREET FLOODING

OLDER ART STUDENTS

WRONG SIDE OF THE TRACKS

STREET CRIME GALLERY

CRAFTSMAN ARCHITECTURE DILAPIDATION PROJECT

ST. PATRICK'S DAY PARKING

STARVING ART STUDENTS

TERMITE COLONIES

OUTDOOR STREET CAMERA TV STUDIO

CREATIVE ZONING TRIALS

CRACK MANSIONS

STREET FLOODING

BROKE-ASS

ACADEMIC DEFICIENCY INITIATIVE

BUSINESS LICENSE-FREE ZONE

OBNOXIOUS TRAIN

HIPSTER WANNABES

LIFE-IN-YOUR-HANDS ALLEY

LONGEST-TO-BUILD-ROAD IN THE USA

ART SCHOOL OCCUPATION SECTOR

RICH-ASS

NON-HIPSTERS WITH MONEY

NEARLY BROKE-ASS

WHERE THE BODIES ARE HIDDEN

STORM WATER RUNOFF FISHING AREA

↑

OSTRACIZED FILM OFFICE

DODGY BASEBALL TEAM

SNOOTY SHOPPERS

RACIAL DIVIDING LINE

HIPSTERS WITH MONEY

WAFTING BAKED GOODS AND ROTTEN EGGS

HIPSTERS WITH SOME KIDS AND SOME MONEY

HIPSTERS WITH NO KIDS OR MONEY

TINY EQUESTRIAN PRACTICE YARDS

↓

MOSQUITO BREEDING GROUNDS

HIPSTERS WITH KIDS AND NO MONEY

NEW YEAR'S EVE FIREARM CELEBRATIONS

NORTH JACKSONVILLE ↓

SEEDY 1950'S PRESERVATION AND PROTECTION AREA

NEARLY BROKE-ASS

"I once saw some graffiti that read, 'No more false profits.' I can guarantee that the person who spray-painted that message is receiving no profits."
DELIZA D.

AQUIFER DRILLING
EXPERIMENTS

LNG BOMB
STORAGE
FACILITY

SAVANNAH
GEORGIA

TOXIC GASES

DOLLAR STORE
RIPOFF AREA

CEOS

SPERRYS AND
YACHTS

HUMAN TARGET
PRACTICE

HOMELESS
BEAUTIFICATION
CONSORTIUM

ROVING, BORED,
IMPOVERISHED YOUTH
CONGREGATION POINT

CRIMINAL
THOROUGHFARES

OUTDOOR
GUN RANGE

PROPERTY VALUE
REDUCTION REGION

NON-SNOOTY
SHOPPERS

CHOLESTEROL
ROW

GREAT LOOKING
DEAD PEOPLE

SHORT-SIGHTED
TRAFFIC
PATTERNS

REDNECK BEACH

SPEED TRAP

PAULA DEEN CULT HEADQUARTERS
"Love her or hate her, I only have Paula Deen's amazing recipes to thank for my diabetes."
RHETT H.

HOMELESS BEAUTIFICATION CONSORTIUM
"It's called beauty school, you asshole."
TANYA R.

TINY EQUESTRIAN PRACTICE YARDS
"Ooh, look! Miniature ponies!"
ETHEL S.

Savannah is the dirty little city of the south, where you can drink in the streets, then check out a ghost tour with people covered in sheets. Savannah's downtown Historic District is one of the largest National Historic Landmark Districts in the United States, and includes twenty-two parklike squares. Yet, somehow, parking is still a problem downtown, especially on the weekends. The city is also filled with live oak trees dripping with Spanish moss, much like the arteries of people in town, dripping with butter from Paula Deen's restaurant.

Credit: Eric D.

47

COLUMBUS
GEORGIA

Columbus is the home to Aflac Insurance. Along with being well-covered in case of flood, Columbus, GA is also recognized as the uglier stepsister to Columbus, OH. Although the city lies just across the Chattahoochee River from Phenix, AL (they couldn't afford to add an "o" to their name), don't let the city's proximity to Alabama scare you off. Let the fact that Columbus was one of the most important industrial centers of the Confederacy scare you off. But, don't let that stop you from at least visiting Columbus on your way from Atlanta to whatever the hell is south of Atlanta.

NEW MONEY
"Their money is new, but their fashion is old as hell."
ELIZABETH W.

SCARED
"Not because of the rough neighborhood. No, not that. I'm scared of the long-term consequences of my increasing carbon footprint."
ETHEL R.

RATCHET PIGGLY WIGGLY
"Ambience: 1, product: 11"
DIANE Q.

ALABAMA NOTHINGNESS
"A sad and racist wasteland, but at least it's not Mississippi."
AMY E.

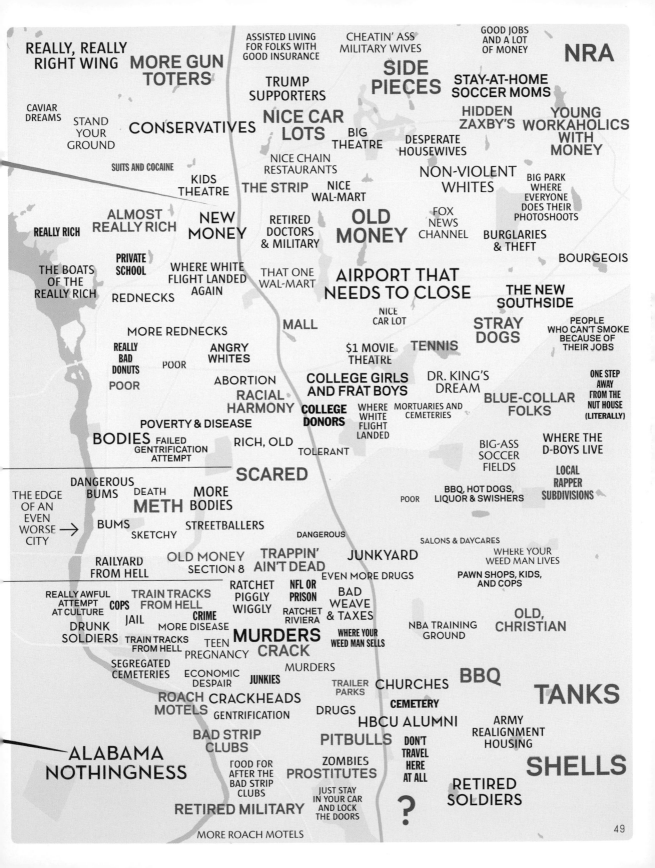

MACON

GEORGIA

Macon, located in the heart of Georgia, rhymes with "Bacon," which may actually explain the state's overwhelming obesity rate. Along with its fondness for a size XXL, 1 in 13 residents has a chance of being the victim of a property crime. Maybe that is what puts it on top of the "Worst Cities to Live in America" list. But in AMC's "The Walking Dead," Macon plays host to Terminus, a place where all who arrive survive. So, maybe there is hope for Macon after all. As long as Macon's historic structures hold up to zombie attacks.

THE MIDDLE CLASS

STRAIGHT FISHIN'

MERCER UNIVERSITY DRIVE:
DRIVE 0 TO 100 MPH,
REAL QUICK

DIRTY LAKE

REAL COUNTRY

THROW ROCKS AT FEDEX AND UPS TRUCKS

"Oh, man. I used to spend hours each day throwing rocks at the delivery trucks as a boy. Still do, just now I get paid to do it."
ELMER T.

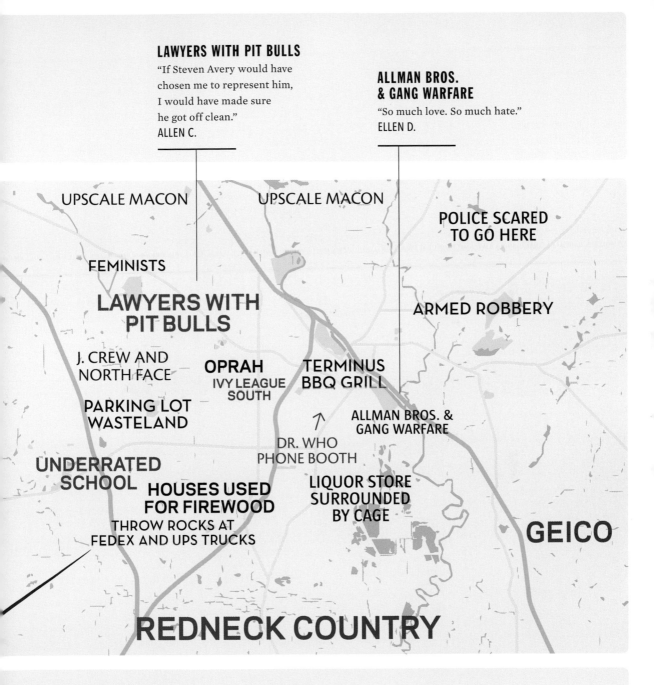

LAWYERS WITH PIT BULLS

"If Steven Avery would have chosen me to represent him, I would have made sure he got off clean."
ALLEN C.

ALLMAN BROS. & GANG WARFARE

"So much love. So much hate."
ELLEN D.

UPSCALE MACON

UPSCALE MACON

POLICE SCARED TO GO HERE

FEMINISTS

LAWYERS WITH PIT BULLS

ARMED ROBBERY

J. CREW AND NORTH FACE

OPRAH
IVY LEAGUE SOUTH

TERMINUS BBQ GRILL

PARKING LOT WASTELAND

ALLMAN BROS. & GANG WARFARE

DR. WHO PHONE BOOTH

UNDERRATED SCHOOL

HOUSES USED FOR FIREWOOD

LIQUOR STORE SURROUNDED BY CAGE

THROW ROCKS AT FEDEX AND UPS TRUCKS

GEICO

REDNECK COUNTRY

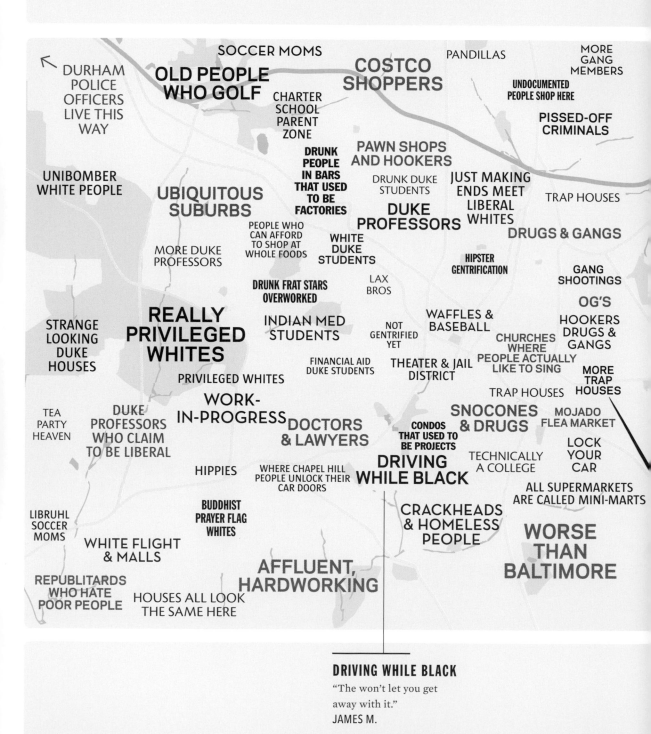

SOCCER MOMS

← DURHAM POLICE OFFICERS LIVE THIS WAY

OLD PEOPLE WHO GOLF

COSTCO SHOPPERS

PANDILLAS

MORE GANG MEMBERS

CHARTER SCHOOL PARENT ZONE

UNDOCUMENTED PEOPLE SHOP HERE

PISSED-OFF CRIMINALS

UNIBOMBER WHITE PEOPLE

UBIQUITOUS SUBURBS

DRUNK PEOPLE IN BARS THAT USED TO BE FACTORIES

PAWN SHOPS AND HOOKERS

DRUNK DUKE STUDENTS

JUST MAKING ENDS MEET LIBERAL WHITES

TRAP HOUSES

DUKE PROFESSORS

PEOPLE WHO CAN AFFORD TO SHOP AT WHOLE FOODS

WHITE DUKE STUDENTS

DRUGS & GANGS

MORE DUKE PROFESSORS

HIPSTER GENTRIFICATION

GANG SHOOTINGS

REALLY PRIVILEGED WHITES

DRUNK FRAT STARS OVERWORKED

INDIAN MED STUDENTS

LAX BROS

WAFFLES & BASEBALL

NOT GENTRIFIED YET

CHURCHES WHERE PEOPLE ACTUALLY LIKE TO SING

OG'S HOOKERS DRUGS & GANGS

STRANGE LOOKING DUKE HOUSES

FINANCIAL AID DUKE STUDENTS

THEATER & JAIL DISTRICT

MORE TRAP HOUSES

PRIVILEGED WHITES

WORK-IN-PROGRESS

TRAP HOUSES

TEA PARTY HEAVEN

DUKE PROFESSORS WHO CLAIM TO BE LIBERAL

DOCTORS & LAWYERS

SNOCONES & DRUGS

MOJADO FLEA MARKET

CONDOS THAT USED TO BE PROJECTS

TECHNICALLY A COLLEGE

LOCK YOUR CAR

HIPPIES

WHERE CHAPEL HILL PEOPLE UNLOCK THEIR CAR DOORS

DRIVING WHILE BLACK

ALL SUPERMARKETS ARE CALLED MINI-MARTS

LIBRUHL SOCCER MOMS

BUDDHIST PRAYER FLAG WHITES

CRACKHEADS & HOMELESS PEOPLE

WORSE THAN BALTIMORE

WHITE FLIGHT & MALLS

AFFLUENT, HARDWORKING

REPUBLITARDS WHO HATE POOR PEOPLE

HOUSES ALL LOOK THE SAME HERE

DRIVING WHILE BLACK

"The won't let you get away with it."
JAMES M.

DURHAM
NORTH CAROLINA

Of the three cities in the Research Triangle, the Dirty D is definitely the worst. Sure, it has an unbeatable basketball team and a very beatable football team, but there are also rampant crime rates, way too many Denny's for any one town, and over-privileged students who think they'll change the world. The worst. At least there is great barbecue?

TRAILERS & METH

TRAILERS & METH

STORAGE UNITS & OLD PEOPLE

WHITE FLIGHT & HICKS

MOVIN' ON UP

WHITE PEOPLE WHOSE RELATIVES WERE IN THE KLAN

SINGLE MOMS

RECESSION STILL NOT OVER HERE

FLEABAG MOTEL & CRACKHEAD ZONE

JUST GETTING BY

TORE UP COMMERCIAL PROPERTY

IDENTICAL SUBDIVISIONS

LITTLE MUMBAI →

HACKERS & NERDS

BIOMEDICAL APARTMENT DWELLERS

WHITE PEOPLE WHOSE RELATIVES WERE IN THE KLAN
"Better than black people whose relatives were in the Klan."
DANNY B.

RECESSION STILL NOT OVER HERE
"Hey! Hey there! Remember us? No one else does! It's still happening!"
CALVIN D.

MORE TRAP HOUSES
"Can't we all just stop using the word 'trap' to describe a house? Trap and house are two very different genres of music."
SHEILA S.

53

CHARLOTTE
NORTH CAROLINA

Charlotte is one of the fastest-growing cities in the country. Which is surprising because Charlotte is home to NASCAR—a sport that consists of rednecks driving in circles for hours. However, it is the number one spectator sport in the world. Charlotte plays a role in the banking and airline industries, both of which are beloved by everyone across America.

CLOSED 90s BUSINESSES
"It's like Circuit City and Kids 'R' Us were murdered, and bled out Capri Sun all over the streets."
MANDY K.

REDNECKS & JESUS
"Jesus was a redneck. And his name was Dale Earnhardt Jr."
DAWSON R.

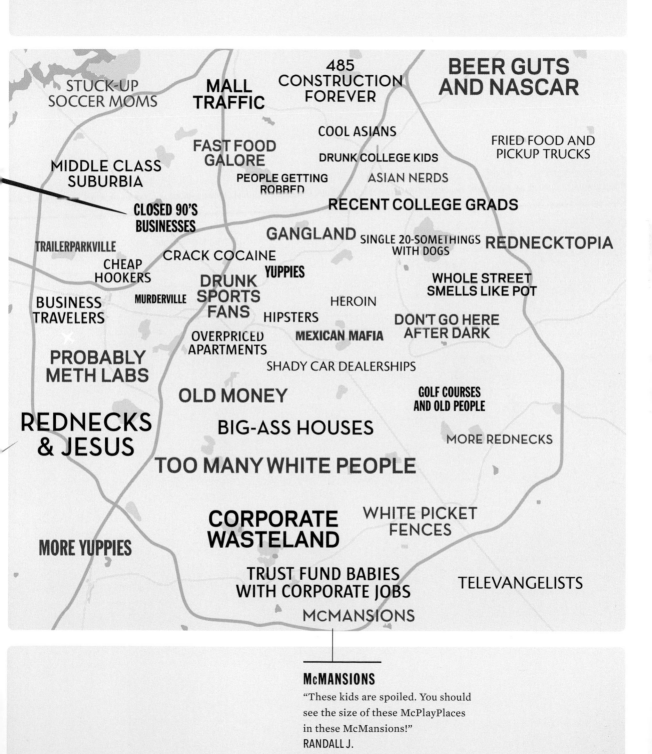

STUCK-UP
SOCCER MOMS

MALL
TRAFFIC

485
CONSTRUCTION
FOREVER

BEER GUTS
AND NASCAR

COOL ASIANS

FRIED FOOD AND
PICKUP TRUCKS

FAST FOOD
GALORE

DRUNK COLLEGE KIDS

MIDDLE CLASS
SUBURBIA

PEOPLE GETTING
ROBBED

ASIAN NERDS

CLOSED 90'S
BUSINESSES

RECENT COLLEGE GRADS

GANGLAND

SINGLE 20-SOMETHINGS
WITH DOGS

REDNECKTOPIA

TRAILERPARKVILLE

CRACK COCAINE

CHEAP
HOOKERS

YUPPIES

WHOLE STREET
SMELLS LIKE POT

DRUNK
SPORTS
FANS

MURDERVILLE

HEROIN

BUSINESS
TRAVELERS

HIPSTERS

DON'T GO HERE
AFTER DARK

OVERPRICED
APARTMENTS

MEXICAN MAFIA

PROBABLY
METH LABS

SHADY CAR DEALERSHIPS

OLD MONEY

GOLF COURSES
AND OLD PEOPLE

REDNECKS
& JESUS

BIG-ASS HOUSES

MORE REDNECKS

TOO MANY WHITE PEOPLE

CORPORATE
WASTELAND

WHITE PICKET
FENCES

MORE YUPPIES

TRUST FUND BABIES
WITH CORPORATE JOBS

TELEVANGELISTS

MCMANSIONS

McMANSIONS

"These kids are spoiled. You should
see the size of these McPlayPlaces
in these McMansions!"
RANDALL J.

CHAPEL HILL

NORTH CAROLINA

Of the three cities in the Research Triangle, Chapel Thrill is the hippy. Chapel Hill is a liberal city in a (just barely, but not Trumpishly) conservative state. It is host to old rich white people and college basketball players who get "A" grades for fake classes like "Planets That Look Like A Basketball" and "Math?"

GUNS AND COWS
"Go together like a horse and carriage."
FLOYD J.

GUNS AND COWS

I.T. GUYS

MOMMY NEEDS A VALIUM
"I sold that phrase to Hallmark. Number-one Mother's Day card three years in a row!"
JULIA S.

GENDER NEUTRAL PRONOUNS USED HERE

PEOPLE WHO EAT FARRO

LESS DIRTY HIPPIES

Credit: Molly

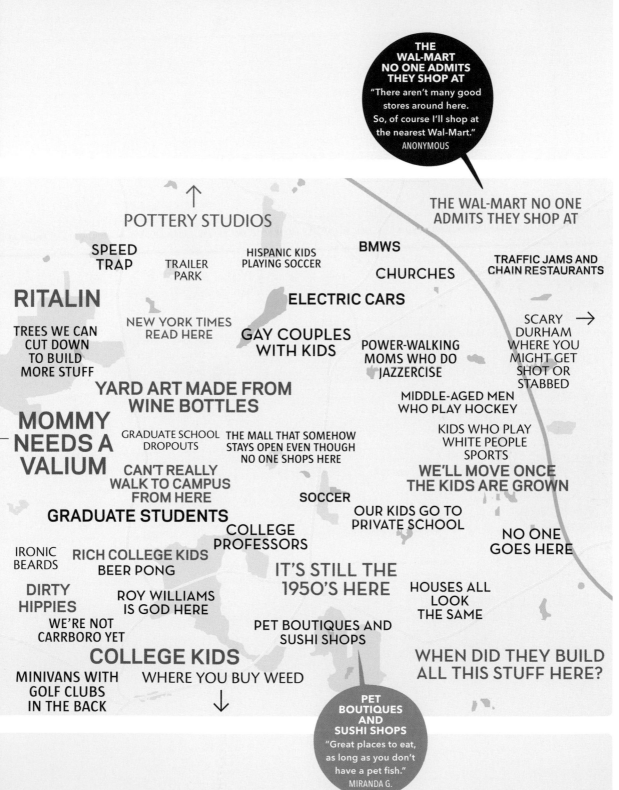

THE WAL-MART NO ONE ADMITS THEY SHOP AT

THE WAL-MART NO ONE ADMITS THEY SHOP AT
"There aren't many good stores around here. So, of course I'll shop at the nearest Wal-Mart."
ANONYMOUS

↑
POTTERY STUDIOS

SPEED TRAP

TRAILER PARK

HISPANIC KIDS PLAYING SOCCER

BMWS

CHURCHES

TRAFFIC JAMS AND CHAIN RESTAURANTS

RITALIN

NEW YORK TIMES READ HERE

ELECTRIC CARS

SCARY DURHAM WHERE YOU MIGHT GET SHOT OR STABBED →

TREES WE CAN CUT DOWN TO BUILD MORE STUFF

GAY COUPLES WITH KIDS

POWER-WALKING MOMS WHO DO JAZZERCISE

YARD ART MADE FROM WINE BOTTLES

MIDDLE-AGED MEN WHO PLAY HOCKEY

— MOMMY NEEDS A VALIUM

GRADUATE SCHOOL DROPOUTS

THE MALL THAT SOMEHOW STAYS OPEN EVEN THOUGH NO ONE SHOPS HERE

KIDS WHO PLAY WHITE PEOPLE SPORTS

CAN'T REALLY WALK TO CAMPUS FROM HERE

WE'LL MOVE ONCE THE KIDS ARE GROWN

SOCCER

OUR KIDS GO TO PRIVATE SCHOOL

GRADUATE STUDENTS

COLLEGE PROFESSORS

NO ONE GOES HERE

IRONIC BEARDS

RICH COLLEGE KIDS BEER PONG

IT'S STILL THE 1950'S HERE

HOUSES ALL LOOK THE SAME

DIRTY HIPPIES

ROY WILLIAMS IS GOD HERE

WE'RE NOT CARRBORO YET

PET BOUTIQUES AND SUSHI SHOPS

WHEN DID THEY BUILD ALL THIS STUFF HERE?

COLLEGE KIDS

WHERE YOU BUY WEED

MINIVANS WITH GOLF CLUBS IN THE BACK

↓

PET BOUTIQUES AND SUSHI SHOPS
"Great places to eat, as long as you don't have a pet fish."
MIRANDA G.

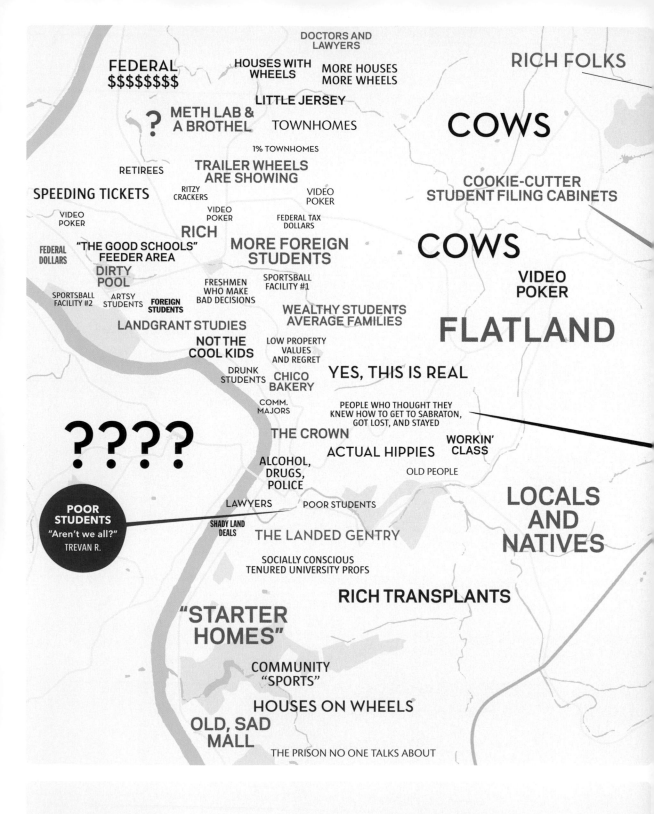

MORGANTOWN
WEST VIRGINIA

Morgantown is known as the home of West Virginia University, which is often forgotten due to the sheer amount of alcohol that is consumed on campus. In West Virginia, you have to be careful not to drink too much, though, or you may end up hooking up with a relative. Just make sure to avoid the half-naked girls puking in the snow while carrying their heels. If you don't like the outdoors, drinking, or getting stoned, you may find it tough to spend much time in Morgantown. However, don't forget that one of the town's primary features/downfalls is that it is just over an hour drive to Pittsburgh.

CHATTANOOGA
TENNESSEE

Chattanooga is most widely known through Glenn Miller's "Chattanooga Choo Choo" train song, belting out 'Woo, woo, Chattanooga there you are!' Of course, Chattanooga is also the site of the first Coca-Cola bottling company and the home of the otherworldly dessert: Moon Pies. If the town's humid air doesn't get you moist and sweaty like a southern sow, the pollen will make you sneeze your eyes out. The town is also bordered by two mountains: "Lookout" and "Signal." You can't say the settlers of Chattanooga didn't provide people fair warning about moving there.

STRANGELY NORMAL
"If you're able to live in Hixson, you can sleep soundly knowing that you're surrounded by normal young Democrats with kids, and you're not far from the safe Wal-Mart. It is the ideal place to live."
VIC H.

GOLF & STINK
"The Moccasin Bend Golf Club is right next to the water treatment plant. If the wind is blowing in just the right direction, you are in for quite a treat out on the course. More like playing eighteen assholes."
TONY T.

Credit: Logan C.

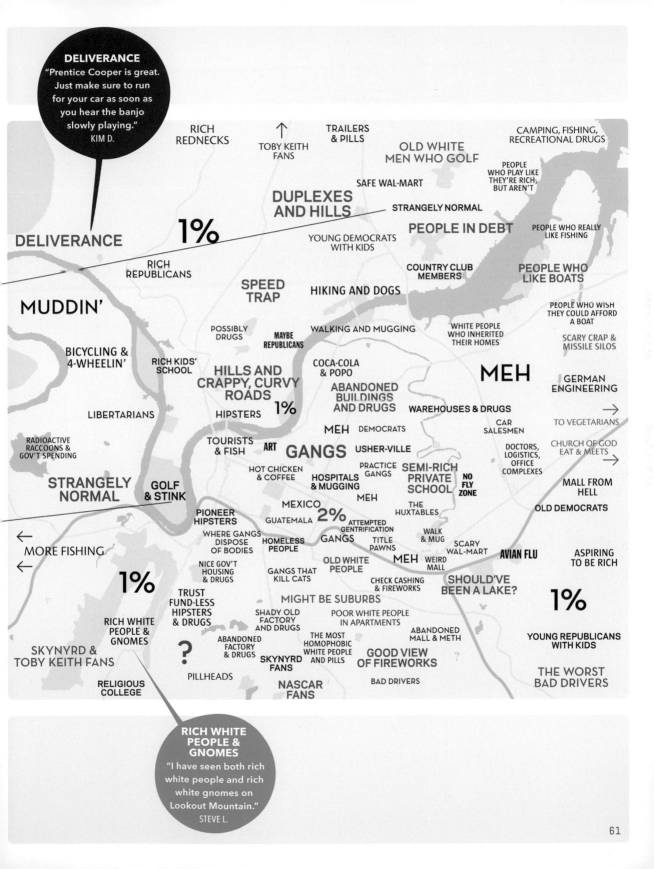

DELIVERANCE
"Prentice Cooper is great. Just make sure to run for your car as soon as you hear the banjo slowly playing."
KIM D.

RICH REDNECKS

↑ TOBY KEITH FANS

TRAILERS & PILLS

OLD WHITE MEN WHO GOLF

CAMPING, FISHING, RECREATIONAL DRUGS

SAFE WAL-MART

PEOPLE WHO PLAY LIKE THEY'RE RICH, BUT AREN'T

DELIVERANCE

DUPLEXES AND HILLS

1%

STRANGELY NORMAL

PEOPLE IN DEBT

PEOPLE WHO REALLY LIKE FISHING

YOUNG DEMOCRATS WITH KIDS

RICH REPUBLICANS

COUNTRY CLUB MEMBERS

PEOPLE WHO LIKE BOATS

MUDDIN'

SPEED TRAP

HIKING AND DOGS

PEOPLE WHO WISH THEY COULD AFFORD A BOAT

POSSIBLY DRUGS

MAYBE REPUBLICANS

WALKING AND MUGGING

WHITE PEOPLE WHO INHERITED THEIR HOMES

SCARY CRAP & MISSILE SILOS

BICYCLING & 4-WHEELIN'

RICH KIDS' SCHOOL

HILLS AND CRAPPY, CURVY ROADS

COCA-COLA & POPO

MEH

GERMAN ENGINEERING

1%

ABANDONED BUILDINGS AND DRUGS

WAREHOUSES & DRUGS

LIBERTARIANS

HIPSTERS

MEH

DEMOCRATS

CAR SALESMEN

→ TO VEGETARIANS

RADIOACTIVE RACCOONS & GOV'T SPENDING

TOURISTS & FISH

ART

GANGS

USHER-VILLE

DOCTORS, LOGISTICS, OFFICE COMPLEXES

CHURCH OF GOD EAT & MEETS →

HOT CHICKEN & COFFEE

HOSPITALS & MUGGING

PRACTICE GANGS

SEMI-RICH PRIVATE SCHOOL

NO FLY ZONE

MALL FROM HELL

STRANGELY NORMAL

GOLF & STINK

MEXICO

MEH

THE HUXTABLES

OLD DEMOCRATS

PIONEER HIPSTERS

GUATEMALA

2%

ATTEMPTED GENTRIFICATION

WALK & MUG

WHERE GANGS DISPOSE OF BODIES

HOMELESS PEOPLE

GANGS

TITLE PAWNS

SCARY WAL-MART

AVIAN FLU

ASPIRING TO BE RICH

← MORE FISHING

NICE GOV'T HOUSING & DRUGS

OLD WHITE PEOPLE

MEH

WEIRD MALL

←

GANGS THAT KILL CATS

CHECK CASHING & FIREWORKS

SHOULD'VE BEEN A LAKE?

1%

1%

TRUST FUND-LESS HIPSTERS & DRUGS

MIGHT BE SUBURBS

YOUNG REPUBLICANS WITH KIDS

RICH WHITE PEOPLE & GNOMES

?

SHADY OLD FACTORY AND DRUGS

POOR WHITE PEOPLE IN APARTMENTS

ABANDONED MALL & METH

SKYNYRD & TOBY KEITH FANS

ABANDONED FACTORY & DRUGS

THE MOST HOMOPHOBIC WHITE PEOPLE AND PILLS

GOOD VIEW OF FIREWORKS

THE WORST BAD DRIVERS

RELIGIOUS COLLEGE

PILLHEADS

SKYNYRD FANS

NASCAR FANS

BAD DRIVERS

RICH WHITE PEOPLE & GNOMES
"I have seen both rich white people and rich white gnomes on Lookout Mountain."
STEVE L.

61

KNOXVILLE
TENNESSEE

Knoxville was the first capital of Tennessee, before whatever the capital of Tennessee is now. Johnny Knoxville is the official representative of Knoxville, a city filled with jackasses. And the city is home to the University of Tennessee Volunteers, named for the people who volunteered to live in the city when no one else would. But seriously, Knoxville is one of the largest cities in the Appalachian region and, in recent years, has positioned itself as a bastion of Appalachian culture (read: guns, big trucks, camo, and chew). And in 2015, Forbes ranked Knoxville as one of the top five most affordable cities to live in the U.S. Take that, every other city in Tennessee!

FELLINI KROGER

"It's hard to describe the Fellini Kroger to someone who hasn't been there. It provides a perfect snapshot of the surrounding area in the style of walking into a bar in one of the Star Wars movies. You will find some eccentric characters in there regardless of the time of day."
BRUCE B.

AWKWARDLY PLACED STRIP CLUB

"The Mouse's Ear strip club is almost impossible to find. Do I go through the car wash? Behind the car wash? Or is it behind the urgent care? You really have to work hard to get there."
KENNY H.

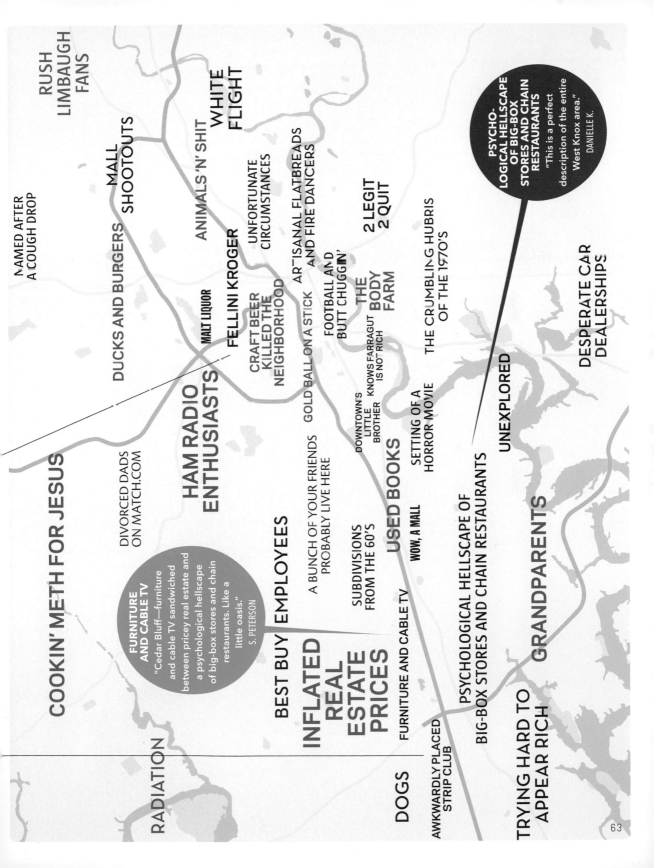

RADIATION

COOKIN' METH FOR JESUS

NAMED AFTER A COUGH DROP

RUSH LIMBAUGH FANS

DUCKS AND BURGERS

MALL SHOOTOUTS

WHITE FLIGHT

ANIMALS 'N' SHIT

MALT LIQUOR

FELLINI KROGER

UNFORTUNATE CIRCUMSTANCES

ARTISANAL FLATBREADS AND FIRE DANCERS

CRAFT BEER KILLED THE NEIGHBORHOOD

2 LEGIT 2 QUIT

FOOTBALL AND BUTT CHUGGIN'

THE BODY FARM

THE CRUMBLING HUBRIS OF THE 1970'S

PSYCHO-LOGICAL HELLSCAPE OF BIG-BOX STORES AND CHAIN RESTAURANTS

"This is a perfect description of the entire West Knox area."

DANIELLE K.

DIVORCED DADS ON MATCH.COM

HAM RADIO ENTHUSIASTS

GOLD BALL ON A STICK

DOWNTOWN'S LITTLE BROTHER

KNOWS FARRAGUT IS NOT RICH

SETTING OF A HORROR MOVIE

UNEXPLORED

DESPERATE CAR DEALERSHIPS

FURNITURE AND CABLE TV

"Cedar Bluff—furniture and cable TV sandwiched between pricey real estate and a psychological hellscape of big-box stores and chain restaurants. Like a little oasis."

S. PETERSON

EMPLOYEES

BEST BUY

INFLATED REAL ESTATE PRICES

A BUNCH OF YOUR FRIENDS PROBABLY LIVE HERE

SUBDIVISIONS FROM THE 60'S

USED BOOKS

WOW, A MALL

FURNITURE AND CABLE TV

PSYCHOLOGICAL HELLSCAPE OF BIG-BOX STORES AND CHAIN RESTAURANTS

GRANDPARENTS

DOGS

AWKWARDLY PLACED STRIP CLUB

TRYING HARD TO APPEAR RICH

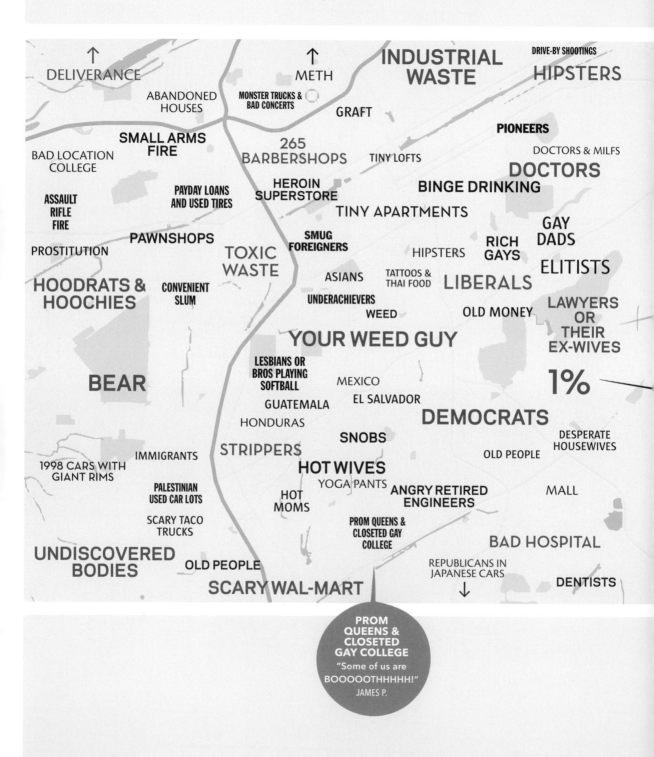

↑
DELIVERANCE

ABANDONED HOUSES

↑
METH

MONSTER TRUCKS & BAD CONCERTS

INDUSTRIAL WASTE

DRIVE-BY SHOOTINGS

HIPSTERS

GRAFT

SMALL ARMS FIRE

265 BARBERSHOPS

TINY LOFTS

PIONEERS

DOCTORS & MILFS

DOCTORS

BAD LOCATION COLLEGE

ASSAULT RIFLE FIRE

PAYDAY LOANS AND USED TIRES

HEROIN SUPERSTORE

BINGE DRINKING

TINY APARTMENTS

PROSTITUTION

PAWNSHOPS

SMUG FOREIGNERS

GAY DADS

RICH GAYS

ELITISTS

HOODRATS & HOOCHIES

CONVENIENT SLUM

TOXIC WASTE

ASIANS

TATTOOS & THAI FOOD

LIBERALS

UNDERACHIEVERS

WEED

OLD MONEY

LAWYERS OR THEIR EX-WIVES

YOUR WEED GUY

LESBIANS OR BROS PLAYING SOFTBALL

MEXICO

EL SALVADOR

1%

BEAR

GUATEMALA

HONDURAS

DEMOCRATS

DESPERATE HOUSEWIVES

IMMIGRANTS

STRIPPERS

SNOBS

OLD PEOPLE

1998 CARS WITH GIANT RIMS

PALESTINIAN USED CAR LOTS

HOT WIVES

YOGA PANTS

HOT MOMS

ANGRY RETIRED ENGINEERS

MALL

SCARY TACO TRUCKS

PROM QUEENS & CLOSETED GAY COLLEGE

BAD HOSPITAL

UNDISCOVERED BODIES

OLD PEOPLE

REPUBLICANS IN JAPANESE CARS
↓

DENTISTS

SCARY WAL-MART

PROM QUEENS & CLOSETED GAY COLLEGE
"Some of us are BOOOOOTHHHHH!"
JAMES P.

BIRMINGHAM
ALABAMA

WIDOWS AND COOL COUPLES

"I live in 'Widows and Cool Couples,' but I am neither. Dammit. Does that mean I have to move to 'Lawyers or Their Ex-wives?'"
TOMMY D.

LAWYERS OR THEIR EX-WIVES

"Whichever one wasn't killed in the divorce lives here."
MICHAEL N.

1%

"The 1 percent in Birmingham are just the people that have more gold in their mouths than the rest of us."
KATHERINE A.

Birmingham is famous for being the birthplace of the American Civil Rights movement and for holding the record for most American Idol winners. Historically, Birmingham's major industries were steel and iron, but with general trends in recent years, the city has found more prosperity transitioning to become a multi-million dollar cocaine and heroin empire. And it is a fantastic city to build your own drug empire, as it is *Forbes* 2015 most affordable city in the U.S.

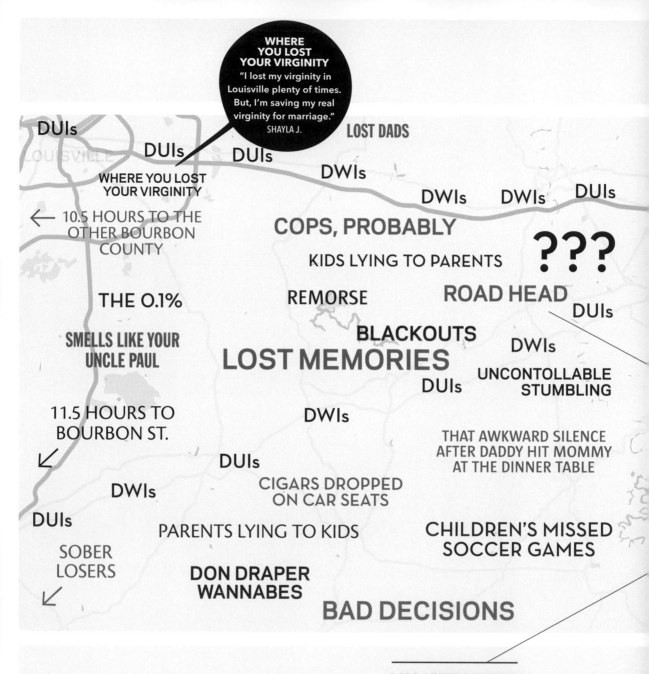

WHERE
YOU LOST
YOUR VIRGINITY

"I lost my virginity in Louisville plenty of times. But, I'm saving my real virginity for marriage."
SHAYLA J.

DUIs

LOUISVILLE

DUIs

DUIs

WHERE YOU LOST YOUR VIRGINITY

← 10.5 HOURS TO THE OTHER BOURBON COUNTY

LOST DADS

DWIs

DWIs DWIs DUIs

COPS, PROBABLY

KIDS LYING TO PARENTS

???

THE 0.1%

REMORSE

ROAD HEAD

DUIs

SMELLS LIKE YOUR UNCLE PAUL

BLACKOUTS
LOST MEMORIES

DUIs

DWIs

UNCONTOLLABLE STUMBLING

11.5 HOURS TO BOURBON ST.

DWIs

THAT AWKWARD SILENCE AFTER DADDY HIT MOMMY AT THE DINNER TABLE

DWIs

DUIs

CIGARS DROPPED ON CAR SEATS

DUIs

PARENTS LYING TO KIDS

CHILDREN'S MISSED SOCCER GAMES

SOBER LOSERS

DON DRAPER WANNABES

BAD DECISIONS

DADS LEAVING FAMILIES

"This map totally explains why my dad moved thirty minutes southeast of us after he and my mom got divorced. He got caught cheating at an Olive Garden. Now, when we go back to Olive Garden, we're there, but we're not family."
RUSSELL K.

BOURBON TRAIL

KENTUCKY

In the 1700s, farmers learned that they could easily convert corn and other grains into whiskey in order to transport them through the mountains and prevent them from rotting along the way. With that discovery, it is a surprise corn hasn't become extinct in this country. Today, America's signature bourbon industry has helped to create 9,000 jobs, and destroys nearly 10,000 lives each year due to alcohol-impaired driving crashes. The region is in the heart of Kentucky, and when people aren't drinking bourbon, they're riding horses. Thanks to DUIs, uncontrollable stumbling, blackouts, and dads leaving families, the Bourbon Trail is the wealthy white man's trail of tears.

WHISKEY DICK

PISSED PANTS

DUIs

DUIs

DWIs

LEXINGTON

FAILED ROADSIDE TESTS

DADS LEAVING FAMILIES

TO PEOPLE WITH LIVES AND JOBS

CRIPPLING SELF-DOUBT

ROAD HEAD
"There is nothing better than getting road head. Just watch out for the speed bumps if you are one of those guys who is into girls with teeth."
NICK S.

PALM COAST

FLORIDA

Palm Coast was developed in 1969 by a community development organization, and incorporated in 1999. Since the city was mass-produced, its health is as embalmed as the inhabitants who leave the city. Palm Coast is a tropical casket where old people go to die. Many have even coaxed their children to move south to the city because of the beautiful weather and coast, and have trapped them there only to grow old and die as well. Despite the death, the city has had one of the highest rates of population growth in the United States since 1990.

D-AVERAGE STUDENTS WHO THINK THEY'RE SMART
"Joke's on you—it's 'their.'"
BRIAN R.,
DAYTONA STATE '17

HOMELESS PEOPLE WHO LIVE IN TENTS
"Aren't all homeless people intense?"
CLAIRE S.

DON'T GO HERE BY YOURSELF
"A few years ago in Graham Swamp, a few 70-year-old men were caught publicly masturbating in the swamp in broad daylight. Turns out, the only alligator you need to watch out for in the swamp is a cock-o-dile."
ROGER C.

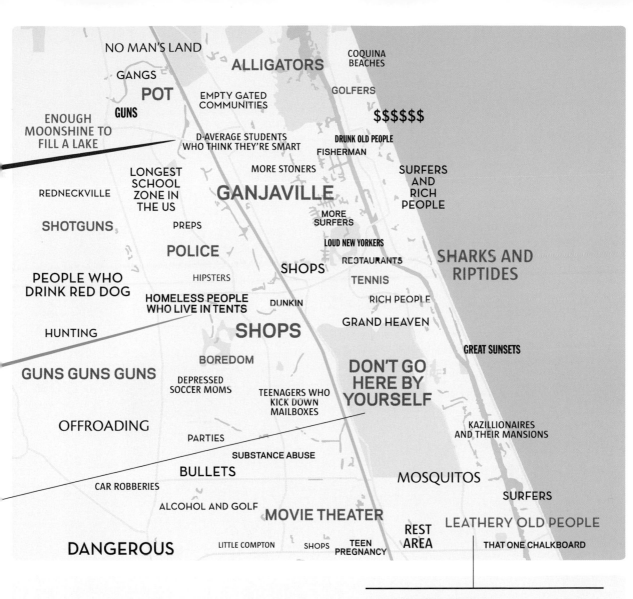

NO MAN'S LAND

GANGS

POT

GUNS

ENOUGH MOONSHINE TO FILL A LAKE

ALLIGATORS

COQUINA BEACHES

GOLFERS

EMPTY GATED COMMUNITIES

$$$$$$

D-AVERAGE STUDENTS WHO THINK THEY'RE SMART

DRUNK OLD PEOPLE

FISHERMAN

MORE STONERS

LONGEST SCHOOL ZONE IN THE US

REDNECKVILLE

GANJAVILLE

SURFERS AND RICH PEOPLE

MORE SURFERS

SHOTGUNS

PREPS

LOUD NEW YORKERS

POLICE

RESTAURANTS

SHARKS AND RIPTIDES

SHOPS

PEOPLE WHO DRINK RED DOG

HIPSTERS

TENNIS

HOMELESS PEOPLE WHO LIVE IN TENTS

DUNKIN

RICH PEOPLE

HUNTING

SHOPS

GRAND HEAVEN

BOREDOM

GREAT SUNSETS

GUNS GUNS GUNS

DEPRESSED SOCCER MOMS

TEENAGERS WHO KICK DOWN MAILBOXES

DON'T GO HERE BY YOURSELF

OFFROADING

PARTIES

KAZILLIONAIRES AND THEIR MANSIONS

SUBSTANCE ABUSE

BULLETS

MOSQUITOS

CAR ROBBERIES

SURFERS

ALCOHOL AND GOLF

MOVIE THEATER

REST AREA

LEATHERY OLD PEOPLE

DANGEROUS

LITTLE COMPTON

SHOPS

TEEN PREGNANCY

THAT ONE CHALKBOARD

LEATHERY OLD PEOPLE

"One time at Flagler Beach, we saw the oldest, leatheriest-looking man I've ever seen. All the sun he'd been exposed to over the years had done a number on his body. As we watched him eat a snack, I couldn't help seeing potato chips being inserted into the opening of an old Coach wallet."
MATT G.

MIAMI
FLORIDA

If the city was a nightclub, it would charge a $1,000 cover. Miami is more Cuba than Cuba itself and if you aren't Cuban, you are tan enough to pass. The Capital of Latin America and Cruise Capital of the world has a vibrant culture and fantastic food. Miami has rich people celebrating the luxurious nightlife, and poor people just trying to stay alive at night. But, if you aren't on a beach, are you even really alive?

TEEPEES AND CHEAP SMOKES

"I haven't been very far west of Miami, but seeing this map definitely gets me excited to go to the Everglades for the alligators, snakes, toothless bikers, dead bodies, and cheap smokes. Where do I sign up for a boat tour?"

ROD A.

GLOCK GLOCK

"Miami is all about image—what you wear, what you drive, what clubs you can get in to, who you know, who you've murdered."

BRIAN S.

Credit: Anonymous

DEAD BODIES & FELONS HIDING

ALLIGATORS AND SNAKES

TOOTHLESS DIRTBIKERS

TEEPEES AND CHEAP SMOKES

MORE ALLIGATORS AND SNAKES

RANDOM LOCALS WHO GO TO KNAUS BERRY FARM FOR THE CINNAMON BUNS

TOTAL NACOS

INDIAN RESERVATIONS

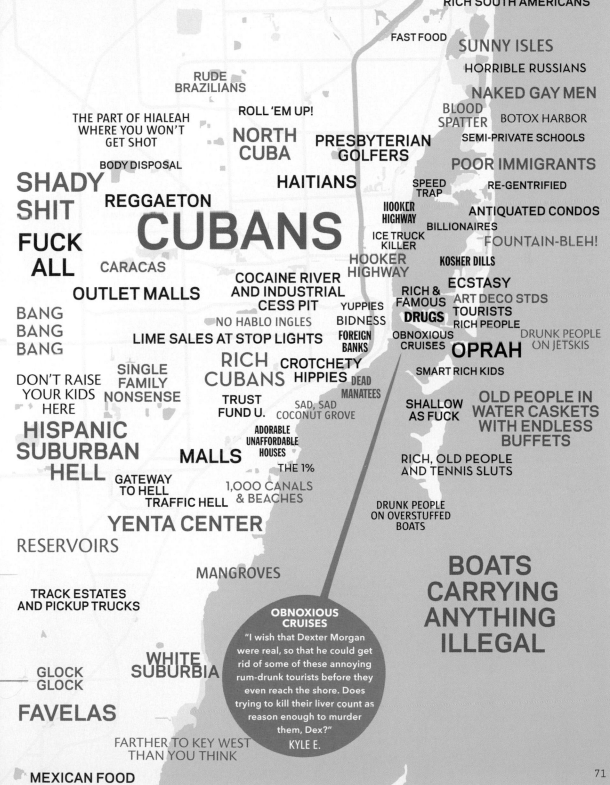

SHRINKING MIDDLE CLASS

RICH SOUTH AMERICANS

FAST FOOD

SUNNY ISLES

HORRIBLE RUSSIANS

RUDE BRAZILIANS

NAKED GAY MEN

BLOOD SPATTER   BOTOX HARBOR

ROLL 'EM UP!

THE PART OF HIALEAH WHERE YOU WON'T GET SHOT

SEMI-PRIVATE SCHOOLS

NORTH CUBA

PRESBYTERIAN GOLFERS

POOR IMMIGRANTS

BODY DISPOSAL

HAITIANS

RE-GENTRIFIED

SHADY

SPEED TRAP

SHIT

REGGAETON

HOOKER HIGHWAY

ANTIQUATED CONDOS

BILLIONAIRES

FUCK

CUBANS

ICE TRUCK KILLER

FOUNTAIN-BLEH!

ALL

CARACAS

HOOKER HIGHWAY

KOSHER DILLS

OUTLET MALLS

COCAINE RIVER AND INDUSTRIAL CESS PIT

ECSTASY

RICH & FAMOUS

ART DECO STDS

TOURISTS

BANG

YUPPIES

DRUGS

RICH PEOPLE

BANG

NO HABLO INGLES

BIDNESS

DRUNK PEOPLE ON JETSKIS

BANG

LIME SALES AT STOP LIGHTS

FOREIGN BANKS

OBNOXIOUS CRUISES

OPRAH

DON'T RAISE YOUR KIDS HERE

SINGLE FAMILY NONSENSE

RICH CUBANS

CROTCHETY HIPPIES

SMART RICH KIDS

DEAD MANATEES

TRUST FUND U.

SAD, SAD COCONUT GROVE

SHALLOW AS FUCK

OLD PEOPLE IN WATER CASKETS WITH ENDLESS BUFFETS

HISPANIC SUBURBAN HELL

MALLS

ADORABLE UNAFFORDABLE HOUSES

THE 1%

RICH, OLD PEOPLE AND TENNIS SLUTS

GATEWAY TO HELL

1,000 CANALS & BEACHES

TRAFFIC HELL

YENTA CENTER

DRUNK PEOPLE ON OVERSTUFFED BOATS

RESERVOIRS

MANGROVES

BOATS CARRYING ANYTHING ILLEGAL

TRACK ESTATES AND PICKUP TRUCKS

OBNOXIOUS CRUISES

"I wish that Dexter Morgan were real, so that he could get rid of some of these annoying rum-drunk tourists before they even reach the shore. Does trying to kill their liver count as reason enough to murder them, Dex?"

KYLE E.

GLOCK GLOCK

WHITE SUBURBIA

FAVELAS

FARTHER TO KEY WEST THAN YOU THINK

MEXICAN FOOD

NEW ORLEANS
LOUISIANA

STRIP CLUBS THAT GO ALL THE WAY

STRIP CLUBS THAT GO ALL THE WAY

"When they say that the strip clubs in East New Orleans go all the way, they mean they go all the way. I've been married to one of those strippers for over five years now."
ANTOINE R.

DRUNKS

"I've seen friends lose phones, wallets, virginity, dignity, and more on Bourbon Street. The only way you can guarantee saving any of those things is to stay away altogether. But life is all about taking risks."
LAUREN H.

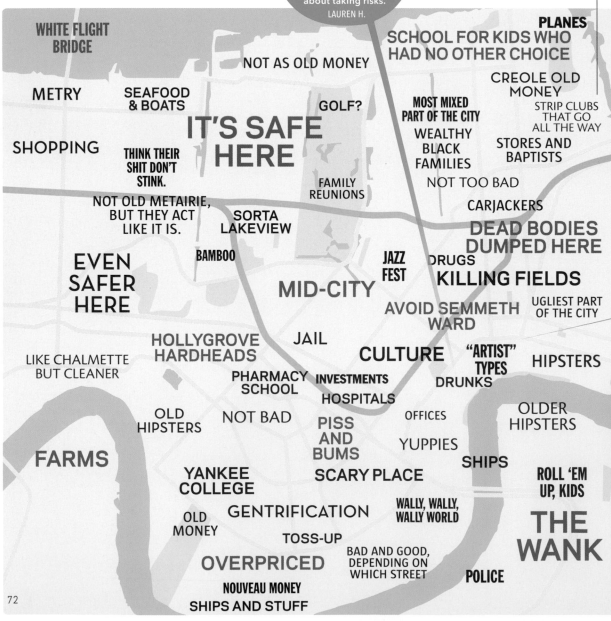

WHITE FLIGHT BRIDGE

PLANES

SCHOOL FOR KIDS WHO HAD NO OTHER CHOICE

NOT AS OLD MONEY

CREOLE OLD MONEY

METRY

SEAFOOD & BOATS

GOLF?

MOST MIXED PART OF THE CITY

STRIP CLUBS THAT GO ALL THE WAY

SHOPPING

THINK THEIR SHIT DON'T STINK.

IT'S SAFE HERE

WEALTHY BLACK FAMILIES

STORES AND BAPTISTS

FAMILY REUNIONS

NOT TOO BAD

NOT OLD METAIRIE, BUT THEY ACT LIKE IT IS.

SORTA LAKEVIEW

CARJACKERS

DEAD BODIES DUMPED HERE

BAMBOO

JAZZ FEST

DRUGS

KILLING FIELDS

EVEN SAFER HERE

MID-CITY

AVOID SEMMETH WARD

UGLIEST PART OF THE CITY

LIKE CHALMETTE BUT CLEANER

HOLLYGROVE HARDHEADS

JAIL

CULTURE

"ARTIST" TYPES

HIPSTERS

PHARMACY SCHOOL

INVESTMENTS

DRUNKS

OLD HIPSTERS

NOT BAD

HOSPITALS

PISS AND BUMS

OFFICES

OLDER HIPSTERS

YUPPIES

FARMS

YANKEE COLLEGE

SCARY PLACE

SHIPS

ROLL 'EM UP, KIDS

OLD MONEY

GENTRIFICATION

WALLY, WALLY, WALLY WORLD

THE WANK

TOSS-UP

OVERPRICED

BAD AND GOOD, DEPENDING ON WHICH STREET

POLICE

NOUVEAU MONEY

SHIPS AND STUFF

New Orleans is a city that knows its priorities: food, drinking, partying, and boobs. NOLA is famous for its jazz music, Creole food, Mardi Gras festival, and hurricanes that will blow you away. While this historic southern city is one of the most dangerous in America, that doesn't mean you shouldn't take the risk of an all-night bender followed by the world's best beignets. Your liver and fat rolls will thank you for it.

Credit: CM

IMPROVING

WEALTHY
BLACK FAMILIES

LITTLE VIETNAM

HOOD, AND
PROUD OF IT!

NASA

ILLEGAL CAR RACES

MORE BODIES

SCRAP YARDS

"ARTIST" TYPES
"New Orleans: Come for the jazz and Cajun food. Stay for the beignets, hurricanes, and flourishing murder scene."
RONALD E.

BRAD PITT
HOUSES

FISHING

THE PARISH

HIPSTERS
AND
HOODRATS

OLD CHALMATIONS

WHITE TRASH
"If you don't know what 'Chalmation' means, you've never had scattered gravy, or you never made groceries, you best off going up da road, y'hear?"
JAXSON S.

FEDERAL
CITY

WHITE TRASH

MEH

OIL FIELDS

REALLY
BAD
ROADS

TOO FAR

REALLY BAD

NICE

NICE!

FARMS IN
NOLA?

73

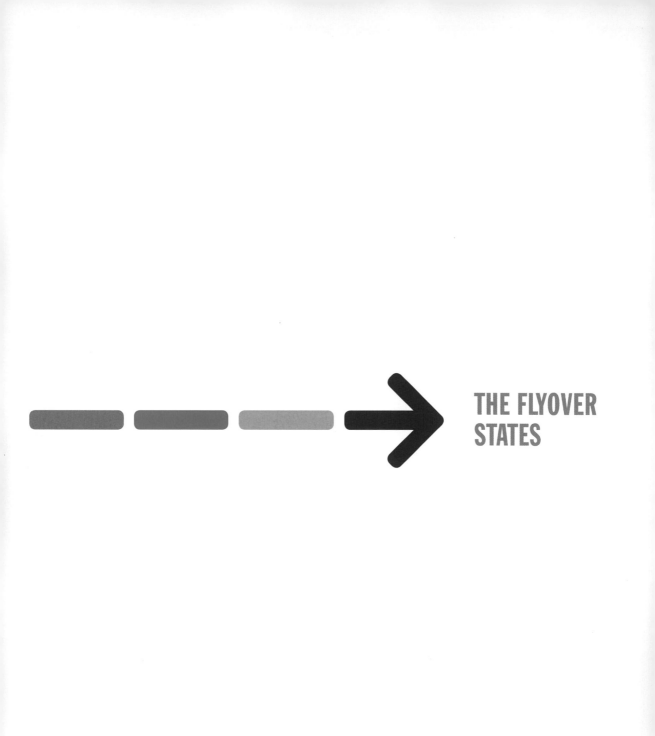

**THE FLYOVER
STATES**

The Midwest is known as America's heartland, and home to the only remaining family values in the country, but most coastal Americans can't tell Omaha from Wichita. So, for you snobs, let me fill you in. These wonderfully square states have played a significant role in the history of corn, deep-fried state fair food, serial killers of the 1950s, and road trips filled with boring white Republicans, and they are the birthplace of tumbleweeds and LeBron James. The Midwest also produces and consumes the majority of the food in the United States in order to keep as many people as possible grounded during tornado season. It is a glorious land.

To the north of the Midwest is our largest regional border with beaver-loving Canada. And with that border comes polite, slightly alcoholic Canadian rednecks who have emigrated to the United States because the free health care and heavenly poutine were not enough. However, the great American north provides solace for those Canucks through its own obsession with hockey, fighting, the great outdoors, and maple syrup. While most people forget about the Midwest because it is flatter than a seventh-grade girl, it is the beef capital of the United States and, most important, it is host to some of the best undiscovered cities that our country has to offer. Detroit has turned an economic apocalypse and crumbling infrastructure into squatter-friendly farming and one of the most affordable cities in America. Milwaukee is stepping out of the shadow of its bigger brother Chicago with a breathtaking art museum and two times the childhood obesity. And I'm pretty sure Cincinnati is going to get that fourth Chipotle open any day now. Fingers crossed.

So, take a look at what the breadbasket of the world has to offer. From "That Fucking Kmart" in Minneapolis to Cleveland's "Polish People and People Who Would Enjoy Being Polish," there is something for everyone to enjoy. And, if you are so lucky as to move to one of these cities, the corn-fed locals will welcome you with open arms and wide smiles. They're not special, I swear. Just especially decent Americans.

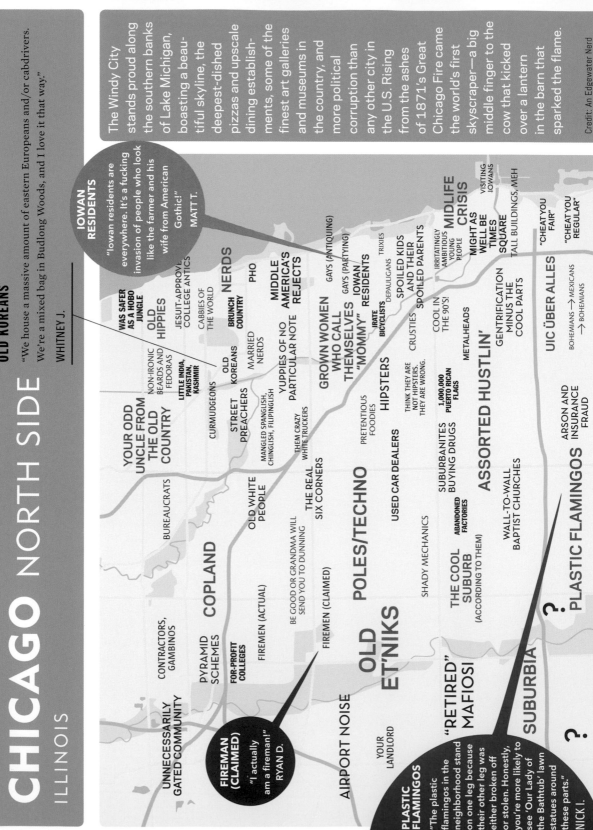

CHICAGO NORTH SIDE
ILLINOIS

OLD KOREANS
"We house a massive amount of eastern Europeans and/or cabdrivers. We're a mixed bag in Budlong Woods, and I love it that way."
WHITNEY J.

The Windy City stands proud along the southern banks of Lake Michigan, boasting a beautiful skyline, the deepest-dished pizzas and upscale dining establishments, some of the finest art galleries and museums in the country, and more political corruption than any other city in the U.S. Rising from the ashes of 1871's Great Chicago Fire came the world's first skyscraper—a big middle finger to the cow that kicked over a lantern in the barn that sparked the flame.

Credit: An Edgewater Nerd

IOWAN RESIDENTS
"Iowan residents are everywhere. It's a fucking invasion of people who look like the farmer and his wife from American Gothic!"
MATT T.

UNNECESSARILY GATED COMMUNITY

CONTRACTORS, GAMBINOS

PYRAMID SCHEMES

COPLAND

FOR-PROFIT COLLEGES

FIREMEN (ACTUAL)

BE GOOD OR GRANDMA WILL SEND YOU TO DUNNING

FIREMEN (CLAIMED)

BUREAUCRATS

YOUR ODD UNCLE FROM THE OLD COUNTRY

NON-IRONIC BEARDS AND FEDORAS

LITTLE INDIA, PAKISTAN, KASHMIR

CURMUDGEONS

OLD KOREANS

STREET PREACHERS

OLD WHITE PEOPLE

MANGLED SPANGLISH, CHINGLISH, FILIPINGLISH

THEM CRAZY WHITE TRUCKERS

THE REAL SIX CORNERS

WAS SAFER AS A HOBO JUNGLE

OLD HIPPIES

JESUIT-APPROVE COLLEGE ANTICS

CABBIES OF THE WORLD

MARRIED NERDS

BRUNCH NERDS

PHO

MIDDLE AMERICA'S REJECTS

YUPPIES OF NO PARTICULAR NOTE

GROWN WOMEN WHO CALL THEMSELVES "MOMMY"

GAYS (ANTIQUING)

GAYS (PARTYING)

IOWAN RESIDENTS

IRATE BICYCLISTS

DEPAULIGANS

TRIXIES

PRETENTIOUS FOODIES

HIPSTERS

THINK THEY ARE NOT HIPSTERS. THEY ARE WRONG.

SPOILED KIDS AND THEIR SPOILED PARENTS

CRUSTIES

COOL IN THE 90'S!

IRRITATINGLY AMBITIOUS YOUNG PEOPLE

METALHEADS

MIDLIFE CRISIS

VISITING IOWANS

MIGHT AS WELL BE TIMES SQUARE

TALL BUILDINGS, MEH

GENTRIFICATION MINUS THE COOL PARTS

"CHEAT YOU FAIR"

"CHEAT YOU REGULAR"

UIC ÜBER ALLES

BOHEMIANS → MEXICANS → BOHEMIANS

USED CAR DEALERS

SHADY MECHANICS

SUBURBANITES BUYING DRUGS

ABANDONED FACTORIES

THE COOL SUBURB (ACCORDING TO THEM)

1,000,000 PUERTO RICAN FLAGS

ASSORTED HUSTLIN'

WALL-TO-WALL BAPTIST CHURCHES

ARSON AND INSURANCE FRAUD

AIRPORT NOISE

YOUR LANDLORD

OLD ET'NIKS

POLES/TECHNO

"RETIRED" MAFIOSI

SUBURBIA

?

PLASTIC FLAMINGOS

?

FIREMAN (CLAIMED)
"I actually am a fireman!"
RYAN D.

PLASTIC FLAMINGOS
"The plastic flamingos in the neighborhood stand on one leg because their other leg was either broken off or stolen. Honestly, you're more likely to see 'Our Lady of the Bathtub' lawn statues around these parts."
NICKI.

CHICAGO SOUTH SIDE

ILLINOIS

Chicago's south side gets a bad rep due to its violent history, gang presence, and crime rates. The city has become divided (even in this book), but the South Side is tough—it is the birthplace of Mr. T and Michelle Obama's arms. Come to South Side for Harold's Chicken Shack. Stay because you've been shot.

Credit: An Edgewater Nerd

WELL, THAT EXPLAINS THE SMELL

FAST EDDIE, SLOW ECONOMY

SHUTTERED STEEL MILLS

FARRAKKAN SPEECHES PLAYING IN STORES

CALLED "PILL HILL" BUT WON'T SELL YOU DRUGS

HEY, WHAT'S THAT SMELL?

BLACK COPS

BLACK NEIGHBORHOODS NOT IN THE NEWS

END O' THE LINE

UNAUTHORIZED GARBAGE DUMPS

SHUTTERED TRAIN/CAR FACTORY

INTELLECTUALS, OBAMA

JAZZ, STATUES, CRIME

FAILED OLYMPIC BID

T-HE WORST KIND OF COLLEGE KIDS

BUPPIES, BLERDS, BLENTRIFICATION

CHINATOWN

CHINESE AMERICATOWN

YOUSE GUYS

RUST BELT HIPSTERS

SHUTTERED STOCKYARDS

BUY YOUR STOLEN STUFF BACK HERE

WARRIORS, COME OUT TO PLAY-AY

LITTLE DETROIT

OTHER WRONG SIDE OF THE TRACKS

COSBY SWEATERS

SKETCHY WHITE PEOPLE IN OTHERWISE MEXICAN HOOD

DURANGO NORTE

WHERE YOUR NO-GOOD COUSIN ENDED UP

COWBOYS AND GUNFIGHTS

ARCHIE BUNKER

SUBURBAN SPRAWL, URBAN CRIME!

WHERE YOUR NO-GOOD COUSIN STARTED OUT

MULTI-RACIAL RACISTS

WRONG SIDE OF THE TRACKS

THE NEW AULD SOD

IRISH PUBS AND ANGRY DRUNKS

PROPERTY OF LARRY DOMINICK

LAND OF MARIACHI BANDS

LOTS AND LOTS OF SEWAGE

STREETS AND SAN LAND

LIKE, ALL THE RAILROAD TRACKS

POLKA HELL

ANGRY LITHUANIAN YELLING

PRETTY BAD MALL

BLUE COLLAR GOONS

KELLY-GREEN REDNECKS

DAY-DRUNK RACIST DADS

?

?

EAST ST. LOUIS
ILLINOIS

East St. Louis may not have the same arch as St. Louis, but it does have twenty times the national average murder rate and is one of the most violent cities in the United States. Even after strikes in the late 1800s and riots in the early 1900s, the city still found a way to later play an integral role in the blues, rock and roll, and jazz scenes, helping to bring up both Miles Davis and Tina Turner. In spite of recent redevelopment projects, the city population still suffers from drastic urban blight, probably because of the murders. But if you love corruption and decaying strip clubs, visiting East St. Louis may be worth the risk.

CAR MUSEUM THAT NO ONE VISITS

"Many tourists stumble upon East St. Louis thinking we're part of St. Louis. They couldn't be more wrong. Does St. Louis have the second tallest fountain in the world? I don't think so. Is St. Louis suffering from massive urban blight? Guess again. Did East St. Louis have to put up with Nelly coming up here? Nope. I think we can all see clearly that East St. Louis is the winner here."

SEAN T.

JUNKYARDS

METH LABS

CORN

CORN

CORN

TRAILER TRASH

PAWN SHOPS

CHICKEN FARMS

REDNECKS

COCKY COPS

RACISTS

STRIP CLUB SWAMP HEAVEN

DEAD BODIES

GEAR HEADS

METH LABS

THE SOUL TRAIN

OLD TAXI CABS

HOT DOG CART VENDORS

BIKER GANG

SMELLS LIKE POOP

GREASY FRIED CHICKEN

RATS

SHOOTINGS

OUTRAGEOUS STRIP CLUBS

ESCAPED CONVICTS

FRINGE

TRAILER PARKS

SPEED TRAP

ILLEGAL DOG FIGHTS

MURDER

NICE HOUSES?

THUGGED-OUT PIMPS

SHOOTINGS

HITMEN FOR HIRE

DRUG MONEY HOUSES

COPPER THIEVES

OLD BLACK MONEY

WELFARE SCAMMERS

SCRAPPERS

STARBUCKS & CHRISTMAS SWEATERS

THE RACIAL DIVIDING LINE

TREE STUMP COLLECTORS

RATS

GOOD WEED

BURNT OUT HOUSES

ZOMBIES

LOTS OF TRAINS

THE SOUL TRAIN

CRACK HOUSES

DEAD BABIES

KINDA NICE HOUSES

MACK DADDY MANSIONS

GOOSE POOP

KICKASS BBQ

BIG RIM PIMP DADDY

TREES

SWAMP

LOWRIDERS AND QUESADILLAS

GARBAGE

CAR MUSEUM THAT NO ONE VISITS

DESPERATE FLEA MARKETS

CRACK WHORES

CHEAP DRUGS

RANDOM ABANDONMENT

GRUNGY, LOWER MIDDLE CLASS ZONE

THE MOLDY PARK

MIGHT BE HAUNTED

AVID BAPTISTS

FUNKY TOWN

SWAMP MONSTERS

REDNECK ENCLAVE SURROUNDED BY SWAMPS AND FILTH

THE SLABS

SHITTY STRIP CLUBS

METH LABS

MILES DAVIS

STINKY SWAMP

DISMAL SWAMP

REDNECK RACEWAY

DEAD BODIES

CHOP SHOPS

SWAMP

RETURNING TO NATURE

CRAZY HOOKERS

CHEAP HOOKERS

SHITTY DRUGS

VOO DOO

ROVING TEENAGE GANGS

FREE SEX

DRUG DEALERS

THE NEW DOWNTOWN

FAKE WEED

OLD TIRES

FACTORY THAT SMELLS LIKE FARTS

LITTER

JUNGLE EVERYWHERE

JESUS FREAKS

ILLITERACY

RANDOM JUNK

STREETS CRUMBLING AWAY TO NOTHINGNESS

ROTTEN SHACKS

SCORCHED EARTH

CHEMICAL BURN

CHEAP STRIP CLUBS

OVERGROWN GHOST TOWN

HOMELESS CAMPERS

BROWN OUT ZONE

HOBOS

CLASSY PIMPS

RUINS

24/7 MUGGINGS

RATS

SPEEDY HOUSING PROJECT

RATTY OLD MANSIONS

ILLEGAL DRAG RACES

STAGNANT PONDS

TOXIC WASTELAND

WHITE PEOPLE

DEAD DOGS

INDUSTRIAL CLEANUP

WILD DOG PACKS

CASINO TOWN

RV TOURISTS

CRACKHEAD ZOMBIES

CAR THIEVES

THE HOMELESS HOTEL

SOUL FOOD

SEEDY

CHEAP TATTOOS

GIANT GEODESIC DOME

MEAN, VICIOUS DOGS

URBAN PRAIRIE

TOURISTS

POOP

TINA TURNER PLAYED HERE

STREETS OF EMPTINESS

GOOD DRUGS

GUNSHOTS

SHACKS

HICKS

HOMELESS HIDEOUT

THE MEGA FOUNTAIN

DEAD BODIES

SCARY STRIP CLUB

WILD DOGS

HITCHHIKERS

WEIRD STRIP CLUBS

INDUSTRIAL WASTELAND

THE BIKER METAL BAR

FACTORY THAT SMELLS LIKE FARTS

"The factories on Missouri Avenue always smell like they're producing farts. But, what if the people who live nearby are actually farting all the time, and it smells like factories?"
Dani V.

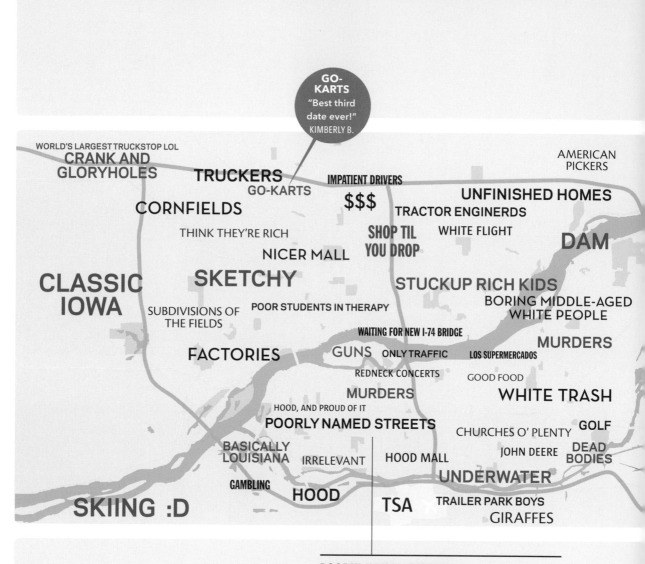

GO-KARTS
"Best third date ever!"
KIMBERLY B.

WORLD'S LARGEST TRUCKSTOP LOL
CRANK AND GLORYHOLES

AMERICAN PICKERS

TRUCKERS
GO-KARTS

IMPATIENT DRIVERS

UNFINISHED HOMES

CORNFIELDS

$$$

TRACTOR ENGINERDS

THINK THEY'RE RICH

SHOP TIL YOU DROP

WHITE FLIGHT

DAM

NICER MALL

CLASSIC IOWA

SKETCHY

STUCKUP RICH KIDS

SUBDIVISIONS OF THE FIELDS

POOR STUDENTS IN THERAPY

BORING MIDDLE-AGED WHITE PEOPLE

WAITING FOR NEW I-74 BRIDGE

MURDERS

FACTORIES

GUNS

ONLY TRAFFIC

LOS SUPERMERCADOS

REDNECK CONCERTS

GOOD FOOD

MURDERS

WHITE TRASH

HOOD, AND PROUD OF IT
POORLY NAMED STREETS

CHURCHES O' PLENTY

GOLF

BASICALLY LOUISIANA

IRRELEVANT

HOOD MALL

JOHN DEERE

DEAD BODIES

GAMBLING

HOOD

UNDERWATER

SKIING :D

TSA

TRAILER PARK BOYS

GIRAFFES

POORLY NAMED STREETS:

"Saying your address is on the corner of 24 ½ St. and 24 St. means the pizza guy will always be thirty minutes late. I haven't paid for a pizza in five years."
JOEL G.

QUAD CITIES
IOWA AND ILLINOIS

The Quad Cities are comprised of Davenport and Bettendorf, IA and Rock Island, Moline, and East Moline, IL, who have joined forces to try and become one relevant region. Now, you may realize that is five cities. Yet, Quad Citians can actually count—the name of the region came from the rising popularity of four riverside towns in the 1930s. Bettendorf rose to popularity later, but the "Quad Cities" name had already stuck (classic Bettendorf). Contrary to popular belief, the famous hip-hop group Quad City DJs have nothing to do with the cities. However, as a consolation prize, the area serves as the headquarters for John Deere.

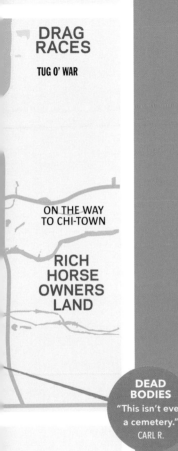

DRAG RACES

TUG O' WAR

ON THE WAY TO CHI-TOWN

RICH HORSE OWNERS LAND

DEAD BODIES
"This isn't even a cemetery."
CARL R.

DRUNK EVERY WEEKEND
"'Drunk Every Weekend' could be Detroit's official slogan. But that wouldn't account for all the rampant bankruptcy."
WILL C.

KLAN

WATCH YOUR BACK, TED NUGENT MIGHT SHOOT YOU

TEETH OPTIONAL

METH ENTREPRENEURS

ALCOHOLICS WITH BAD TASTE

ARABS ENJOYING NATURE

COUNTRY MUSIC CAPITAL OF THE MIDWEST

MILLIONAIRES WHO LIKE COUNTRY MUSIC

PEOPLE WITH TRUCKS

HOCKEY FANS

ISRAEL

GAZA

WEST BANK

METH LABS

GREAT WEED!

TURNING A LITTLE BLACK

MORE PEOPLE WITH TRUCKS

WHITES WHO USE TO LIVE IN REDFORD

CHEAPSKATES WHO DON'T MIND THE COMMUTE TO ANN ARBOR

EXTREMELY WHITE

BIPOLAR TEA PARTY ACTIVISTS

STILL RURAL!

MORE JUGGALOS

PREGNANT CHRISTIAN TEENS

BECOMING LESS RURAL EVERY SECOND

INTENSELY BORING

GREAT WEED!

PRETTY DARN WHITE

TONS OF LESBIANS

PHD BARISTAS

WHERE MANY GARAGE ROCKERS SPENT TROUBLED CHILDHOODS

TECH MILLIONAIRES

MORE NANNIES GIVING BLOWJOBS TRUSTAFARIANS

SLIGHTLY LESS WHITE

DETROIT
MICHIGAN

Detroit is the poorest city in America. While $1 million can buy you a 700-square-foot apartment in San Francisco, $1 million can buy you Detroit. But, the city has character and soul. It isn't what the media and news

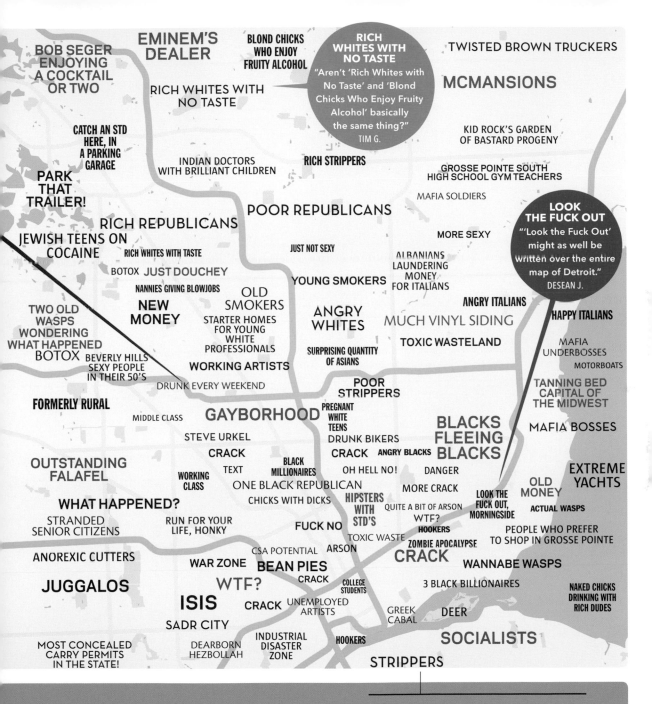

BOB SEGER ENJOYING A COCKTAIL OR TWO

EMINEM'S DEALER

BLOND CHICKS WHO ENJOY FRUITY ALCOHOL

TWISTED BROWN TRUCKERS

MCMANSIONS

RICH WHITES WITH NO TASTE

RICH WHITES WITH NO TASTE
"Aren't 'Rich Whites with No Taste' and 'Blond Chicks Who Enjoy Fruity Alcohol' basically the same thing?"
TIM G.

CATCH AN STD HERE, IN A PARKING GARAGE

KID ROCK'S GARDEN OF BASTARD PROGENY

INDIAN DOCTORS WITH BRILLIANT CHILDREN

RICH STRIPPERS

GROSSE POINTE SOUTH HIGH SCHOOL GYM TEACHERS

PARK THAT TRAILER!

MAFIA SOLDIERS

POOR REPUBLICANS

LOOK THE FUCK OUT
"'Look the Fuck Out' might as well be written over the entire map of Detroit."
DESEAN J.

RICH REPUBLICANS

MORE SEXY

JEWISH TEENS ON COCAINE

RICH WHITES WITH TASTE

JUST NOT SEXY

ALBANIANS LAUNDERING MONEY FOR ITALIANS

BOTOX JUST DOUCHEY

YOUNG SMOKERS

NANNIES GIVING BLOWJOBS

NEW MONEY

OLD SMOKERS

ANGRY WHITES

ANGRY ITALIANS

HAPPY ITALIANS

TWO OLD WASPS WONDERING WHAT HAPPENED

STARTER HOMES FOR YOUNG WHITE PROFESSIONALS

MUCH VINYL SIDING

TOXIC WASTELAND

MAFIA UNDERBOSSES

BOTOX

BEVERLY HILLS SEXY PEOPLE IN THEIR 50'S

SURPRISING QUANTITY OF ASIANS

MOTORBOATS

WORKING ARTISTS

DRUNK EVERY WEEKEND

POOR STRIPPERS

TANNING BED CAPITAL OF THE MIDWEST

FORMERLY RURAL

MIDDLE CLASS

GAYBORHOOD

PREGNANT WHITE TEENS

BLACKS FLEEING BLACKS

MAFIA BOSSES

STEVE URKEL

DRUNK BIKERS

CRACK

CRACK

ANGRY BLACKS

OUTSTANDING FALAFEL

WORKING CLASS

TEXT

BLACK MILLIONAIRES

OH HELL NO!

DANGER

OLD MONEY

EXTREME YACHTS

ONE BLACK REPUBLICAN

MORE CRACK

LOOK THE FUCK OUT, MORNINGSIDE

ACTUAL WASPS

WHAT HAPPENED?

CHICKS WITH DICKS

HIPSTERS WITH STD'S

QUITE A BIT OF ARSON

WTF?

STRANDED SENIOR CITIZENS

RUN FOR YOUR LIFE, HONKY

FUCK NO

HOOKERS

PEOPLE WHO PREFER TO SHOP IN GROSSE POINTE

TOXIC WASTE

ZOMBIE APOCALYPSE

ANOREXIC CUTTERS

CSA POTENTIAL

ARSON

CRACK

WANNABE WASPS

WAR ZONE

BEAN PIES

JUGGALOS

WTF?

CRACK

COLLEGE STUDENTS

3 BLACK BILLIONAIRES

NAKED CHICKS DRINKING WITH RICH DUDES

ISIS

CRACK

UNEMPLOYED ARTISTS

GREEK CABAL

DEER

SADR CITY

MOST CONCEALED CARRY PERMITS IN THE STATE!

DEARBORN HEZBOLLAH

INDUSTRIAL DISASTER ZONE

HOOKERS

SOCIALISTS

STRIPPERS

says it is. The city is rebuilding itself to the tune of Eminem and the Lions. It will rise from the ashes. So, much like tourists visiting Detroit, look the fuck out.

STRIPPERS

"Everybody knows that the best strippers are Canadian. Detroit is one of the few American cities where you can venture down south to get a taste of the great north. Yes, it's hard to believe I am somebody's father."
CHRIS G.

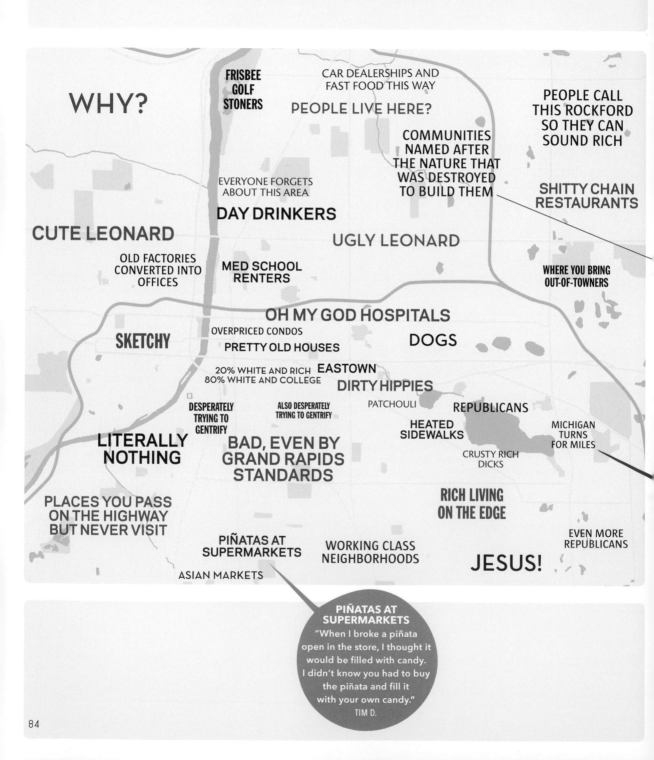

WHY?

FRISBEE GOLF STONERS

CAR DEALERSHIPS AND FAST FOOD THIS WAY

PEOPLE LIVE HERE?

PEOPLE CALL THIS ROCKFORD SO THEY CAN SOUND RICH

COMMUNITIES NAMED AFTER THE NATURE THAT WAS DESTROYED TO BUILD THEM

EVERYONE FORGETS ABOUT THIS AREA

SHITTY CHAIN RESTAURANTS

DAY DRINKERS

CUTE LEONARD

UGLY LEONARD

OLD FACTORIES CONVERTED INTO OFFICES

MED SCHOOL RENTERS

WHERE YOU BRING OUT-OF-TOWNERS

OH MY GOD HOSPITALS

SKETCHY

OVERPRICED CONDOS

PRETTY OLD HOUSES

DOGS

20% WHITE AND RICH
80% WHITE AND COLLEGE

EASTOWN

DIRTY HIPPIES

PATCHOULI

REPUBLICANS

DESPERATELY TRYING TO GENTRIFY

ALSO DESPERATELY TRYING TO GENTRIFY

HEATED SIDEWALKS

MICHIGAN TURNS FOR MILES

LITERALLY NOTHING

BAD, EVEN BY GRAND RAPIDS STANDARDS

CRUSTY RICH DICKS

RICH LIVING ON THE EDGE

PLACES YOU PASS ON THE HIGHWAY BUT NEVER VISIT

EVEN MORE REPUBLICANS

PIÑATAS AT SUPERMARKETS

WORKING CLASS NEIGHBORHOODS

JESUS!

ASIAN MARKETS

PIÑATAS AT SUPERMARKETS
"When I broke a piñata open in the store, I thought it would be filled with candy. I didn't know you had to buy the piñata and fill it with your own candy."
TIM D.

GRAND RAPIDS
MICHIGAN

Grand Rapids is the second largest city in Michigan, which easily makes it the best city in Michigan. The city is nicknamed "Furniture City" because of its strong support of the couch potato community during the latter half of the nineteenth century, and is still a leading city in office furniture, the most exciting type of furniture. In 2013, Grand Rapids was declared "Beer City USA" due to its many prominent breweries and supporting taxi companies in the area. The city is also home to ArtPrize, the world's largest art competition determined by public voting, which is a lot like Grand Rapids Idol, but for art.

COMMUNITIES NAMED AFTER THE NATURE THAT WAS DESTROYED BUILDING THEM

"Everything here is named after the nature we destroyed: Huron Manor, Aspen Lakes, Dollar Tree."
MAXWELL S.

MICHIGAN TURNS FOR MILES

"The Michigan left turn was created to confuse the shit out of people and cause accidents across the state."
KEVIN R.

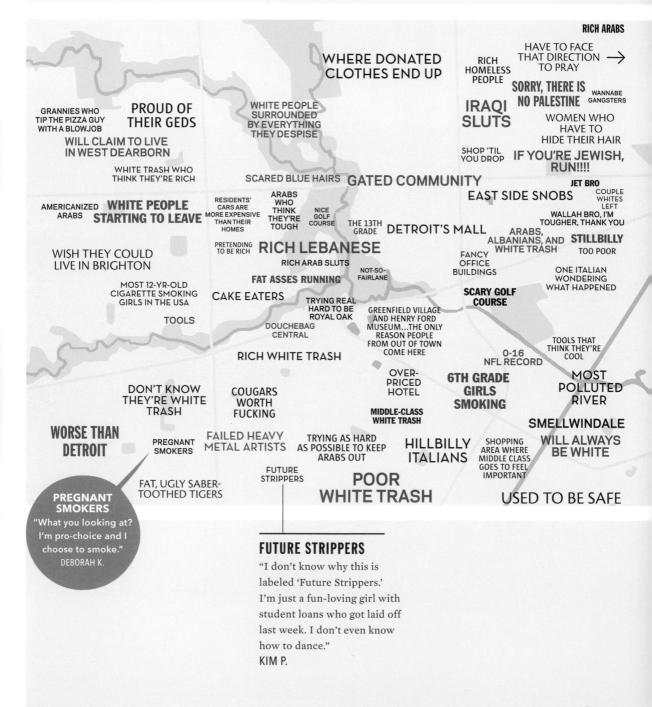

RICH ARABS

HAVE TO FACE THAT DIRECTION TO PRAY →

WHERE DONATED CLOTHES END UP

RICH HOMELESS PEOPLE

SORRY, THERE IS NO PALESTINE

WANNABE GANGSTERS

GRANNIES WHO TIP THE PIZZA GUY WITH A BLOWJOB

PROUD OF THEIR GEDS

WHITE PEOPLE SURROUNDED BY EVERYTHING THEY DESPISE

IRAQI SLUTS

WOMEN WHO HAVE TO HIDE THEIR HAIR

WILL CLAIM TO LIVE IN WEST DEARBORN

SHOP 'TIL YOU DROP

IF YOU'RE JEWISH, RUN!!!!

WHITE TRASH WHO THINK THEY'RE RICH

SCARED BLUE HAIRS

GATED COMMUNITY

JET BRO

EAST SIDE SNOBS

COUPLE WHITES LEFT

AMERICANIZED ARABS

WHITE PEOPLE STARTING TO LEAVE

RESIDENTS' CARS ARE MORE EXPENSIVE THAN THEIR HOMES

ARABS WHO THINK THEY'RE TOUGH

NICE GOLF COURSE

THE 13TH GRADE

DETROIT'S MALL

WALLAH BRO, I'M TOUGHER, THANK YOU

ARABS, ALBANIANS, AND WHITE TRASH

STILLBILLY TOO POOR

WISH THEY COULD LIVE IN BRIGHTON

PRETENDING TO BE RICH

RICH LEBANESE

FANCY OFFICE BUILDINGS

ONE ITALIAN WONDERING WHAT HAPPENED

RICH ARAB SLUTS

NOT-SO-FAIRLANE

MOST 12-YR-OLD CIGARETTE SMOKING GIRLS IN THE USA

FAT ASSES RUNNING

SCARY GOLF COURSE

CAKE EATERS

TRYING REAL HARD TO BE ROYAL OAK

TOOLS

DOUCHEBAG CENTRAL

GREENFIELD VILLAGE AND HENRY FORD MUSEUM...THE ONLY REASON PEOPLE FROM OUT OF TOWN COME HERE

TOOLS THAT THINK THEY'RE COOL

RICH WHITE TRASH

0-16 NFL RECORD

OVER-PRICED HOTEL

6TH GRADE GIRLS SMOKING

MOST POLLUTED RIVER

DON'T KNOW THEY'RE WHITE TRASH

COUGARS WORTH FUCKING

MIDDLE-CLASS WHITE TRASH

SMELLWINDALE

WILL ALWAYS BE WHITE

WORSE THAN DETROIT

PREGNANT SMOKERS

FAILED HEAVY METAL ARTISTS

TRYING AS HARD AS POSSIBLE TO KEEP ARABS OUT

HILLBILLY ITALIANS

SHOPPING AREA WHERE MIDDLE CLASS GOES TO FEEL IMPORTANT

FUTURE STRIPPERS

FAT, UGLY SABER-TOOTHED TIGERS

POOR WHITE TRASH

USED TO BE SAFE

PREGNANT SMOKERS

"What you looking at? I'm pro-choice and I choose to smoke."
DEBORAH K.

FUTURE STRIPPERS

"I don't know why this is labeled 'Future Strippers.' I'm just a fun-loving girl with student loans who got laid off last week. I don't even know how to dance."
KIM P.

DEARBORN
MICHIGAN

Dearborn is the world headquarters of Ford Motor Company, creator of the world-famous Pinto and Edsel cars. The city also has the largest percentage of Arabs in America, which means the baba ghanoush is to die for, and nearly everyone in Dearborn is racially profiled in the Detroit airport.

BARS ON WINDOWS

PACKS OF WILD DOGS

POOR LEBANESE

LIFE EXPECTANCY IS 30

DRIVE-IN MOVIE

HOOKERS AS FAR AS THE EYE CAN SEE

WHERE ARAB WEED IS GROWN

JIMMY HOFFA'S GRAVE

COPS ARE SCARED TO GO HERE

RICH YEMENIS

MEXICAN HOOKERS THAT LOOK LIKE MEN

NO ENGLISH SPOKEN HERE

WHERE DETROIT COPS COOK METH

POOR YEMENIS

POLLUTION

WHERE 14-YR-OLDS LEARN TO BE HOOKERS

USED TO BE ITALIAN

FREE BLOWJOBS

HOOKERS

COPS ARE SCARED TO GO HERE
"It's not because of the crime or meth heads. Just with the ghost of Jimmy Hoffa haunting the place and those damn wild dogs running around, it's just not safe."
SGT. BILL THOMAS

MINNEAPOLIS ST. PAUL
MINNESOTA

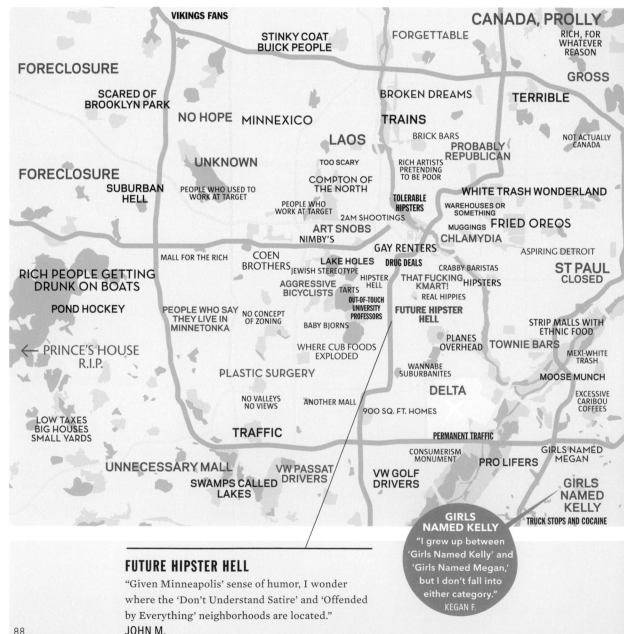

VIKINGS FANS

STINKY COAT BUICK PEOPLE

FORGETTABLE

CANADA, PROLLY

RICH, FOR WHATEVER REASON

FORECLOSURE

GROSS

SCARED OF BROOKLYN PARK

BROKEN DREAMS

TERRIBLE

NO HOPE   MINNEXICO

TRAINS

LAOS

BRICK BARS

PROBABLY REPUBLICAN

NOT ACTUALLY CANADA

UNKNOWN

TOO SCARY

RICH ARTISTS PRETENDING TO BE POOR

FORECLOSURE

SUBURBAN HELL

PEOPLE WHO USED TO WORK AT TARGET

COMPTON OF THE NORTH

WHITE TRASH WONDERLAND

WAREHOUSES OR SOMETHING

PEOPLE WHO WORK AT TARGET

TOLERABLE HIPSTERS

MUGGINGS   FRIED OREOS

2AM SHOOTINGS

ART SNOBS

CHLAMYDIA

NIMBY'S

MALL FOR THE RICH

GAY RENTERS

COEN BROTHERS

LAKE HOLES

DRUG DEALS

ASPIRING DETROIT

JEWISH STEREOTYPE

CRABBY BARISTAS

ST PAUL CLOSED

RICH PEOPLE GETTING DRUNK ON BOATS

HIPSTER HELL

THAT FUCKING KMART!

HIPSTERS

AGGRESSIVE BICYCLISTS   TARTS

OUT-OF-TOUCH UNIVERSITY PROFESSORS

REAL HIPPIES

POND HOCKEY

NO CONCEPT OF ZONING

PEOPLE WHO SAY THEY LIVE IN MINNETONKA

BABY BJORNS

FUTURE HIPSTER HELL

STRIP MALLS WITH ETHNIC FOOD

PLANES OVERHEAD

TOWNIE BARS

← PRINCE'S HOUSE R.I.P.

WHERE CUB FOODS EXPLODED

MEXI-WHITE TRASH

PLASTIC SURGERY

WANNABE SUBURBANITES

MOOSE MUNCH

NO VALLEYS NO VIEWS

ANOTHER MALL

DELTA

EXCESSIVE CARIBOU COFFEES

900 SQ. FT. HOMES

LOW TAXES BIG HOUSES SMALL YARDS

TRAFFIC

PERMANENT TRAFFIC

GIRLS NAMED MEGAN

CONSUMERISM MONUMENT

UNNECESSARY MALL

VW PASSAT DRIVERS

PRO LIFERS

SWAMPS CALLED LAKES

VW GOLF DRIVERS

GIRLS NAMED KELLY

TRUCK STOPS AND COCAINE

GIRLS NAMED KELLY
"I grew up between 'Girls Named Kelly' and 'Girls Named Megan,' but I don't fall into either category."
KEGAN F.

FUTURE HIPSTER HELL
"Given Minneapolis' sense of humor, I wonder where the 'Don't Understand Satire' and 'Offended by Everything' neighborhoods are located."
JOHN M.

Ahh, the Twin Cities. Two great metropolises divided by a river, but bound by frozen temperatures and Mary Tyler Moore. The Twin cities have over twenty lakes, so the only problem you'll have is picking which one you want to throw the body into. But all kidding aside, Minneapolis and St. Paul are national treasures, two cubic zirconias in America's urban crown.

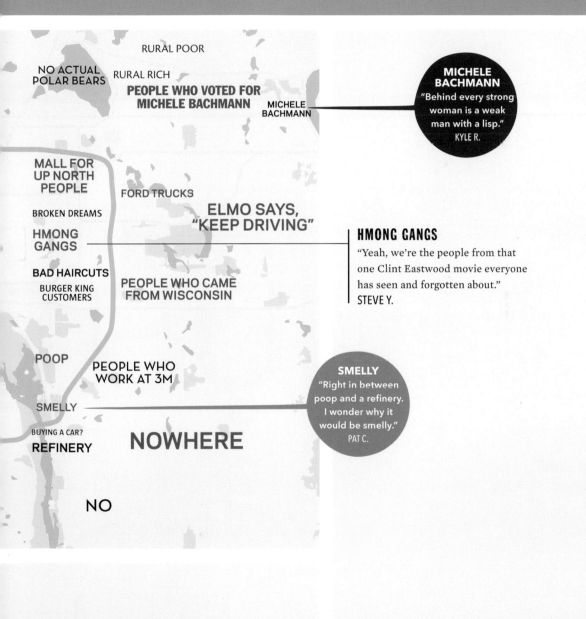

RURAL POOR

NO ACTUAL
POLAR BEARS

RURAL RICH

**PEOPLE WHO VOTED FOR
MICHELE BACHMANN**

MICHELE
BACHMANN

**MICHELE
BACHMANN**
"Behind every strong
woman is a weak
man with a lisp."
KYLE R.

**MALL FOR
UP NORTH
PEOPLE**

FORD TRUCKS

ELMO SAYS,
"KEEP DRIVING"

BROKEN DREAMS

**HMONG
GANGS**

HMONG GANGS
"Yeah, we're the people from that
one Clint Eastwood movie everyone
has seen and forgotten about."
STEVE Y.

BAD HAIRCUTS

BURGER KING
CUSTOMERS

**PEOPLE WHO CAME
FROM WISCONSIN**

POOP

PEOPLE WHO
WORK AT 3M

SMELLY
"Right in between
poop and a refinery.
I wonder why it
would be smelly."
PAT C.

SMELLY

BUYING A CAR?

REFINERY

NOWHERE

NO

FARGO
NORTH DAKOTA

KIDDING

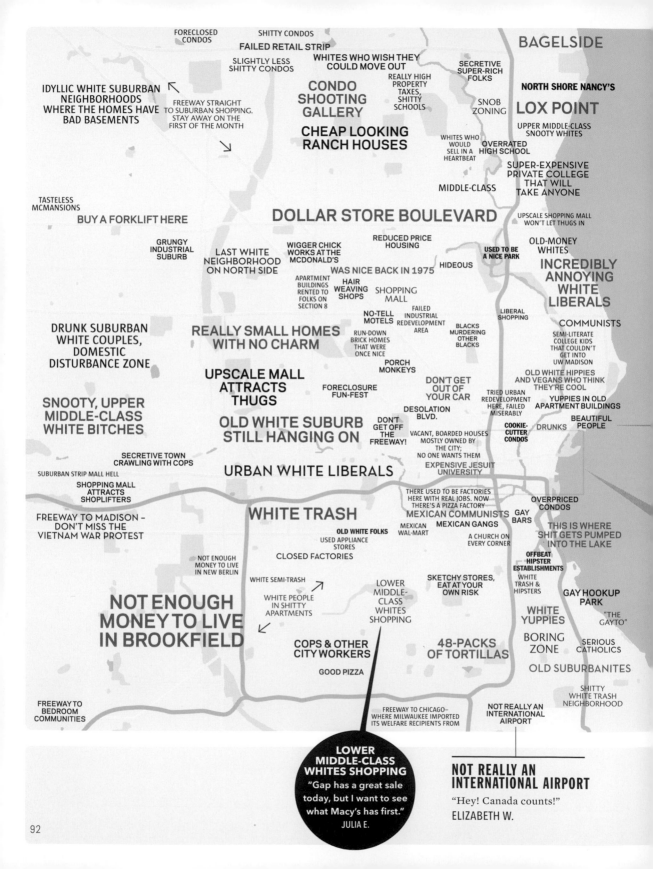

FORECLOSED CONDOS

SHITTY CONDOS

FAILED RETAIL STRIP

WHITES WHO WISH THEY COULD MOVE OUT

SECRETIVE SUPER-RICH FOLKS

BAGELSIDE

SLIGHTLY LESS SHITTY CONDOS

REALLY HIGH PROPERTY TAXES, SHITTY SCHOOLS

NORTH SHORE NANCY'S

IDYLLIC WHITE SUBURBAN NEIGHBORHOODS WHERE THE HOMES HAVE BAD BASEMENTS

FREEWAY STRAIGHT TO SUBURBAN SHOPPING. STAY AWAY ON THE FIRST OF THE MONTH

CONDO SHOOTING GALLERY

SNOB ZONING

LOX POINT

UPPER MIDDLE-CLASS SNOOTY WHITES

CHEAP LOOKING RANCH HOUSES

WHITES WHO WOULD SELL IN A HEARTBEAT

OVERRATED HIGH SCHOOL

MIDDLE-CLASS

SUPER-EXPENSIVE PRIVATE COLLEGE THAT WILL TAKE ANYONE

TASTELESS MCMANSIONS

BUY A FORKLIFT HERE

DOLLAR STORE BOULEVARD

UPSCALE SHOPPING MALL WON'T LET THUGS IN

GRUNGY INDUSTRIAL SUBURB

LAST WHITE NEIGHBORHOOD ON NORTH SIDE

WIGGER CHICK WORKS AT THE MCDONALD'S

REDUCED PRICE HOUSING

USED TO BE A NICE PARK

OLD-MONEY WHITES

INCREDIBLY ANNOYING WHITE LIBERALS

WAS NICE BACK IN 1975

HIDEOUS

APARTMENT BUILDINGS RENTED TO FOLKS ON SECTION 8

HAIR WEAVING SHOPS

SHOPPING MALL

LIBERAL SHOPPING

NO-TELL MOTELS

FAILED INDUSTRIAL REDEVELOPMENT AREA

BLACKS MURDERING OTHER BLACKS

COMMUNISTS

SEMI-LITERATE COLLEGE KIDS THAT COULDN'T GET INTO UW MADISON

DRUNK SUBURBAN WHITE COUPLES, DOMESTIC DISTURBANCE ZONE

REALLY SMALL HOMES WITH NO CHARM

RUN-DOWN BRICK HOMES THAT WERE ONCE NICE

PORCH MONKEYS

OLD WHITE HIPPIES AND VEGANS WHO THINK THEY'RE COOL

UPSCALE MALL ATTRACTS THUGS

FORECLOSURE FUN-FEST

DON'T GET OUT OF YOUR CAR

TRIED URBAN REDEVELOPMENT HERE, FAILED MISERABLY

YUPPIES IN OLD APARTMENT BUILDINGS

SNOOTY, UPPER MIDDLE-CLASS WHITE BITCHES

OLD WHITE SUBURB STILL HANGING ON

DON'T GET OFF THE FREEWAY!

DESOLATION BLVD.

COOKIE-CUTTER CONDOS

BEAUTIFUL PEOPLE

DRUNKS

VACANT, BOARDED HOUSES MOSTLY OWNED BY THE CITY; NO ONE WANTS THEM

SECRETIVE TOWN CRAWLING WITH COPS

URBAN WHITE LIBERALS

EXPENSIVE JESUIT UNIVERSITY

SUBURBAN STRIP MALL HELL

SHOPPING MALL ATTRACTS SHOPLIFTERS

THERE USED TO BE FACTORIES HERE WITH REAL JOBS. NOW THERE'S A PIZZA FACTORY

OVERPRICED CONDOS

FREEWAY TO MADISON – DON'T MISS THE VIETNAM WAR PROTEST

WHITE TRASH

MEXICAN COMMUNISTS

GAY BARS

THIS IS WHERE SHIT GETS PUMPED INTO THE LAKE

OLD WHITE FOLKS

MEXICAN WAL-MART

MEXICAN GANGS

NOT ENOUGH MONEY TO LIVE IN NEW BERLIN

USED APPLIANCE STORES

A CHURCH ON EVERY CORNER

OFFBEAT HIPSTER ESTABLISHMENTS

CLOSED FACTORIES

WHITE TRASH & HIPSTERS

WHITE SEMI-TRASH

NOT ENOUGH MONEY TO LIVE IN BROOKFIELD

WHITE PEOPLE IN SHITTY APARTMENTS

LOWER MIDDLE-CLASS WHITES SHOPPING

SKETCHY STORES, EAT AT YOUR OWN RISK

GAY HOOKUP PARK

WHITE YUPPIES

"THE GAYTO"

COPS & OTHER CITY WORKERS

48-PACKS OF TORTILLAS

BORING ZONE

SERIOUS CATHOLICS

GOOD PIZZA

OLD SUBURBANITES

FREEWAY TO BEDROOM COMMUNITIES

FREEWAY TO CHICAGO– WHERE MILWAUKEE IMPORTED ITS WELFARE RECIPIENTS FROM

NOT REALLY AN INTERNATIONAL AIRPORT

SHITTY WHITE TRASH NEIGHBORHOOD

LOWER MIDDLE-CLASS WHITES SHOPPING

"Gap has a great sale today, but I want to see what Macy's has first."

JULIA E.

NOT REALLY AN INTERNATIONAL AIRPORT

"Hey! Canada counts!"

ELIZABETH W.

MILWAUKEE
WISCONSIN

If beer is Milwaukee's Best, being named the most segregated city in the country is certainly Milwaukee's Worst. But Chicago Jr. has come a long way, being named as the seventh most dangerous city in America in 2015. The gem city of the Great Lakes offers a lot of activities in the summer, but people resort to binge drinking and unrestrained cheese-curd consumption to pass time in the winter.

WHITEFOLKS BAY

BEAUTIFUL PEOPLE
"I'm a 6 in New York, a 4 in LA and an 11 in Milwaukee."
JOSH R.

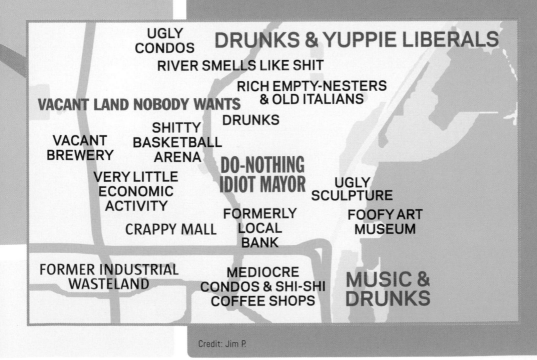

UGLY CONDOS

DRUNKS & YUPPIE LIBERALS

RIVER SMELLS LIKE SHIT

RICH EMPTY-NESTERS & OLD ITALIANS

VACANT LAND NOBODY WANTS

DRUNKS

VACANT BREWERY

SHITTY BASKETBALL ARENA

DO-NOTHING IDIOT MAYOR

VERY LITTLE ECONOMIC ACTIVITY

UGLY SCULPTURE

FORMERLY LOCAL BANK

FOOFY ART MUSEUM

CRAPPY MALL

FORMER INDUSTRIAL WASTELAND

MEDIOCRE CONDOS & SHI-SHI COFFEE SHOPS

MUSIC & DRUNKS

Credit: Jim P.

TAVERNS, SO MANY TAVERNS

OLD PEOPLE

PRETTY OKAY PIZZA AND BURRITOS

ABANDONED MALL

ARTISTS

WAKING UP IN BUGATTIS

WEIRD HIPSTERS, MUSIC

OLD PEOPLE

SAUSAGE

YOU'LL PROBABLY DIE

COWBOY BARS, MOSTLY DESERTED

EXTREMELY LARGE RICH PEOPLE HOUSES

FADED GRANDEUR

IF YOU SWIM IN HERE, YOU WILL DIE

INDUSTRIAL WASTELAND

PROBABLY MONEY

WEIRD MARINAS

GOOD PIZZA

ALMOST CERTAIN DEATH

PROBABLY EITHER MONEY OR NOT

SURPRISINGLY PLEASANT

POINTLESS AIRPORT NOBODY LIKES OR USES, EXCEPT LEBRON JAMES

INEXPLICABLY SLOVENIANS

MILE AFTER MILE OF RETAIL BULLSHIT

CORNED BEEF

COOL CEMETERY

SALT MINE (APPROX)

ASIANS

DOCTORS

MED STUDENTS

POOR COLLEGE STUDENTS

RICH COLLEGE STUDENTS

WHITE PEOPLE WITH SMALL HOUSES

MARKETING EXECS

ITALIANS

HIPPIES

WHOLE FOODS, FOR THE LIBERALS

FRATBOYLANDIA

NOTHING. LITERALLY NOTHING.

ASIAN MED STUDENTS

LIBERALS

BEARDED HIPSTERS

BEER

REALLY POOR COLLEGE STUDENTS

RICH PEOPLE

RICHER PEOPLE

DRIVE SLLLOOOOWW

NORTH FACE, PROBABLY

POLISH PEOPLE AND PEOPLE WHO WOULD ENJOY BEING POLISH

HIPSTERS

ARTISTS

VELODROME OR SOMETHING

MAYBE FIVE HUNGARIANS STILL GOOD RESTAURANTS

REALLY GODDAMN RICH PEOPLE

POOL YOU'RE NOT ALLOWED IN

PBS ENTHUSIASTS

PUNK ROCK MUSIC

HOT DOGS

LIBERALS

ARTISTS

BOWLING. NOTHING BUT BOWLING.

PUERTO RICANS

BIG, DUMB MALL

SLUMMING HIPSTERS

LITTLE CAESARS AND BOOST MOBILES

FANCY WHITE PEOPLE

GERMANS AND PUERTO RICANS AND MEXICANS, OH MY

HILLBILLIES?

BRIMSTONE, ASHES, ACRID SCENTS, OLD TIRES, WEIRD-COLORED WATER, DELIGHTFUL NATURE TRAIL

POOR WHITE AND BLACK PEOPLE

TAVERNS

LESS FANCY WHITE PEOPLE

POOR WHITE PEOPLE

CREEPY HORSE-RACING TRACK

DREW CAREY

THRIFTSTORE-LANDIA

POSSIBLY SAUSAGE

WORLD'S CREEPIEST ABANDONED MALL

OLD PEOPLE

OLD PEOPLE

OLD PEOPLE

PACKS OF STRAY DOGS

OLD PEOPLE

BEER

OLD PEOPLE

UKRAINIANS

AIRPORTLANDIA

WHITE PEOPLE WEARING SOCK SUSPENDERS

GRILLED CHEESE

↓ LEBRON JAMES

CLEVELAND
OHIO

Most of us know the city as "The C Word," but whatever you call it, Cleveland rocks! And they have the Cleveland Browns and Lebron James to prove it. They also have the Rock and Roll Hall of Fame, awarded to the city because it is the hometown of Nine Inch Nails and Bone Thugs-N-Harmony. The city hosted the 2014 Gay Games and the 2016 Republican National Convention. So, it is safe to say the city is confused. Come visit "The Mistake on the Lake," and let Cleveland set you on fire, just like they set the Cuyahoga River on fire in 1969.

FOREST CREATURES

MAYBE AMISH

RETAILAGEDDON

APPLES

ALMOST CERTAIN DEATH
"Cleveland is a really great place to live if you mind your own fucking business."
KEN G.

ONLY WORTH THE FISHING

INSANELY RICH PEOPLE

AMISH-LIKE

THE ONLY TRADER JOE'S FOR 9,000 MILES

OLD PEOPLE

FROU FROU RICH PEOPLE AND RICH PEOPLE ACCESSORIES

FROU FROU RICH PEOPLE AND RICH PEOPLE ACCESSORIES
"Frou Frou is also the name of my toy poodle."
EVELYN T.

COLUMBUS

OHIO

Columbus is the home to *The* Ohio State University, one of the largest universities and best college football teams in the nation. It's city policy to stab Michigan fans. Along with a gigantic university, Columbus is also the home to Wendy's and White Castle, which help to make students as big as the university. Although never accused of being the most glamorous place to be, Abercrombie and Fitch is headquartered here, adding a lot of jobs and shirtless guys to the biggest small town in America. Best of all, "The Columbus Experiment" of 1908 produced the world's first water plant to apply filtration and softening. So, you can rest assured that Columbus isn't Flint.

Credit: Eric

↑
TO AMISH COUNTRY

SUBURBAN HELL

STRIP MALL-A-PALOOZA!

CALL CENTERS

DIVORCED DAD CONDOS

← TO BERKELEY

?

FUCK IF I KNOW

THE BMV

ACTUALLY SORTA UNDERRATED

MORE WHITE TRASH

NO ONE COMES HERE AFTER 5 PM
"I went to River South one time after 5 p.m. It was so uneventful, I can't think of a reason for you to include anything about it on a map of Columbus or even in your book. I'm serious. I'm bored even talking about it."
KEVIN C.

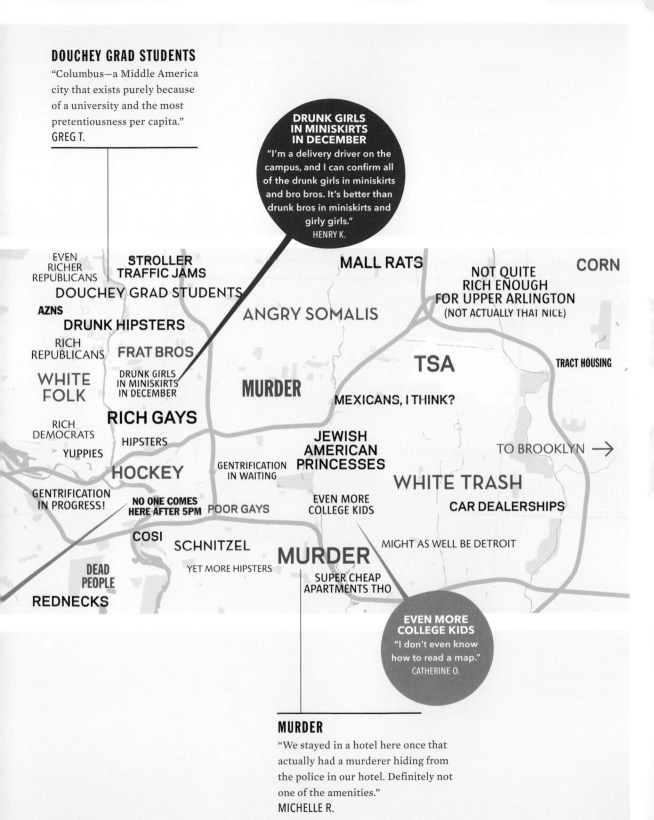

DOUCHEY GRAD STUDENTS

"Columbus—a Middle America city that exists purely because of a university and the most pretentiousness per capita."
GREG T.

DRUNK GIRLS IN MINISKIRTS IN DECEMBER

"I'm a delivery driver on the campus, and I can confirm all of the drunk girls in miniskirts and bro bros. It's better than drunk bros in miniskirts and girly girls."
HENRY K.

EVEN RICHER REPUBLICANS

STROLLER TRAFFIC JAMS

DOUCHEY GRAD STUDENTS

MALL RATS

NOT QUITE RICH ENOUGH FOR UPPER ARLINGTON (NOT ACTUALLY THAT NICE)

CORN

AZNS

DRUNK HIPSTERS

ANGRY SOMALIS

RICH REPUBLICANS

FRAT BROS

TSA

TRACT HOUSING

WHITE FOLK

DRUNK GIRLS IN MINISKIRTS IN DECEMBER

MURDER

MEXICANS, I THINK?

RICH DEMOCRATS

RICH GAYS

HIPSTERS

JEWISH AMERICAN PRINCESSES

TO BROOKLYN →

YUPPIES

HOCKEY

GENTRIFICATION IN WAITING

WHITE TRASH

GENTRIFICATION IN PROGRESS!

NO ONE COMES HERE AFTER 5PM

POOR GAYS

EVEN MORE COLLEGE KIDS

CAR DEALERSHIPS

COSI

SCHNITZEL

MURDER

MIGHT AS WELL BE DETROIT

DEAD PEOPLE

YET MORE HIPSTERS

SUPER CHEAP APARTMENTS THO

REDNECKS

EVEN MORE COLLEGE KIDS

"I don't even know how to read a map."
CATHERINE O.

MURDER

"We stayed in a hotel here once that actually had a murderer hiding from the police in our hotel. Definitely not one of the amenities."
MICHELLE R.

97

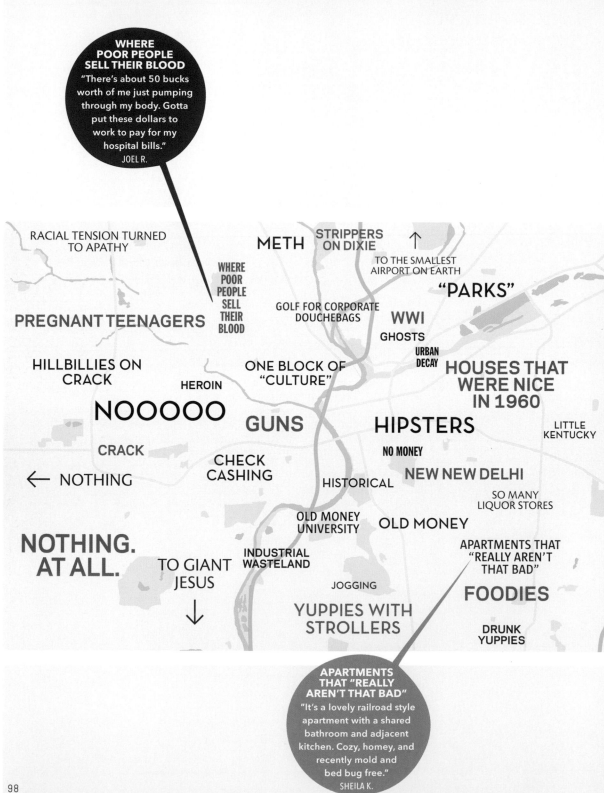

WHERE POOR PEOPLE SELL THEIR BLOOD
"There's about 50 bucks worth of me just pumping through my body. Gotta put these dollars to work to pay for my hospital bills."
JOEL R.

RACIAL TENSION TURNED TO APATHY

METH

STRIPPERS ON DIXIE

↑

TO THE SMALLEST AIRPORT ON EARTH

"PARKS"

WHERE POOR PEOPLE SELL THEIR BLOOD

GOLF FOR CORPORATE DOUCHEBAGS

WWI

GHOSTS

PREGNANT TEENAGERS

URBAN DECAY

HILLBILLIES ON CRACK

ONE BLOCK OF "CULTURE"

HOUSES THAT WERE NICE IN 1960

HEROIN

LITTLE KENTUCKY

NOOOOO

GUNS

HIPSTERS

NO MONEY

CRACK

CHECK CASHING

NEW NEW DELHI

← NOTHING

HISTORICAL

SO MANY LIQUOR STORES

OLD MONEY UNIVERSITY

OLD MONEY

NOTHING. AT ALL.

TO GIANT JESUS

INDUSTRIAL WASTELAND

APARTMENTS THAT "REALLY AREN'T THAT BAD"

JOGGING

↓

FOODIES

YUPPIES WITH STROLLERS

DRUNK YUPPIES

APARTMENTS THAT "REALLY AREN'T THAT BAD"
"It's a lovely railroad style apartment with a shared bathroom and adjacent kitchen. Cozy, homey, and recently mold and bed bug free."
SHEILA K.

DAYTON
OHIO

Dayton is the birthplace of the Wright Brothers and aviation, and the Air Force employs nearly half of the city today. So, you could say the future of Dayton is up in the air! But seriously, the future of Dayton is pretty bright, as indicated by the inebriated students at one of the nation's top party schools: University of Dayton. While Dayton's population has been rapidly declining over the past four decades, the city has been redeeming itself in recent years, with the establishment of minor league baseball team, the Dayton Dragons, aimed at solving the city's most drastic issues.

AIR FORCE—
THE ONLY
EMPLOYER
IN DAYTON

LOWER
MIDDLE CLASS
UNIVERSITY

HIPPIE
VILLAGE
→

MYSTERIOUS
MILITARY
ACTIVITY

NEW
MONEY

SHOPPING
FOR RICH
ASSHOLES

NEW MONEY
"We have a hot tub right next to our outdoor televisions so we can grill, catch the games, and take a soak all at once."
BRUCE T.

TOLEDO
OHIO

Toledo is most notably known as the armpit of Ohio. Others simply call it "avoidable" and give it 1 out of 5 stars. While traffic, even during rush hour, is nearly nonexistent, that isn't the kind of traffic the city needs to worry about. Toledo is the fourth largest recruitment site for human trafficking in the United States. But, the cost of living is low and it is the closest major city to Cedar Point amusement park. And aren't roller coasters what life is really all about? The city is also redeemed by its name rhyming with such a cool word as "torpedo."

CITY FOUNDED BY PEOPLE STUCK IN TRAFFIC

CAR DEALERSHIPS AND NOT MUCH ELSE

MORE "SHOPPING"

SO NICE YOU'LL FORGET IT'S TOLEDO:
"This is the best place in town. Right next to the Arby's and across the street from Wendy's. The scent of processed lunch meats, the breeze off the river, and light at sunset reminds me of Paris."
JOAN A.

← TO "AIRPORT"

MORE SHOPPING FOR RICH ASSHOLES:
"They even put the Express right next to the Victoria's Secret. I hate rich people."
MADELINE W.

MORE SHOPPING FOR RICH ASSHOLES

HIPSTERS:
"I came to Toledo to avoid hipsters. How the hell did they get here?"
TREVOR H.

STRIP CLUBS AND INDUSTRIAL WASTE

WHERE POOR KIDS SPEND WEEKENDS

HOUR-LONG TRAFFIC JAM

TO CITY THAT MAKES TOLEDO LOOK AWESOME (DETROIT)

DEL TACO

HIPSTERS

HIDE YO KIDS HIDE YO WIFE

OLD MONEY AND "KAKISTOCRACY"

PEOPLE STILL WAITING FOR CLEAN WATER

HOMELESS

URBAN DECAY TURNED INTO APATHY

POOR?

FARMLAND?

TOSTADAS AND CHALUPAS

TO CEDAR POINT AND ISLANDS

MAYOR OPAL'S "MANSION"

MORE INDUSTRIAL WASTE

WHERE POOR PEOPLE SPEND MONDAYS

WHERE PEOPLE WASTE THEIR PAYCHECKS

SO NICE YOU'LL FORGET IT'S TOLEDO

SPEED TRAP IN THE MIDDLE OF WHERE YOU'RE GOING

SLOWENS

MIDDLE-CLASS YUPPIES

PEOPLE TRAPPED BY TRAINS

"HISTORY" AND CULTURE

NEW MONEY

TO CRAZY COLLEGE PARTIES

TORNADO ALLEY

SHOPPING FOR RICH ASSHOLES

CINCINNATI

OHIO

Cincinnati Chili makes up 65% of the food consumed in the city. So that explains the smell. People say that Cincinnati isn't that bad, which is a promising quality for any city to have. But, luckily its rivals are Cleveland and Columbus. So, grading on a curve makes Cincy nearly the fifth best city in the state. But, much like the Bengals, you have to struggle through the tough times to be almost rewarded with the good times. Cincinnati's culture and food scene is strongly influenced by its German heritage, and the city hosts the largest Oktoberfest celebration outside of Munich. In October, it's time dip your schnitzel in some sauerkraut, and get ready for Cincinnati to show you its wurst.

CASINOS AND DIFFERENT ALCOHOL!:
"You can still gamble just over the state line, and they even offer mixed drinks with ethyl, isopropyl and diacetone."
KENNETH L.

WHITES ON WEEKENDS

CORN

NOTHING HAPPENS OUT HERE

CORN

CORN

CORN

WHAT IS SAYLER PARK, EVEN? IT'S WEIRD

CASINOS AND DIFFERENT ALCOHOL!

FARMS AND NOTHING

FLEA MARKET/ WHITE PEOPLE

LITERALLY NOTHING

AIRPLANE NOISES

MCMANSIONS

RICH, OLD WHITE PEOPLE
"I've got news for you, America. We're not going anywhere anytime soon. We're old, but not that old."
EARL R.

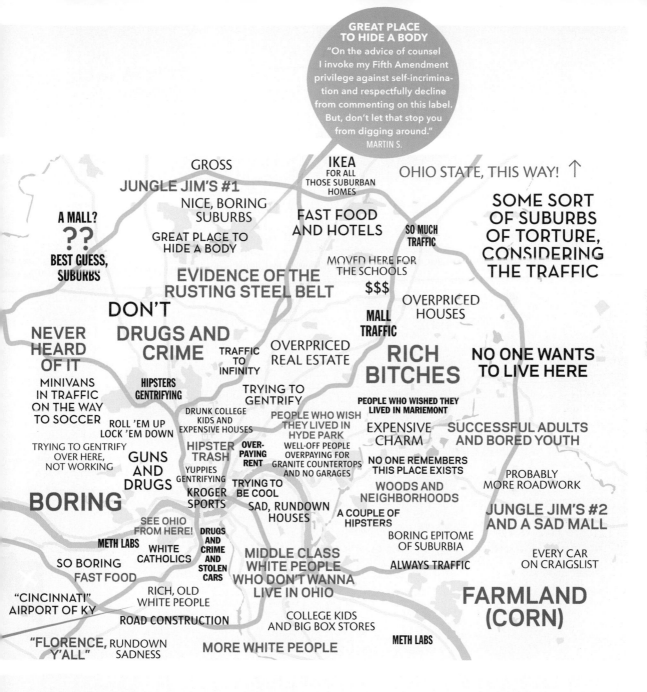

GREAT PLACE TO HIDE A BODY

"On the advice of counsel I invoke my Fifth Amendment privilege against self-incrimination and respectfully decline from commenting on this label. But, don't let that stop you from digging around."
MARTIN S.

GROSS

JUNGLE JIM'S #1

IKEA FOR ALL THOSE SUBURBAN HOMES

OHIO STATE, THIS WAY! ↑

NICE, BORING SUBURBS

A MALL?
??
BEST GUESS, SUBURBS

GREAT PLACE TO HIDE A BODY

FAST FOOD AND HOTELS

SO MUCH TRAFFIC

SOME SORT OF SUBURBS OF TORTURE, CONSIDERING THE TRAFFIC

MOVED HERE FOR THE SCHOOLS

EVIDENCE OF THE RUSTING STEEL BELT

$$$

OVERPRICED HOUSES

DON'T DRUGS AND CRIME

MALL TRAFFIC

NEVER HEARD OF IT

TRAFFIC TO INFINITY

OVERPRICED REAL ESTATE

RICH BITCHES

NO ONE WANTS TO LIVE HERE

MINIVANS IN TRAFFIC ON THE WAY TO SOCCER

HIPSTERS GENTRIFYING

TRYING TO GENTRIFY

PEOPLE WHO WISHED THEY LIVED IN MARIEMONT

ROLL 'EM UP LOCK 'EM DOWN

DRUNK COLLEGE KIDS AND EXPENSIVE HOUSES

PEOPLE WHO WISH THEY LIVED IN HYDE PARK

EXPENSIVE CHARM

SUCCESSFUL ADULTS AND BORED YOUTH

TRYING TO GENTRIFY OVER HERE, NOT WORKING

GUNS AND DRUGS

HIPSTER TRASH

OVER-PAYING RENT

WELL-OFF PEOPLE OVERPAYING FOR GRANITE COUNTERTOPS AND NO GARAGES

NO ONE REMEMBERS THIS PLACE EXISTS

PROBABLY MORE ROADWORK

YUPPIES GENTRIFYING

BORING

KROGER SPORTS

TRYING TO BE COOL

WOODS AND NEIGHBORHOODS

JUNGLE JIM'S #2 AND A SAD MALL

SAD, RUNDOWN HOUSES

A COUPLE OF HIPSTERS

SEE OHIO FROM HERE!

DRUGS AND CRIME AND STOLEN CARS

BORING EPITOME OF SUBURBIA

EVERY CAR ON CRAIGSLIST

METH LABS

WHITE CATHOLICS

MIDDLE CLASS WHITE PEOPLE WHO DON'T WANNA LIVE IN OHIO

ALWAYS TRAFFIC

SO BORING

FAST FOOD

"CINCINNATI" AIRPORT OF KY

RICH, OLD WHITE PEOPLE

FARMLAND (CORN)

ROAD CONSTRUCTION

COLLEGE KIDS AND BIG BOX STORES

"FLORENCE, Y'ALL"

RUNDOWN SADNESS

MORE WHITE PEOPLE

METH LABS

103

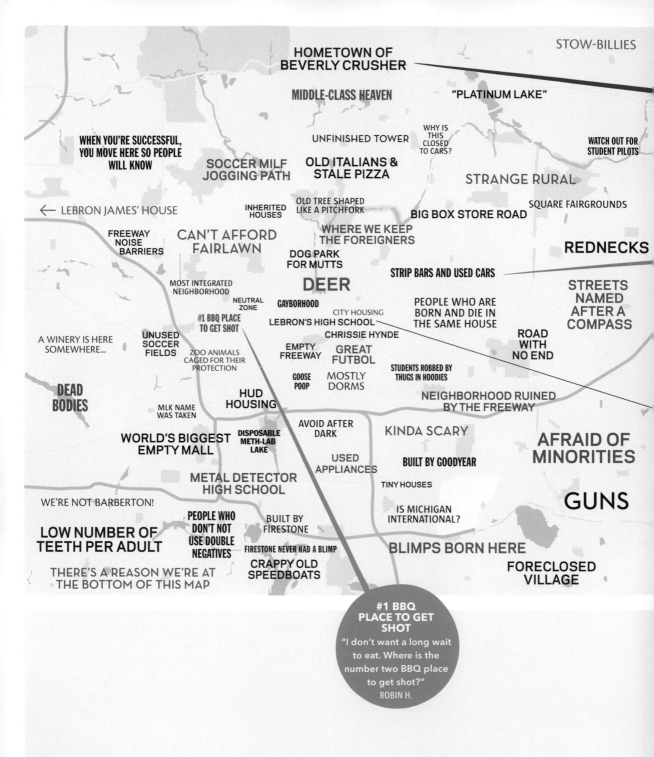

STOW-BILLIES

HOMETOWN OF
BEVERLY CRUSHER

MIDDLE-CLASS HEAVEN

"PLATINUM LAKE"

UNFINISHED TOWER

WHY IS THIS CLOSED TO CARS?

WATCH OUT FOR STUDENT PILOTS

WHEN YOU'RE SUCCESSFUL, YOU MOVE HERE SO PEOPLE WILL KNOW

SOCCER MILF JOGGING PATH

OLD ITALIANS & STALE PIZZA

STRANGE RURAL

← LEBRON JAMES' HOUSE

INHERITED HOUSES

OLD TREE SHAPED LIKE A PITCHFORK

BIG BOX STORE ROAD

SQUARE FAIRGROUNDS

FREEWAY NOISE BARRIERS

CAN'T AFFORD FAIRLAWN

WHERE WE KEEP THE FOREIGNERS

REDNECKS

DOG PARK FOR MUTTS

STRIP BARS AND USED CARS

STREETS NAMED AFTER A COMPASS

MOST INTEGRATED NEIGHBORHOOD

DEER

NEUTRAL ZONE

GAYBORHOOD

PEOPLE WHO ARE BORN AND DIE IN THE SAME HOUSE

#1 BBQ PLACE TO GET SHOT

CITY HOUSING

LEBRON'S HIGH SCHOOL

ROAD WITH NO END

A WINERY IS HERE SOMEWHERE...

UNUSED SOCCER FIELDS

ZOO ANIMALS CAGED FOR THEIR PROTECTION

CHRISSIE HYNDE

EMPTY FREEWAY

GREAT FUTBOL

STUDENTS ROBBED BY THUGS IN HOODIES

GOOSE POOP

MOSTLY DORMS

DEAD BODIES

MLK NAME WAS TAKEN

HUD HOUSING

NEIGHBORHOOD RUINED BY THE FREEWAY

AVOID AFTER DARK

KINDA SCARY

AFRAID OF MINORITIES

WORLD'S BIGGEST EMPTY MALL

DISPOSABLE METH-LAB LAKE

USED APPLIANCES

BUILT BY GOODYEAR

METAL DETECTOR HIGH SCHOOL

TINY HOUSES

GUNS

WE'RE NOT BARBERTON!

IS MICHIGAN INTERNATIONAL?

PEOPLE WHO DON'T NOT USE DOUBLE NEGATIVES

BUILT BY FIRESTONE

LOW NUMBER OF TEETH PER ADULT

FIRESTONE NEVER HAD A BLIMP

BLIMPS BORN HERE

FORECLOSED VILLAGE

THERE'S A REASON WE'RE AT THE BOTTOM OF THIS MAP

CRAPPY OLD SPEEDBOATS

#1 BBQ PLACE TO GET SHOT
"I don't want a long wait to eat. Where is the number two BBQ place to get shot?"
ROBIN H.

AKRON
OHIO

Akron was once the rubber capital of the world, giving birth to the American trucking industry and its cocaine addiction by housing all four of the major tire companies. It is also the birthplace of both King James (LeBron, not the Bible guy) and the almighty Steph Curry. Is it a coincidence that basketballs are rubber and the town boasts two of the best basketball players ever? If that isn't Illuminati, I don't know what is. Then again, Akron hosts the annual Soap Box Derby World Championship. So, the city probably isn't *that* Illuminati.

HOMETOWN OF BEVERLY CRUSHER
"You might as well put 'hot red-headed MILF from the three hundred years in the future' right here."
STEVEN A.

STRIP BARS AND USED CARS
"Honest to God, I met a stripper named 'Toyota' once. Who could ask for anything more?"
TERRELL W.

LEBRON'S HIGH SCHOOL:
"LeBron was born here and played high school basketball here, but can't even win us a championship up the road in Cleveland. I don't know if I'm more depressed that the Cavs haven't won a championship yet, or that I still live in Akron."
NICK T.

WICHITA

KANSAS

Wichita is the aircraft capital of the world, which is funny because not too many people want to fly here. But, Kansas is the crescent roll of the breadbasket, and along with concealed weapons at church, the city also has one of the best sandwiches and root beer floats ever in existence at the NuWay Cafe. Wichita was also the birthplace of Pizza Hut in 1958, which probably should have been called Pizza Shack given the original building in which it was housed. The origin of Pizza Hut, White Castle, and Rent-A-Center? Now that's something to be proud about!

ANNOYING SOCCER MOMS
"Shouldn't we just call them 'Soccer Moms' because they are all annoying?"
GERALD T.

THE ONLY WAY TO ESCAPE:
"You have to fly out of Wichita to get above the tornadoes that would otherwise prevent you from leaving if you chose to drive."
ANTHONY L.

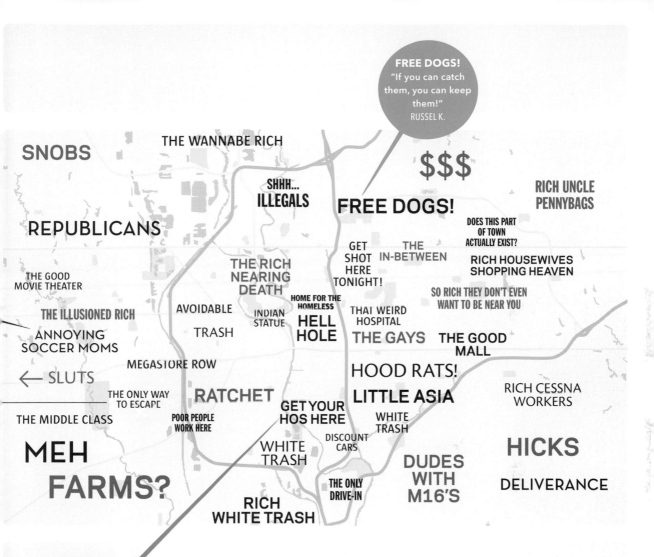

FREE DOGS!
"If you can catch them, you can keep them!"
RUSSEL K.

SNOBS

THE WANNABE RICH

$$$

RICH UNCLE PENNYBAGS

SHHH...
ILLEGALS

FREE DOGS!

REPUBLICANS

DOES THIS PART OF TOWN ACTUALLY EXIST?

GET SHOT HERE TONIGHT!

THE IN-BETWEEN

RICH HOUSEWIVES SHOPPING HEAVEN

THE GOOD MOVIE THEATER

THE RICH NEARING DEATH

SO RICH THEY DON'T EVEN WANT TO BE NEAR YOU

THE ILLUSIONED RICH

AVOIDABLE

HOME FOR THE HOMELESS

THAI WEIRD HOSPITAL

ANNOYING SOCCER MOMS

TRASH

INDIAN STATUE

HELL HOLE

THE GAYS

THE GOOD MALL

← SLUTS

MEGASTORE ROW

HOOD RATS!

THE ONLY WAY TO ESCAPE

RATCHET

LITTLE ASIA

RICH CESSNA WORKERS

THE MIDDLE CLASS

POOR PEOPLE WORK HERE

GET YOUR HOS HERE

WHITE TRASH

MEH

WHITE TRASH

DISCOUNT CARS

DUDES WITH M16'S

HICKS

FARMS?

THE ONLY DRIVE-IN

DELIVERANCE

RICH WHITE TRASH

GET YOUR HOS HERE
"I went to Home Depot and got a hose and some hos."
JADEN T.

OMAHA

NEBRASKA

Omaha is the least Nebraskan city in Nebraska. It is famous for hosting the College World Series and it is home to one of the nation's best zoos. Omaha has a special sense of community and sharing because its STD rates are twice the national average. Notable Omaha inventions include TV dinners, Raisin Bran, and the Reuben sandwich. So, the city is just one big resting home. But, a city that gave birth to Warren Buffet, Malcom X, and 311 can't be all that bad. Heck, just try the city's steaks. Don't worry though, you don't have to go there to get them. They'll ship them right to you.

PEOPLE THAT THINK THEY'RE RICH:
"I don't think it, I know it. I have a time share in Tahoe, an Apple watch, and a flatscreen mounted in each bedroom and bathroom. Get your facts straight."
TODD G.

STILL HAS DIRT ROADS

STILL BUTTHURT ABOUT GETTING ANNEXED

TRAILER TRASH

PEOPLE SCARED TO GO DOWNTOWN

GOLF-OBSESSED OLD MEN

PEOPLE THAT THINK THEY'RE RICH

WANNABE RICH PEOPLE THAT THINK THEY'RE "COUNTRY" FOR LIVING IN A SUBURB

Credit: Nathan T.

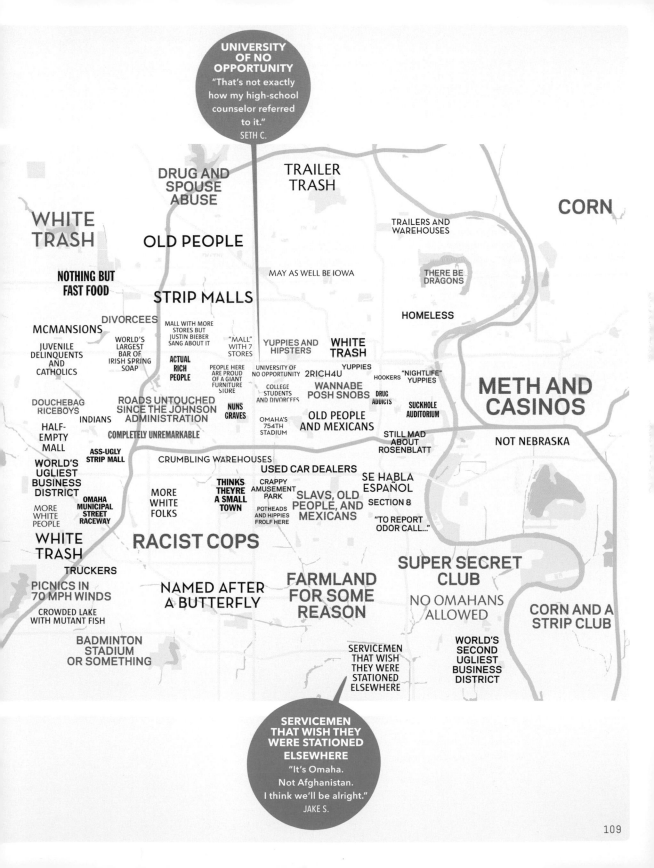

UNIVERSITY OF NO OPPORTUNITY
"That's not exactly how my high-school counselor referred to it."
SETH C.

DRUG AND SPOUSE ABUSE

TRAILER TRASH

CORN

WHITE TRASH

OLD PEOPLE

TRAILERS AND WAREHOUSES

THERE BE DRAGONS

MAY AS WELL BE IOWA

NOTHING BUT FAST FOOD

STRIP MALLS

HOMELESS

DIVORCEES

MCMANSIONS

MALL WITH MORE STORES BUT JUSTIN BIEBER SANG ABOUT IT

"MALL" WITH 7 STORES

YUPPIES AND HIPSTERS

WHITE TRASH

JUVENILE DELINQUENTS AND CATHOLICS

WORLD'S LARGEST BAR OF IRISH SPRING SOAP

ACTUAL RICH PEOPLE

PEOPLE HERE ARE PROUD OF A GIANT FURNITURE STORE

UNIVERSITY OF NO OPPORTUNITY

YUPPIES

2RICH4U

"NIGHTLIFE" YUPPIES

HOOKERS

METH AND CASINOS

DOUCHEBAG RICEBOYS

COLLEGE STUDENTS AND DIVORCEES

WANNABE POSH SNOBS

DRUG ADDICTS

SUCKHOLE AUDITORIUM

INDIANS

ROADS UNTOUCHED SINCE THE JOHNSON ADMINISTRATION

NUNS GRAVES

OMAHA'S 754TH STADIUM

OLD PEOPLE AND MEXICANS

HALF-EMPTY MALL

COMPLETELY UNREMARKABLE

STILL MAD ABOUT ROSENBLATT

NOT NEBRASKA

WORLD'S UGLIEST BUSINESS DISTRICT

ASS-UGLY STRIP MALL

CRUMBLING WAREHOUSES

USED CAR DEALERS

SE HABLA ESPAÑOL

MORE WHITE PEOPLE

OMAHA MUNICIPAL STREET RACEWAY

MORE WHITE FOLKS

THINKS THEY'RE A SMALL TOWN

CRAPPY AMUSEMENT PARK

SLAVS, OLD PEOPLE, AND MEXICANS

SECTION 8

"TO REPORT ODOR CALL..."

POTHEADS AND HIPPIES FROLF HERE

WHITE TRASH

RACIST COPS

SUPER SECRET CLUB

TRUCKERS

PICNICS IN 70 MPH WINDS

NAMED AFTER A BUTTERFLY

FARMLAND FOR SOME REASON

NO OMAHANS ALLOWED

CORN AND A STRIP CLUB

CROWDED LAKE WITH MUTANT FISH

BADMINTON STADIUM OR SOMETHING

SERVICEMEN THAT WISH THEY WERE STATIONED ELSEWHERE

WORLD'S SECOND UGLIEST BUSINESS DISTRICT

SERVICEMEN THAT WISH THEY WERE STATIONED ELSEWHERE
"It's Omaha. Not Afghanistan. I think we'll be alright."
JAKE S.

CHEYENNE
WYOMING

Cheyenne puts the "why" in "Wyoming." It is like the town of Fort Collins, CO took a shit and the miserable Wyoming winds blew it north of the border. Although hardly a hopping city and tourist attraction, it does serve as the official firework retailer for the state of Colorado. And at one point, the city was nicknamed "Magic City of the Plains" due to the construction of the Union Pacific Railroad that brought rapid growth to the area. The city's growth has clearly sustained, as trains are still the primary mode of transportation used by people in the United States.

WIND! WIND! WIND!
"The wind in Cheyenne can get so bad sometimes, with the right size of tumbleweed the whole town would be demolished."
MYRA W.

SNOW CHI MINH TRAIL
"It's just a freeway covered in snow, used for transporting supplies and arms between Cheyenne and the Vietnamese-owned town with a population of one—Buford."
PATRICK E.

AREA 51

WIND!

WIND!

NAZI BUNKERED HILL

LINCOLN'S DISEMBODIED HEAD

IT'S PRONOUNCED "VEDA-VOO!"

BROWN 'N' GOLD!!!

REPUBLICRATS

TRIPLE-RIGGIN' TRUCKERS

SNOW DRIFTS IN JUNE

SNOW CHI MINH TRAIL

"BUFORD" IN VIETNAMESE

Credit: Andy F.

DOZEN BLACK PEOPLE
"If you think there are no black people in this town, you should meet the six Asian people that live here."
TYLER J.

DARN-NEAR CHUGWATER

COYBOYETTES

REAGAN'S AGING NUCLEAR STOCKPILE

TEA PARTY ON!

THE KID WHO SHOT HIS DAD

ACTUAL RANCHES WITH COWS

FORD F-350+

COUNTRY AND WESTERN

FRIENDS OF DICK (CHENEY)

NRA

FORD F250

"BLACK HELICOPTERS"

DOCTOR, LAWYER, PORSCHE!

FAUX-Y FOLKS

RATTLESNAKE GANGS

TANKS!

RECOVERING DEMOCRATS

THAT 70'S SHOW

OIL MONEY

FORD F-150

WHEAT!

WIND!

MY EX-GIRLFRIEND

SKATES & BALLS

'MERICA, DAMNIT!

THAT TORNADER

STRAT BRATS

70'S HOMES 50'S MINDSET

TRAILERETTES

KONSERVATIVE KUNTRY KLUBBERS

WHERE SEARS IS FANCY

W.A.N.G.

STRIP MAULED

PRE-FABULOUS HOMES

ANGRY MILITARY WIVES

CHEYENNE'S SOCIETY

EX-STRATS!

BIBLETHUMPERS

DAIRY-AIR SMELLS

STRATS!

BEAST RIDGE

TRAILERS!

WELFARE REPUBLICAN'S

NUC-U-LAR

THREE HIPPIES

METH MADNESS

NEBRASKA CORNHOLES

SKYNET IS SELF-AWARE

VINYL QUONSET HOMES

BUREAU-CANS

NEARLY A STRIP!

GUNS GUNS GUNS

WRONG SIDE OF THE TRACKS

DANCES WITH SNAKES

WINDRANCH

DOZEN BLACK PEOPLE

MARY-IN-A-BATHTUB

SPORTING GOODS

IOWANS IN WINNEBAGOS

METH'D UP TRUCKERS

PROM NIGHT

LOW RIDERS

NO TROCAS

REFINERY STANK

TOXIC GROUNDWATER PLUME

CABALLEROS CON TROCAS

LAST CHANCE COWBOY COLLEGE

SEWAGE FOR GREELEY

LAST DEMOCRAT HEADED SOUTH

SANITY AND GOOD WEED

LOT LIZARDS

"CREEPY" COLORADO

DARK SMOKE

COLORADANS BUYING FIREWORKS

MAS TRAILERS

STATELINE STRIPPERS AND LOTTERY TICKETS

COLORADANS BUYING FIREWORKS

"The Colorado border is our local equivalent of the Mexican border. Coloradans come up here for their fireworks and we go down there to get our weed and beer. It's a trade that I am OK with."
LUKE S.

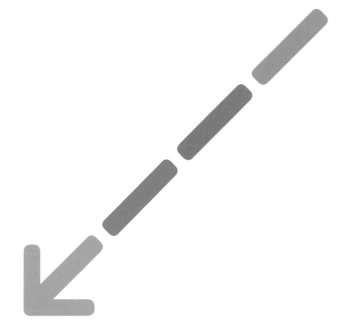

THE OUTLAWED
SOUTHWEST

Mountains, legalized marijuana, deserts, illegal immigrants, Texas, legalized marijuana—the American Southwest has it all! Historically, it is a land for the adventurous, settled by the Northeast's misfits who set off for California but found themselves stuck in Albuquerque. Contrary to popular belief, the region is full of hardworking folk, just most of the work goes undocumented. Yes, this is the home of the Mexican-American border, host to the nation's most active trade routes, with tens of thousands of cargo trucks crisscrossing the border each day and thousands of people hopping fences each night.

This fine parcel of country is famous for its excruciating heat in the summers (but it's a dry heat, right?), with a tourist destination fittingly named Death Valley and a well-earned nickname of "the devil's playground." Just throw some cheese all over it and you've got yourself a melty enchilada. Much of the landscape is reminiscent of Mars. So much so that most of the aliens decide to touch down here and probe people who are stoned enough that no one will believe them. But that doesn't mean you can escape the cold here. The northern part of the area provides a high (really high) mountain range prime for skiing, overpopulation, and nosebleeds.

Remember Native Americans? Neither do we, but the Southwest features some of the nation's finest casinos. Remember the Alamo? Of course you do. That's here, too! The Southwest is also home to Oklahoma City's "Gay Electricians," Salt Lake City's "Mormon Silos," El Paso's "El Shithole," and so much more.

Whether you like meth, states that meet at four corners, or people who take barbeque almost as seriously as they take football and guns, everyone can find a reason to love the Southwest. Plus, everything can be made into a taco.

DENVER
COLORADO

Denver was the most moved-to city in the United States in 2015, and it is no secret why. Denver weed receives weed 300 weed days weed of weed sunshine weed a weed year weed. It is hard to find anyone who hates Denver, aside from Tom Brady and Cam Newton. But, good luck moving to the Queen City of the Plains, because everyone else already did, and they have raised the housing prices so much to ensure you don't move there. Just remember one of Denver's lesser-known mottos: "Denver sucks, and it's always cold and snowy. Don't move here."

NOTHING

"'Nothing' is a misrepresentation. I'd call it 'Little Algiers Meets Korean Yuppies Meets Your Weed Guy.' Then there's that creepy Russian banya just north of the mosque that has mob guys in velour pantsuits mumbling into their cell phones, and spooky Slavic hookers walking back and forth."
RACHEL B.

SOBROS AND HOS

"Baker, South Broadway: if you're looking to see a group of popped collars waiting in line for brunch while a homeless guy peeing gets ignored by two bearded dudes making vegan ice cream, this is the spot."
ADAM C-H

DRUNK/HOMELESS/WEED

"I knew that Denver had finally reached the tipping point with legal marijuana when I walked out of a dispensary and there was a little Girl Scout and her mom selling cookies right outside. They sold way more cookies than the dispensary sold weed. I bet that girl is retired by age seven."
PAUL S.

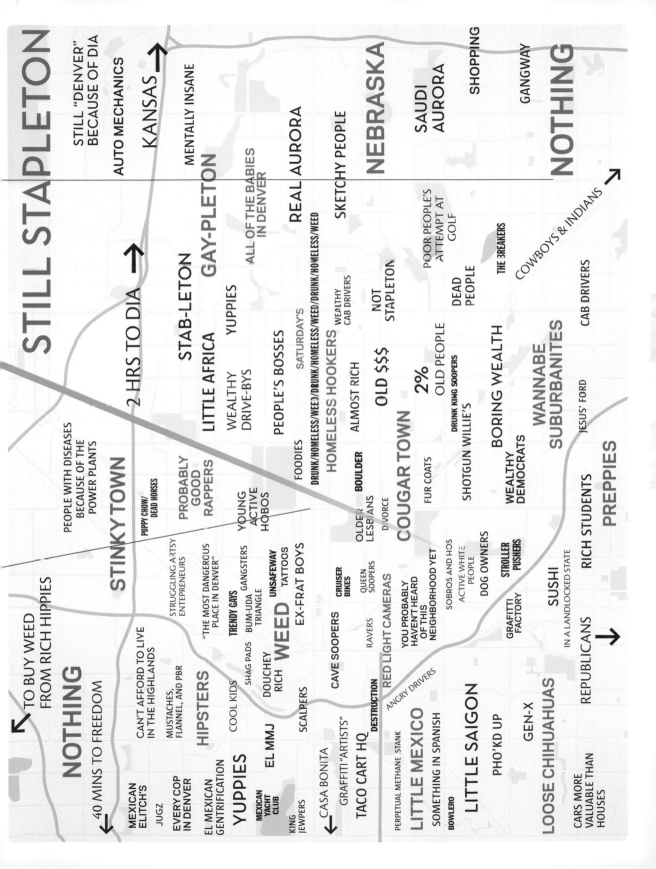

FORT COLLINS

COLORADO

Fort Collins was a farm town known as the "Lamb Feeding Capital of the World" in the early 1900s, which has since evolved into the nickname "Fort Fun" because of the double-digit number of microbreweries you can find there and the loose sorority girls wandering College Ave. after midnight. The town is a poor man's Boulder, but still just as white and batshit liberal.

WANNABE BOULDER
"Fort Collins is just a more affordable and family-friendly Boulder with more cattle and less rape."
NINA B.

BFE

COWPOKES AND FAKE HORSE VAGINAS

WTF STADIUM

PEOPLE WHO CAN'T AFFORD A REAL VACATION

HIPPIES & WEED
"Let's face it. This is the whole state, guys."
BEN G.

HIPPIES & WEED

LANCE ARMSTRONG WANNABES WITH TWO TESTICLES

Credit: Amy L.

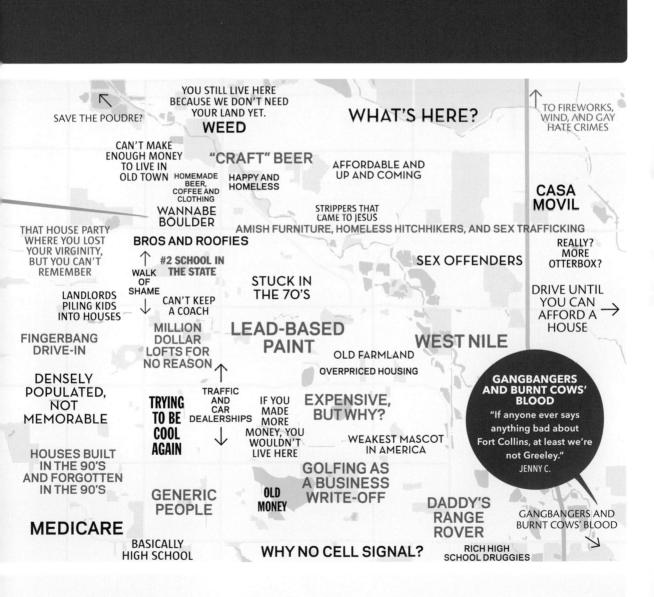

SAVE THE POUDRE?

YOU STILL LIVE HERE BECAUSE WE DON'T NEED YOUR LAND YET.

WEED

WHAT'S HERE?

TO FIREWORKS, WIND, AND GAY HATE CRIMES

CAN'T MAKE ENOUGH MONEY TO LIVE IN OLD TOWN

"CRAFT" BEER

HOMEMADE BEER, COFFEE AND CLOTHING

HAPPY AND HOMELESS

AFFORDABLE AND UP AND COMING

CASA MOVIL

WANNABE BOULDER

STRIPPERS THAT CAME TO JESUS

AMISH FURNITURE, HOMELESS HITCHHIKERS, AND SEX TRAFFICKING

REALLY? MORE OTTERBOX?

THAT HOUSE PARTY WHERE YOU LOST YOUR VIRGINITY, BUT YOU CAN'T REMEMBER

BROS AND ROOFIES

↑ #2 SCHOOL IN THE STATE

WALK OF SHAME

SEX OFFENDERS

DRIVE UNTIL YOU CAN AFFORD A HOUSE →

LANDLORDS PILING KIDS INTO HOUSES

↓ CAN'T KEEP A COACH

STUCK IN THE 70'S

MILLION DOLLAR LOFTS FOR NO REASON

LEAD-BASED PAINT

WEST NILE

FINGERBANG DRIVE-IN

OLD FARMLAND

OVERPRICED HOUSING

GANGBANGERS AND BURNT COWS' BLOOD

"If anyone ever says anything bad about Fort Collins, at least we're not Greeley."
JENNY C.

DENSELY POPULATED, NOT MEMORABLE

↑ TRAFFIC AND CAR DEALERSHIPS

TRYING TO BE COOL AGAIN

IF YOU MADE MORE MONEY, YOU WOULDN'T LIVE HERE

EXPENSIVE, BUT WHY?

WEAKEST MASCOT IN AMERICA

↓

HOUSES BUILT IN THE 90'S AND FORGOTTEN IN THE 90'S

GOLFING AS A BUSINESS WRITE-OFF

GENERIC PEOPLE

OLD MONEY

DADDY'S RANGE ROVER

GANGBANGERS AND BURNT COWS' BLOOD ↓

MEDICARE

BASICALLY HIGH SCHOOL

WHY NO CELL SIGNAL?

RICH HIGH SCHOOL DRUGGIES

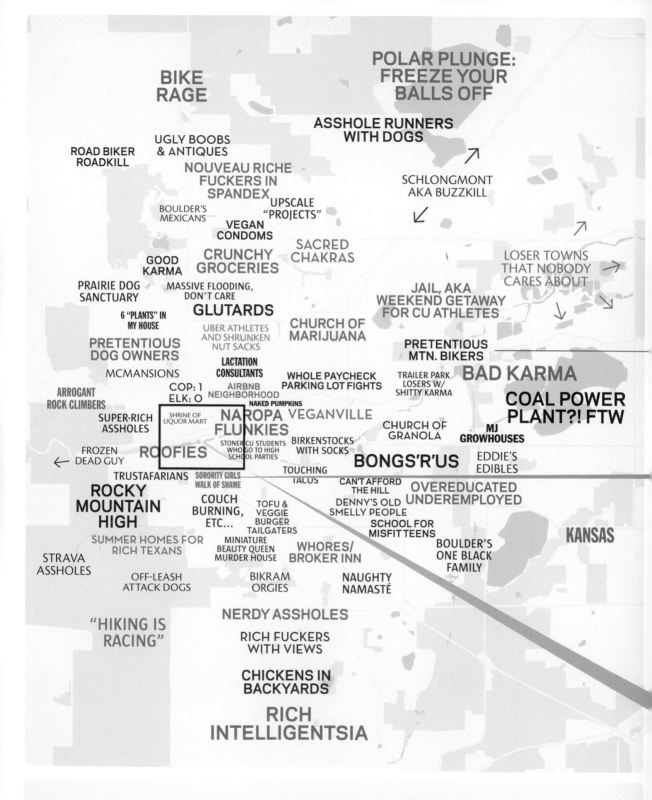

BOULDER
COLORADO

Boulder, Colorado: a 25-square-mile bubble surrounded by reality. Whether it is because of the outdoor activities, CU-Boulder's 420 extravaganza, the booming startup scene, or the elitist utopian douchebag vibes, people yearn to live in the healthiest, most highly educated, and probably whitest city in the United States. Come for the legalized weed and organic quinoa, and stay for the orgasm meditation and crotch-hugging cycling shorts.

PRETENTIOUS MOUNTAIN BIKERS

"The worst part about living in one of the healthiest and most active cities in the United States is that you always feel like a lazy piece of shit. Good thing this healthy, active city is also one of the highest cities in the U.S."
ANDY J.

TRUSTAFARIANS
"I just wish Boulder had more white people."
NOBODY

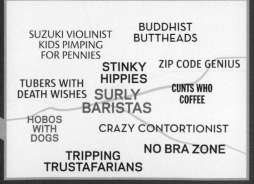

SUZUKI VIOLINIST KIDS PIMPING FOR PENNIES

BUDDHIST BUTTHEADS

ZIP CODE GENIUS

STINKY HIPPIES

TUBERS WITH DEATH WISHES

CUNTS WHO COFFEE

SURLY BARISTAS

HOBOS WITH DOGS

CRAZY CONTORTIONIST

NO BRA ZONE

TRIPPING TRUSTAFARIANS

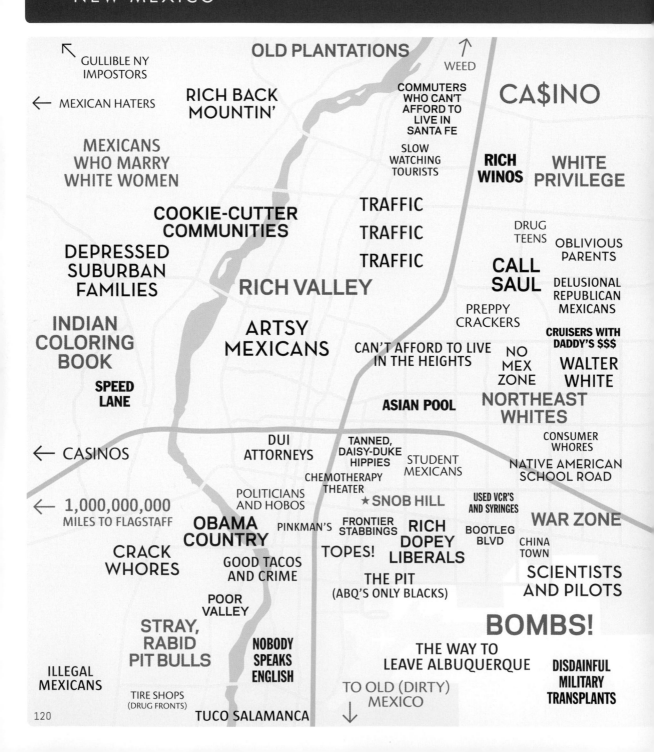

ALBUQUERQUE
NEW MEXICO

GULLIBLE NY IMPOSTORS

MEXICAN HATERS

OLD PLANTATIONS

WEED

COMMUTERS WHO CAN'T AFFORD TO LIVE IN SANTA FE

CA$INO

RICH BACK MOUNTIN'

MEXICANS WHO MARRY WHITE WOMEN

SLOW WATCHING TOURISTS

RICH WINOS

WHITE PRIVILEGE

COOKIE-CUTTER COMMUNITIES

TRAFFIC

TRAFFIC

TRAFFIC

DRUG TEENS

OBLIVIOUS PARENTS

DEPRESSED SUBURBAN FAMILIES

RICH VALLEY

CALL SAUL

DELUSIONAL REPUBLICAN MEXICANS

INDIAN COLORING BOOK

ARTSY MEXICANS

PREPPY CRACKERS

CAN'T AFFORD TO LIVE IN THE HEIGHTS

NO MEX ZONE

CRUISERS WITH DADDY'S $$$

WALTER WHITE

SPEED LANE

NORTHEAST WHITES

ASIAN POOL

CONSUMER WHORES

CASINOS

DUI ATTORNEYS

TANNED, DAISY-DUKE HIPPIES

STUDENT MEXICANS

NATIVE AMERICAN SCHOOL ROAD

CHEMOTHERAPY THEATER

1,000,000,000 MILES TO FLAGSTAFF

POLITICIANS AND HOBOS

★ SNOB HILL

USED VCR'S AND SYRINGES

WAR ZONE

OBAMA COUNTRY

PINKMAN'S

FRONTIER STABBINGS

RICH DOPEY LIBERALS

BOOTLEG BLVD

CHINA TOWN

CRACK WHORES

GOOD TACOS AND CRIME

TOPES!

SCIENTISTS AND PILOTS

THE PIT (ABQ'S ONLY BLACKS)

POOR VALLEY

STRAY, RABID PIT BULLS

NOBODY SPEAKS ENGLISH

BOMBS!

THE WAY TO LEAVE ALBUQUERQUE

DISDAINFUL MILITARY TRANSPLANTS

ILLEGAL MEXICANS

TIRE SHOPS (DRUG FRONTS)

TUCO SALAMANCA

TO OLD (DIRTY) MEXICO

GET HIGH
(10,678 FT.)

MIDGET PORN
MUSEUM
★

SHITTY SKIING
FOR PEOPLE
TOO LAZY TO
DRIVE TO TAOS

GOAT FUCKERS

FUTURE SITE
OF FIRE

SHROOMVILLE

1,000,000,000 →
MILES TO AMARILLO

LOOKS
LIKE
CANADA

MILITARY
MEXICANS
←

WINTER UNTIL MAY

RICH REDNECKS

Tumbleweeds and turquoise! The growth of Albuquerque came from the traffic through the town on historic Route 66 and the dry desert climate that served as a safe haven for tuberculosis patients back in the early 20th century. For the 59th largest metropolitan area in the United States, Albuquerque has got it all. You might catch a show at the KiMo theater, which is only slightly haunted, or take the Breaking Bad walking tour, where they give you a bag of crystal meth at the end. Everyone in Albuquerque gets high in October with the International Balloon Fiesta.

Credit: Rusty Rutherford and Curt Fletcher

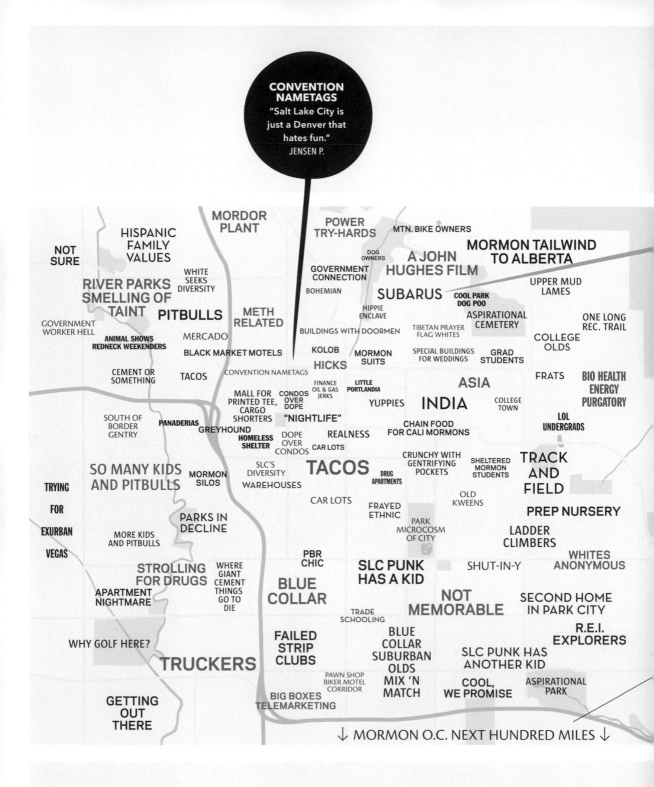

CONVENTION
NAMETAGS
"Salt Lake City is
just a Denver that
hates fun."
JENSEN P.

MORDOR
PLANT

POWER
TRY-HARDS

MTN. BIKE OWNERS

HISPANIC
FAMILY
VALUES

NOT
SURE

DOG
OWNERS

A JOHN
HUGHES FILM

MORMON TAILWIND
TO ALBERTA

WHITE
SEEKS
DIVERSITY

GOVERNMENT
CONNECTION

UPPER MUD
LAMES

RIVER PARKS
SMELLING OF
TAINT

BOHEMIAN

SUBARUS

COOL PARK
DOG POO

METH
RELATED

HIPPIE
ENCLAVE

ASPIRATIONAL
CEMETERY

ONE LONG
REC. TRAIL

PITBULLS

GOVERNMENT
WORKER HELL

BUILDINGS WITH DOORMEN

TIBETAN PRAYER
FLAG WHITES

COLLEGE
OLDS

ANIMAL SHOWS
REDNECK WEEKENDERS

MERCADO

KOLOB

MORMON
SUITS

SPECIAL BUILDINGS
FOR WEDDINGS

GRAD
STUDENTS

BLACK MARKET MOTELS

HICKS

CEMENT OR
SOMETHING

TACOS

CONVENTION NAMETAGS

FINANCE
OIL & GAS
JERKS

LITTLE
PORTLANDIA

ASIA

FRATS

BIO HEALTH
ENERGY
PURGATORY

MALL FOR
PRINTED TEE,
CARGO
SHORTERS

CONDOS
OVER
DOPE

YUPPIES

INDIA

COLLEGE
TOWN

SOUTH OF
BORDER
GENTRY

PANADERIAS

"NIGHTLIFE"

LOL
UNDERGRADS

GREYHOUND

CHAIN FOOD
FOR CALI MORMONS

HOMELESS
SHELTER

DOPE
OVER
CONDOS

REALNESS

CAR LOTS

CRUNCHY WITH
GENTRIFYING
POCKETS

SHELTERED
MORMON
STUDENTS

TRACK
AND
FIELD

SO MANY KIDS
AND PITBULLS

MORMON
SILOS

SLC'S
DIVERSITY

TACOS

DRUG
APARTMENTS

OLD
KWEENS

PREP NURSERY

WAREHOUSES

TRYING

FOR

EXURBAN

VEGAS

MORE KIDS
AND PITBULLS

PARKS IN
DECLINE

CAR LOTS

FRAYED
ETHNIC

PARK
MICROCOSM
OF CITY

LADDER
CLIMBERS

WHERE
GIANT
CEMENT
THINGS
GO TO
DIE

PBR
CHIC

SLC PUNK
HAS A KID

SHUT-IN-Y

WHITES
ANONYMOUS

STROLLING
FOR DRUGS

APARTMENT
NIGHTMARE

BLUE
COLLAR

NOT
MEMORABLE

SECOND HOME
IN PARK CITY

TRADE
SCHOOLING

WHY GOLF HERE?

FAILED
STRIP
CLUBS

BLUE
COLLAR
SUBURBAN
OLDS
MIX 'N
MATCH

R.E.I.
EXPLORERS

TRUCKERS

SLC PUNK HAS
ANOTHER KID

PAWN SHOP
BIKER MOTEL
CORRIDOR

COOL,
WE PROMISE

ASPIRATIONAL
PARK

GETTING
OUT
THERE

BIG BOXES
TELEMARKETING

↓ MORMON O.C. NEXT HUNDRED MILES ↓

SALT LAKE CITY
UTAH

Founded in 1847 by a group of men and women who believe the Garden of Eden is in Missouri, Salt Lake City today is super clean, super white and still super Mormon. The city has given us the Winter Olympics (it's okay if you forgot that happened) and Mitt Romney (also totally okay if you forgot he was a thing once, too). SLC's population is projected to double by 2040. That is a lot of white shirts and black ties.

SUBARUS
"I live in 'Subarus.' To be honest, the entire town could be called Subaru Lake City."
BRIDGET C.

CAN'T GO HERE

MUST OWN CAR TO GO HERE

90'S HIPPIES SAD →

DOCTORS, ETC...

WORSE DOCTORS

AGED RICH

BASEMENT APARTMENTS FOR STUDENTS

COLORADO WAS TOO LIBERAL

MORMON O.C. NEXT HUNDRED MILES
"When you venture outside of Salt Lake City limits, it just gets more and more Mormon-y. It's like when you see the outskirts of any other city filled with crazy suburbanites, except with more prairie garments."
MILES P.

MEXICANS

"The area is actually a total mix of races, ranging from lower middle class to maybe one or two rich people. We might as well call it 'Chex Mex.'"
QUENTIN B.

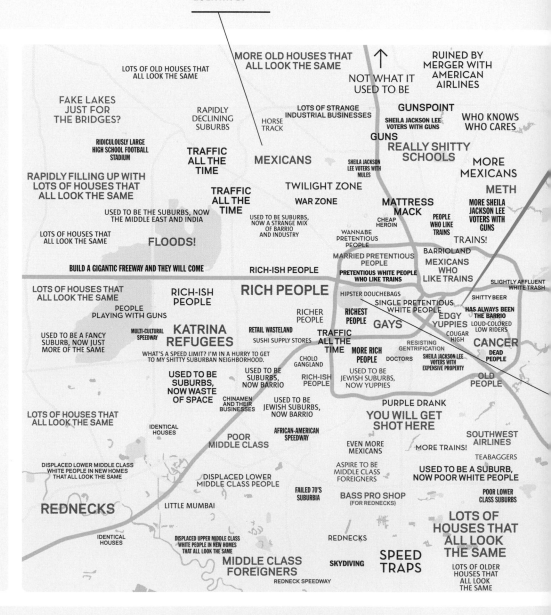

HOUSTON
TEXAS

H-town is the largest city in Texas and the fourth largest in the U.S. Any city that has two freeway loops and never-ending traffic is trying to keep you from escaping. But Houston doesn't take itself too seriously, because no one outside of Houston takes it seriously. The U.S. economy can be up or down, but there is always money to be made in Houston. Unless the oil and gas industry is down. Then, there is absolutely no money to be made in Houston. In 2005, 2.5 million Houstonites left the city, not because of the rising popularity of Austin, but due to Hurricane Rita that ended up leaving little damage to the city. If you love the humidity of the south and the traffic of LA, you will most definitely find something to love in Houston.

EDGY YUPPIES
"It's all DINKs and gays. Once those DINKs whelp a kid, they'll move to the burbs where they feel 'safe' from the minorities and homeless people."
BONNIE M.

STILL PISSED OFF ABOUT BEING ANNEXED

DUELING BANJOS

REDNECKS DIE IN THIS RIVER A LOT

METH
(BUT SOME PEOPLE ARE REALLY RICH)

POOR LOWER CLASS SUBURBS
(PEOPLE ACTUALLY LIVE OUT HERE?)

WHERE BUTANE COMES FROM

ASPIRING MEXICANS

CLOSE TO GOOD JOBS, SHITTY PLACE TO LIVE

TEXAS HISTORY

RICH LOWER CLASS SUBURBS

GOOD JOBS, SHITTY PLACE TO VISIT

WHERE GASOLINE COMES FROM

LOWER CLASS SUBURBS WITH MONEY

JOHN TRAVOLTA

AVOID EYE CONTACT, AVOID GETTING SHOT

VERY RICH LOWER CLASS SUBURBS

RICH LOWER CLASS SUBURBS

NOT AS IMPRESSIVE AS IT USED TO BE, BUT THEY SURE THINK IT IS

ASTRONAUTS AND THEIR SYCOPHANTS

FAKE AMUSEMENT PARK

CAN'T AFFORD TO LIVE IN (THE NICE PART OF) GALVESTON

HIPSTER DOUCHEBAGS
"Does the quote have to be true for you to put it in your book? Really? It doesn't matter? Cool! Then, Houston is the coolest city ever."
AARON G.

DALLAS

TEXAS

Dallas is the city with a little bit of everything and a whole lot of nothing. The city with a love for guns and Jesus that outweighs their crippling obesity epidemic. A little bit of douche and a whole lot of glam. A little bit of oil money and a whole lot of cowboy. A little bit of barbecue and a whole lot of Bush. But, clearly there's more to Dallas than that. The city has more shopping centers per capita than any other city in the United States, and is ranked 6th worldwide amongst cities with the most billionaires. Yee-haw, J.R.!

BUSHVILLE
"Some parts of Dallas are all like, 'Ha-ha-ha,' but yet other parts of Dallas are like so much sad face."
HOLLY F.

LOST COLITIS
"Make sure to read the map closely. 'Colitis' and 'Coitus' are two very different things. And if your coitus is lost, what the fuck are you doing sitting around reading a book with maps in it?"
DARTH S.

OH, CLIFF
"Oak Cliff needs to get rid of all of the gangs, violence, shootings, brutality, stabbings, beatings, savagery, and death."
DANIEL L.

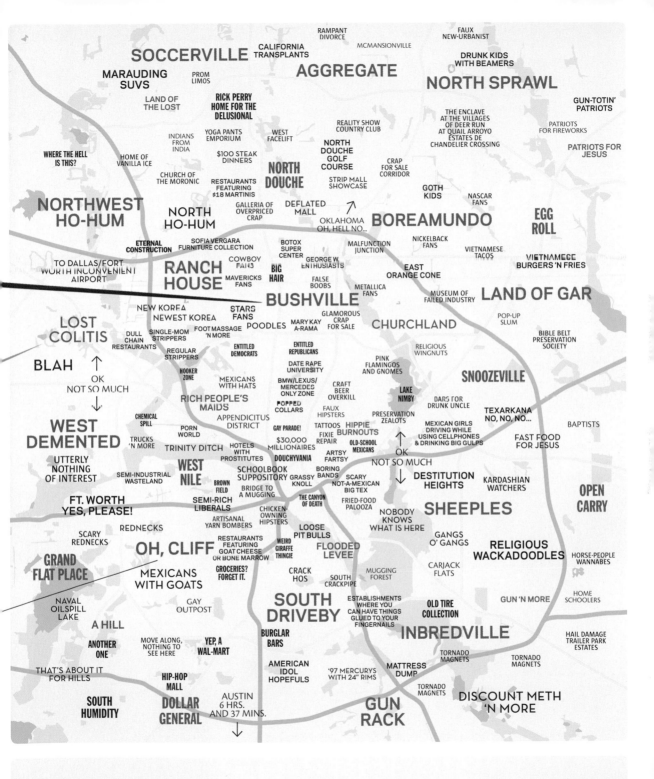

FORT WORTH

TEXAS

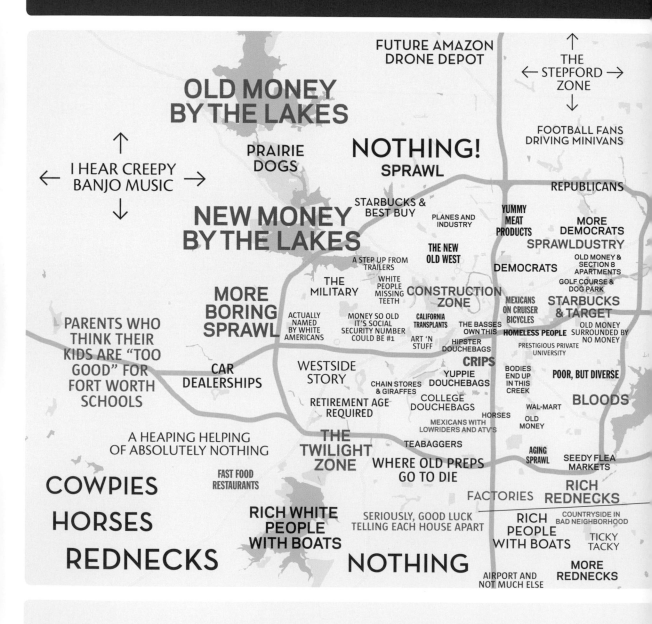

FUTURE AMAZON
DRONE DEPOT

THE
← STEPFORD →
ZONE

OLD MONEY
BY THE LAKES

PRAIRIE
DOGS

NOTHING!
SPRAWL

FOOTBALL FANS
DRIVING MINIVANS

↑
← I HEAR CREEPY →
BANJO MUSIC
↓

REPUBLICANS

STARBUCKS &
BEST BUY

NEW MONEY
BY THE LAKES

PLANES AND
INDUSTRY

YUMMY
MEAT
PRODUCTS

MORE
DEMOCRATS

SPRAWLDUSTRY

THE NEW
OLD WEST

A STEP UP FROM
TRAILERS

OLD MONEY &
SECTION 8
APARTMENTS

DEMOCRATS

GOLF COURSE &
DOG PARK

THE
MILITARY

WHITE
PEOPLE
MISSING
TEETH

CONSTRUCTION
ZONE

MEXICANS
ON CRUISER
BICYCLES

STARBUCKS
& TARGET

MORE
BORING
SPRAWL

ACTUALLY
NAMED
BY WHITE
AMERICANS

MONEY SO OLD
IT'S SOCIAL
SECURITY NUMBER
COULD BE #1

CALIFORNIA
TRANSPLANTS

THE BASSES
OWN THIS

HOMELESS PEOPLE

OLD MONEY
SURROUNDED BY
NO MONEY

ART 'N
STUFF

HIPSTER
DOUCHEBAGS

PRESTIGIOUS PRIVATE
UNIVERSITY

PARENTS WHO
THINK THEIR
KIDS ARE "TOO
GOOD" FOR
FORT WORTH
SCHOOLS

CAR
DEALERSHIPS

WESTSIDE
STORY

CHAIN STORES
& GIRAFFES

CRIPS

YUPPIE
DOUCHEBAGS

BODIES
END UP
IN THIS
CREEK

POOR, BUT DIVERSE

COLLEGE
DOUCHEBAGS

WAL-MART

BLOODS

RETIREMENT AGE
REQUIRED

HORSES

OLD
MONEY

A HEAPING HELPING
OF ABSOLUTELY NOTHING

MEXICANS WITH
LOWRIDERS AND ATV'S

THE
TWILIGHT
ZONE

TEABAGGERS

AGING
SPRAWL

SEEDY FLEA
MARKETS

WHERE OLD PREPS
GO TO DIE

COWPIES

FAST FOOD
RESTAURANTS

FACTORIES

RICH
REDNECKS

HORSES

RICH WHITE
PEOPLE
WITH BOATS

SERIOUSLY, GOOD LUCK
TELLING EACH HOUSE APART

COUNTRYSIDE IN
BAD NEIGHBORHOOD

RICH
PEOPLE
WITH BOATS

TICKY
TACKY

REDNECKS

NOTHING

AIRPORT AND
NOT MUCH ELSE

MORE
REDNECKS

Fort Worth has all of the great aspects of Dallas, without the douchey attitude. The city is nicknamed "Cowtown" because it is a wild-west playground, featuring the Stock Show and world's largest indoor rodeo, the Stockyards, Honky Tonk, and the cowgirl museum. However, the research done by Peter McGraw and Joel Warner in "The Humor Code" found that Fort Worth is the least funny big city in the country. No joke.

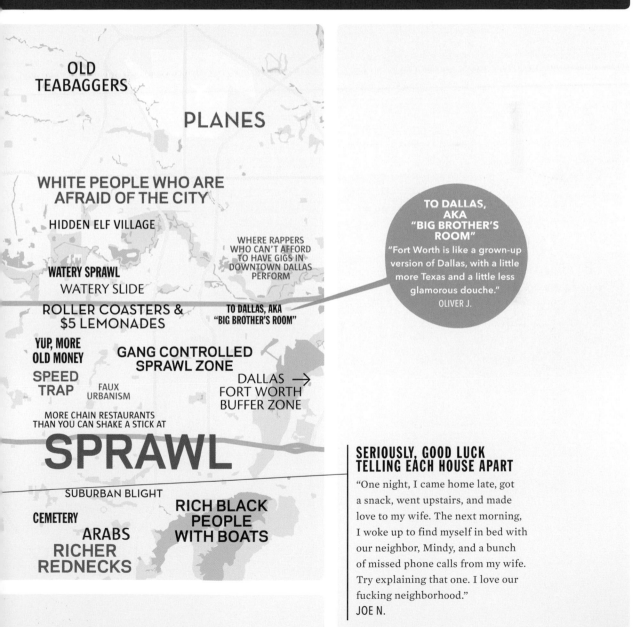

OLD TEABAGGERS

PLANES

WHITE PEOPLE WHO ARE AFRAID OF THE CITY

HIDDEN ELF VILLAGE

WHERE RAPPERS WHO CAN'T AFFORD TO HAVE GIGS IN DOWNTOWN DALLAS PERFORM

WATERY SPRAWL

WATERY SLIDE

ROLLER COASTERS & $5 LEMONADES

TO DALLAS, AKA "BIG BROTHER'S ROOM"

YUP, MORE OLD MONEY

GANG CONTROLLED SPRAWL ZONE

SPEED TRAP

FAUX URBANISM

DALLAS →
FORT WORTH BUFFER ZONE

MORE CHAIN RESTAURANTS THAN YOU CAN SHAKE A STICK AT

SPRAWL

SUBURBAN BLIGHT

CEMETERY

ARABS

RICHER REDNECKS

RICH BLACK PEOPLE WITH BOATS

TO DALLAS, AKA "BIG BROTHER'S ROOM"

"Fort Worth is like a grown-up version of Dallas, with a little more Texas and a little less glamorous douche."

OLIVER J.

SERIOUSLY, GOOD LUCK TELLING EACH HOUSE APART

"One night, I came home late, got a snack, went upstairs, and made love to my wife. The next morning, I woke up to find myself in bed with our neighbor, Mindy, and a bunch of missed phone calls from my wife. Try explaining that one. I love our fucking neighborhood."

JOE N.

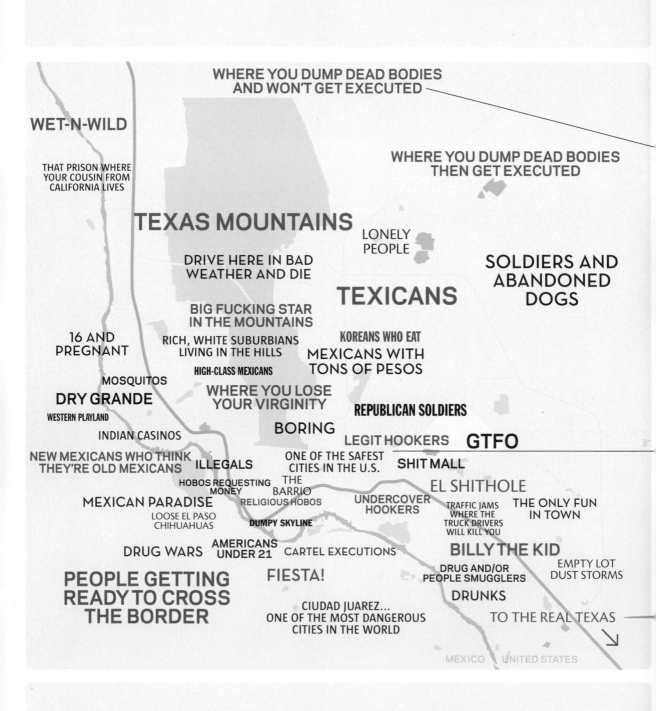

WHERE YOU DUMP DEAD BODIES
AND WON'T GET EXECUTED

WET-N-WILD

THAT PRISON WHERE
YOUR COUSIN FROM
CALIFORNIA LIVES

WHERE YOU DUMP DEAD BODIES
THEN GET EXECUTED

TEXAS MOUNTAINS

LONELY
PEOPLE

SOLDIERS AND
ABANDONED
DOGS

DRIVE HERE IN BAD
WEATHER AND DIE

TEXICANS

BIG FUCKING STAR
IN THE MOUNTAINS

16 AND
PREGNANT

RICH, WHITE SUBURBIANS
LIVING IN THE HILLS

KOREANS WHO EAT

MEXICANS WITH
TONS OF PESOS

HIGH-CLASS MEXICANS

MOSQUITOS

DRY GRANDE

WHERE YOU LOSE
YOUR VIRGINITY

REPUBLICAN SOLDIERS

WESTERN PLAYLAND

INDIAN CASINOS

BORING

LEGIT HOOKERS   GTFO

NEW MEXICANS WHO THINK
THEY'RE OLD MEXICANS   ILLEGALS

ONE OF THE SAFEST
CITIES IN THE U.S.   SHIT MALL

HOBOS REQUESTING
MONEY

THE
BARRIO

EL SHITHOLE

MEXICAN PARADISE

RELIGIOUS HOBOS

UNDERCOVER
HOOKERS

TRAFFIC JAMS
WHERE THE
TRUCK DRIVERS
WILL KILL YOU

THE ONLY FUN
IN TOWN

LOOSE EL PASO
CHIHUAHUAS

DUMPY SKYLINE

DRUG WARS

AMERICANS
UNDER 21

CARTEL EXECUTIONS

BILLY THE KID

EMPTY LOT
DUST STORMS

PEOPLE GETTING
READY TO CROSS
THE BORDER

FIESTA!

DRUG AND/OR
PEOPLE SMUGGLERS

DRUNKS

CIUDAD JUAREZ...
ONE OF THE MOST DANGEROUS
CITIES IN THE WORLD

TO THE REAL TEXAS

MEXICO   UNITED STATES

EL PASO
TEXAS

El Paso is Spanish for "The Paso." Kidding, it's "pass" which is what you say when someone asks if you want to take a trip to El Paso. But seriously, El Paso is home to world caliber art, culture, countless festivals, and the most sophisticated drug smuggling operations the world has ever seen.

WHERE YOU DUMP DEAD BODIES AND WON'T GET EXECUTED

"When murdering someone in El Paso, the difference between dumping the body and getting executed and dumping the body and avoiding execution is driving fifteen minutes north of the city. Hypothetically."
CARL D.

ONE OF THE SAFEST CITIES IN THE U.S.

"How is it that one of the safest cities in the U.S. can be right across the border from one of the most notoriously dangerous cities in the world? At least it's not like you could be out driving around town, accidentally make a wrong turn, end up on the other side of the border, and get killed. Or could you?"
MAX J.

TO THE REAL TEXAS
"I don't think you really want to go there."
JENNIFER L.

SAN ANTONIO

TEXAS

San Antonio is like Austin's Mexican half brother on the junior varsity hipster team. San Antonio's River Walk is overrated and the Alamo is forgettable, but the city hosts the famous San Antonio Stock Show & Rodeo, has one of the best NBA teams, and the Mexican food is muy auténtico. And, the city is home to one of the largest concentrations of military bases in the country, which has given it a nickname of "Military City, USA." Even though Austin takes credit for it (and most other things), San Antonio actually invented one of the most highly revered foods of all time— the breakfast taco.

WANDERING TOURISTS

"Whenever I tell people I'm from San Antonio, they ask, 'Have you been to the River Walk?!' Of course I've been to the River Walk, you idiots. That's the first thing we all do when we move here, and then we only go again when we have friends in town."
JACKIE H.

ART + GOOD FOOD

"The streets of San Antonio were carved out by a drunk Mexican riding a burro."
DAVE

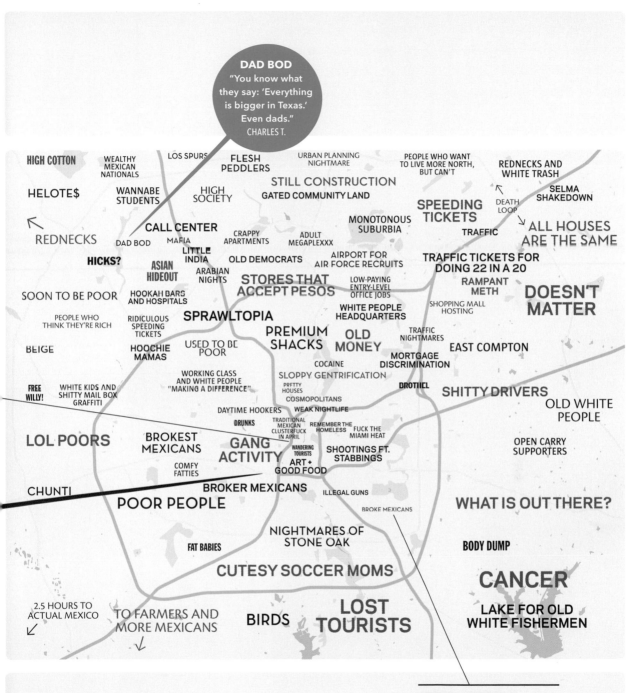

DAD BOD
"You know what they say: 'Everything is bigger in Texas.' Even dads."
CHARLES T.

HIGH COTTON

WEALTHY MEXICAN NATIONALS

LOS SPURS

FLESH PEDDLERS

URBAN PLANNING NIGHTMARE

PEOPLE WHO WANT TO LIVE MORE NORTH, BUT CAN'T

REDNECKS AND WHITE TRASH

HELOTE$

WANNABE STUDENTS

HIGH SOCIETY

STILL CONSTRUCTION

GATED COMMUNITY LAND

SPEEDING TICKETS

DEATH LOOP

SELMA SHAKEDOWN

REDNECKS

CALL CENTER

MONOTONOUS SUBURBIA

TRAFFIC

ALL HOUSES ARE THE SAME

DAD BOD

MAFIA

CRAPPY APARTMENTS

ADULT MEGAPLEXXX

HICKS?

LITTLE INDIA

OLD DEMOCRATS

AIRPORT FOR AIR FORCE RECRUITS

TRAFFIC TICKETS FOR DOING 22 IN A 20

ASIAN HIDEOUT

ARABIAN NIGHTS

STORES THAT ACCEPT PESOS

LOW-PAYING ENTRY-LEVEL OFFICE JOBS

RAMPANT METH

DOESN'T MATTER

SOON TO BE POOR

HOOKAH BARS AND HOSPITALS

WHITE PEOPLE HEADQUARTERS

SHOPPING MALL HOSTING

PEOPLE WHO THINK THEY'RE RICH

RIDICULOUS SPEEDING TICKETS

SPRAWLTOPIA

PREMIUM SHACKS

OLD MONEY

TRAFFIC NIGHTMARES

EAST COMPTON

BEIGE

HOOCHIE MAMAS

USED TO BE POOR

MORTGAGE DISCRIMINATION

COCAINE

SLOPPY GENTRIFICATION

BROTHEL

SHITTY DRIVERS

FREE WILLY!

WHITE KIDS AND SHITTY MAIL BOX GRAFFITI

WORKING CLASS AND WHITE PEOPLE "MAKING A DIFFERENCE"

PRETTY HOUSES

COSMOPOLITANS

OLD WHITE PEOPLE

DAYTIME HOOKERS

WEAK NIGHTLIFE

LOL POORS

BROKEST MEXICANS

DRUNKS

GANG ACTIVITY

TRADITIONAL MEXICAN CLUSTERFUCK IN APRIL

WANDERING TOURISTS

REMEMBER THE HOMELESS

FUCK THE MIAMI HEAT

SHOOTINGS FT. STABBINGS

OPEN CARRY SUPPORTERS

COMFY FATTIES

ART + GOOD FOOD

CHUNTI

BROKER MEXICANS

ILLEGAL GUNS

WHAT IS OUT THERE?

POOR PEOPLE

BROKE MEXICANS

FAT BABIES

NIGHTMARES OF STONE OAK

BODY DUMP

CUTESY SOCCER MOMS

CANCER

2.5 HOURS TO ACTUAL MEXICO

TO FARMERS AND MORE MEXICANS

BIRDS

LOST TOURISTS

LAKE FOR OLD WHITE FISHERMEN

BROKE MEXICANS

"I live in the south side of San Antonio between 'Illegal Guns' and 'Broke Mexicans.' I'm sure it would be a lot quieter around here if I lived between 'Illegal Mexicans' and 'Broke Guns.'"
ANA J.

AUSTIN

TEXAS

Austin is touted as the Live Music Capital of the World because it is has the most live music venues per capita. Where else can you see your favorite band perform in the soup kitchen line at a local homeless shelter, inside a temporary port-o-potty on a construction site, or on a stand-up paddle board in the middle of a river? In 2015, *Forbes* named Austin the nation's biggest boom-town and it has recently received the nickname "Silicon Hills," driven by the strong tech scene filled with jobs that may or may not actually exist. But its infrastruc-ture of two highways, lack of public transportation, and unbikeable streets make it nearly impossible to support the more than 160 people moving there each day (probably assholes from California). Whether you move to Austin or not, please don't.

Credit: Alex, Armando, Brian, James, Joel, John, Scurry, and Trent

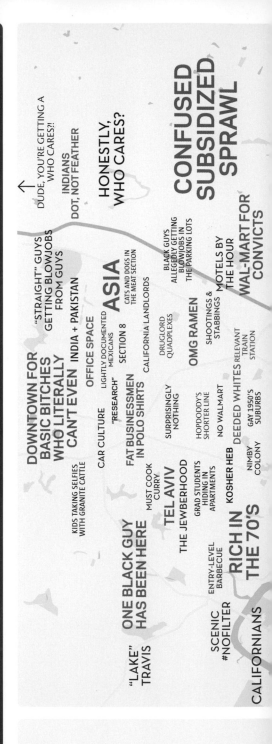

DUDE, YOU'RE GETTING A WHO CARES?!

INDIANS DOT, NOT FEATHER

HONESTLY, WHO CARES?

CONFUSED SUBSIDIZED SPRAWL

"STRAIGHT" GUYS GETTING BLOWJOBS FROM GUYS

DOWNTOWN FOR BASIC BITCHES WHO LITERALLY CAN'T EVEN

INDIA + PAKISTAN

OFFICE SPACE

ASIA

CATS AND DOGS IN THE MEAT SECTION

BLACK GUYS ALLEGEDLY GETTING BLOWJOBS IN THE PARKING LOTS

MOTELS BY THE HOUR

WAL-MART FOR CONVICTS

LIGHTLY DOCUMENTED MEXICANS

SECTION 8

CALIFORNIA LANDLORDS

CAR CULTURE

"RESEARCH"

FAT BUSINESSMEN IN POLO SHIRTS

DRUGLORD QUADPLEXES

OMG RAMEN

SHOOTINGS & STABBINGS

SURPRISINGLY NOTHING

RELEVANT TRAIN STATION

KIDS TAKING SELFIES WITH GRANITE CATTLE

MUST COOK CURRY

HOPDODDY'S SHORTER LINE

NO WALMART

DEEDED WHITES

GAY 1950'S SUBURBS

TEL AVIV

THE JEWBERHOOD

GRAD STUDENTS HIDING IN APARTMENTS

KOSHER HEB

NIMBY COLONY

"LAKE" TRAVIS

ONE BLACK GUY HAS BEEN HERE

ENTRY-LEVEL BARBECUE

RICH IN THE 70'S

SCENIC #NOFILTER

CALIFORNIANS

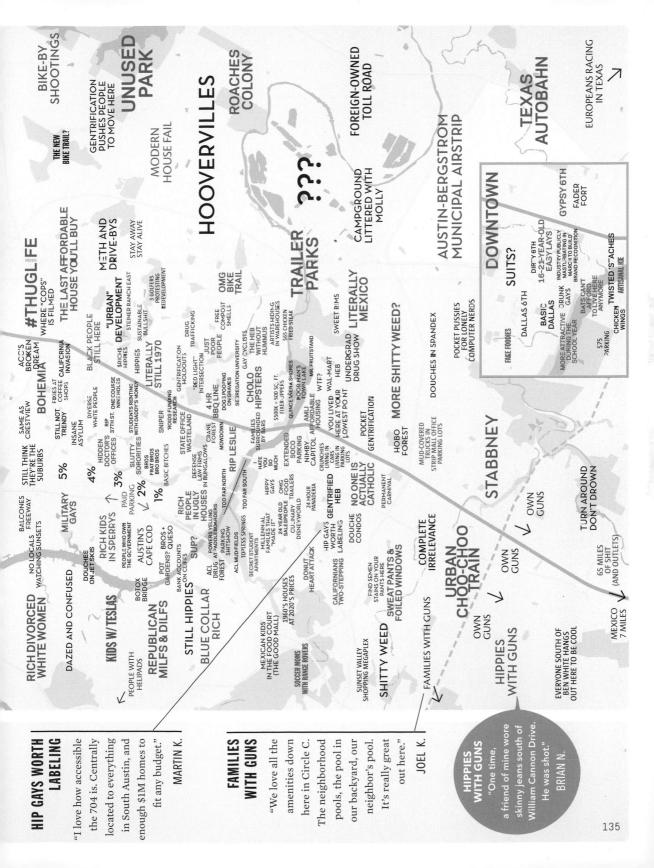

BIKE-BY SHOOTINGS

UNUSED PARK

THE NEW BIKE TRAIL?

GENTRIFICATION PUSHES PEOPLE TO MOVE HERE

MODERN HOUSE FAIL

ROACHES COLONY

HOOVERVILLES

???

FOREIGN-OWNED TOLL ROAD

CAMPGROUND LITTERED WITH MOLLY

AUSTIN-BERGSTROM MUNICIPAL AIRSTRIP

TEXAS AUTOBAHN

EUROPEANS RACING IN TEXAS

#THUGLIFE

WHERE "COPS" IS FILMED

THE LAST AFFORDABLE HOUSE YOU'LL BUY

METH AND DRIVE-BYS

STAY AWAY STAY ALIVE

ACC'S BROKEN DREAM

BOHEMIA

CALIFORNIA INVASION

BLACK PEOPLE STILL HERE

"URBAN" DEVELOPMENT

Steiner Ranch East

$RICH$ HIPPIES

SUSTAINABLE BULLSHIT

3 GOLFERS PROTESTING REDEVELOPMENT

LITERALLY STILL 1970

SAME AS CRESTVIEW

STILL THINK THEY'RE THE SUBURBS

5%

4%

3%

FIXIES AT COFFEE SHOPS

STILL NOT TRENDY

INSANE ASYLUM

DIVERSE WHITE PEOPLE

HIDDEN DOCTOR'S OFFICES

RIP 37TH ST.

ONE COURSE NINE HOLES

STUDENTS RENTING WITH DADDY'S MONEY

GENTRIFICATION HOLDOUTS

DRUG LIGHT TRAFFICKING

"RED LIGHT" INTERSECTION

JUST POOR PEOPLE

FREE COMPOST SMELLS

OMG BIKE TRAIL

DOG'S POOPING ON GRAVES

"ROIDS FUNDING RESEARCH

GAY CYCLISTS

SEGREGATION UNIVERSITY

ARTISTS HIDING IN WAREHOUSES

$65 CHICKEN FRIED STEAK

SWEET RIMS

LITERALLY MEXICO

$500K = 500 SQ. FT. FIXER-UPPERS

QUINCE-ñERA SHORES

Mr. FRUITSTAND

POOR MAN'S TOWN LAKE

WTF?

UNDERGRAD DRUG SHOW

MORE SHITTY WEED?

PAID PARKING

2%

1%

RICH PEOPLE IN UGLY HOUSES ON CLIFFS

SUP?

BANK ACCOUNTS

BASIC BITCHES

DEFENSE LAW FIRMS IN BUNGALOWS

STATE OFFICE WASTELAND

CRANE FOREST

MOWDOWN

RIP LESLIE

4 HR BBQ LINE

FAMILIES SURROUNDED BY BARS

EXTENDED SOCO PARKING

NIMBY CAPITOL

AMLI AFFORDABLE HOUSING

YOU LIVED HERE AT YOUR LOWEST PT

CRUNCHIES LIVING IN CARS

NO ONE IS AT YOUR PT

POCKET GENTRIFICATION

HOBO FOREST

PERMANENT CARNIVAL

MUD-COVERED STRIP MALLS IN OFFICE PARKING LOTS

POCKET PUSSIES FOR LONELY COMPUTER NERDS

DOUCHES IN SPANDEX

TRAILER PARKS

STABBNEY

BALCONES FREEWAY

NO LOCALS WATCHING SUNSETS

MILITARY GAYS

RICH KIDS IN SPERRYS

PEOPLE WHO OWN THE GOVERNMENT

POT GARDENS?

BROS + QUESO

DOUCHES ON JET SKIS

AUSTIN'S CAPE COD

ACL FLOWERS YELLING AT PADDLEBOARDERS

DRUG PARKING FOREST SHITSHOW

ACL MUDFIELDS

TOPLESS SPRINGS

TOO FAR NORTH

TOO FAR SOUTH

SECRET STUDENT APARTMENTS

MILLENNIAL FAMILIES THAT "MADE IT"

24 YEAR OLD CULINARY SALESPEOPLE DISNEYWORLD

HIPPY GAYS

OMG FOOD TRAILERS

HATE YOU SO MUCH

GENTRIFIED HEB

HIP GAYS WORTH LABELING

DOUCHE CONDOS

NO ONE IS ACTUALLY CATHOLIC

COMPLETE IRRELEVANCE

OWN GUNS

TURN AROUND DON'T DROWN

65 MILES OF SHIT (AND OUTLETS)

RICH DIVORCED WHITE WOMEN

DAZED AND CONFUSED

KIDS W/TESLAS

BOTOX BRIDGE

REPUBLICAN MILFS & DILFS

STILL HIPPIES

BLUE COLLAR RICH

PEOPLE WITH HELIPADS

MEXICAN KIDS IN THE FOOD COURT (THE GOOD MALL)

1960'S HOUSES AT 2020'S PRICES

SOCCER MOMS WITH RANGE ROVERS

DONUT HEART ATTACK

CALIFORNIANS TWO-STEPPING

FIND SEMEN STAINS ON YOUR PANTS HERE

SWEAT PANTS & FOILED WINDOWS

CALIFORNIANS WORTH LABELING

SUNSET VALLEY SHOPPING MEGAPLEX

SHITTY WEED

FAMILIES WITH GUNS

URBAN CHOO-CHOO TRAIN

OWN GUNS

HIPPIES WITH GUNS

OWN GUNS

EVERYONE SOUTH OF BEN WHITE HANGS OUT HERE TO BE COOL

MEXICO 7 MILES

DOWNTOWN

SUITS?

DALLAS 6TH

BASIC DALLAS

FAKE FOODIES

MORE ATTRACTIVE DURING THE SCHOOL YEAR

DRUNK GAYS

BATS CAN'T LIVE HERE TOLERATE YOU ANYMORE

$75 PARKING

CHICKEN WINGS

ARTISANAL ICE

TWISTED 'STACHES

DIRTY 6TH

16-21-YEAR-OLD EASY LAYS

INDUSTRY PUBLICLY MASTUBATING IN MARCH TO BUILD BRAND RECOGNITION

GYPSY 6TH

FADER FORT

HIP GAYS WORTH LABELING

"I love how accessible the 704 is. Centrally located to everything in South Austin, and enough $1M homes to fit any budget."

MARTIN K.

FAMILIES WITH GUNS

"We love all the amenities down here in Circle C. The neighborhood pools, the pool in our backyard, our neighbor's pool. It's really great out here."

JOEL K.

HIPPIES WITH GUNS

"One time, a friend of mine wore skinny jeans south of William Cannon Drive. He was shot."

BRIAN N.

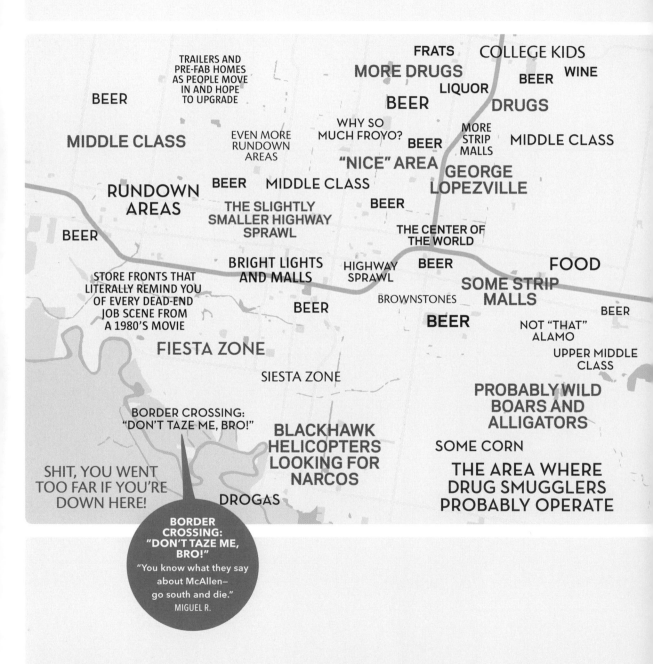

TRAILERS AND PRE-FAB HOMES AS PEOPLE MOVE IN AND HOPE TO UPGRADE

FRATS
COLLEGE KIDS
MORE DRUGS
BEER
WINE
LIQUOR

BEER
BEER
DRUGS

MIDDLE CLASS
EVEN MORE RUNDOWN AREAS
WHY SO MUCH FROYO?
BEER
MORE STRIP MALLS
MIDDLE CLASS

"NICE" AREA
GEORGE LOPEZVILLE

BEER
MIDDLE CLASS

RUNDOWN AREAS
THE SLIGHTLY SMALLER HIGHWAY SPRAWL
BEER

BEER

THE CENTER OF THE WORLD

BRIGHT LIGHTS AND MALLS
HIGHWAY SPRAWL
BEER
FOOD

STORE FRONTS THAT LITERALLY REMIND YOU OF EVERY DEAD-END JOB SCENE FROM A 1980'S MOVIE
BROWNSTONES
SOME STRIP MALLS

BEER
BEER
BEER

NOT "THAT" ALAMO

FIESTA ZONE
UPPER MIDDLE CLASS

SIESTA ZONE

PROBABLY WILD BOARS AND ALLIGATORS

BORDER CROSSING: "DON'T TAZE ME, BRO!"

BLACKHAWK HELICOPTERS LOOKING FOR NARCOS
SOME CORN

SHIT, YOU WENT TOO FAR IF YOU'RE DOWN HERE!
THE AREA WHERE DRUG SMUGGLERS PROBABLY OPERATE

DROGAS

BORDER CROSSING: "DON'T TAZE ME, BRO!"
"You know what they say about McAllen— go south and die."
MIGUEL R.

McALLEN
TEXAS

Despite having some of the highest retail sales per household across the state of Texas, McAllen is one of the poorest metro areas in the nation, where less than 50% of the residents feel safe outside of their homes after dark. It there is a city in this book where you can get shot at, but not know which country it came from, McAllen is it. But, you are probably safe, unless you try to jump the border to get drunk for less than five dollars, and end up playing one of the favorite local drinking games entitled "Getting Kidnapped by the Drug Cartel." Ole!

TOWNS NAMED AFTER WHOEVER BUILT A HOUSE THERE FIRST

EMPTY AREA BEING DEVELOPED INTO A SPRAWL

"RURAL" SETTING FOR IDIOT COWBOY WANNABES

NONE DARE VENTURE HERE

PAWN SHOPS

BEER   WAL-MART

TALLEST BUILDING (IS FOUR STORIES)

PALM TREES

FIREWORKS AND ADMITTEDLY GOOD TACOS

PARTY ZONE AND SKATERS

LESS QUIET NEIGHBORHOOD

QUIET NEIGHBORHOOD

THE 'BURBS

TALLEST BUILDING (IS FOUR STORIES):
"And it's a walk-up."
CARLOS R.

TULSA

OKLAHOMA

Tulsa is the belt buckle of the United States' Bible Belt, working to keep religious America's pants up. The city was known as the oil capital of the world for most of the twentieth century, until a mass exodus of oil companies in 1982 driven by freefalling gas prices and a desire to not be in Oklahoma. Oklahomans are known as Sooners, because the sooner you get here, the sooner you can leave, and while the thrilling new Woodie Guthrie Center for the Arts is worth a look, the overwhelmingly horrible history of the American Indian in Oklahoma will have you looking for the nearest freeway out of town. But don't think too much, Oklahoma is OK!

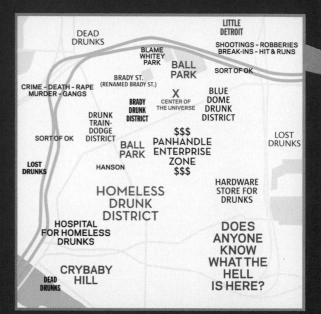

WHITE TRASH ZONE
"Every Tuesday, we just dump all of our trash here."
BRADLEY C.

Credit: Anonymous

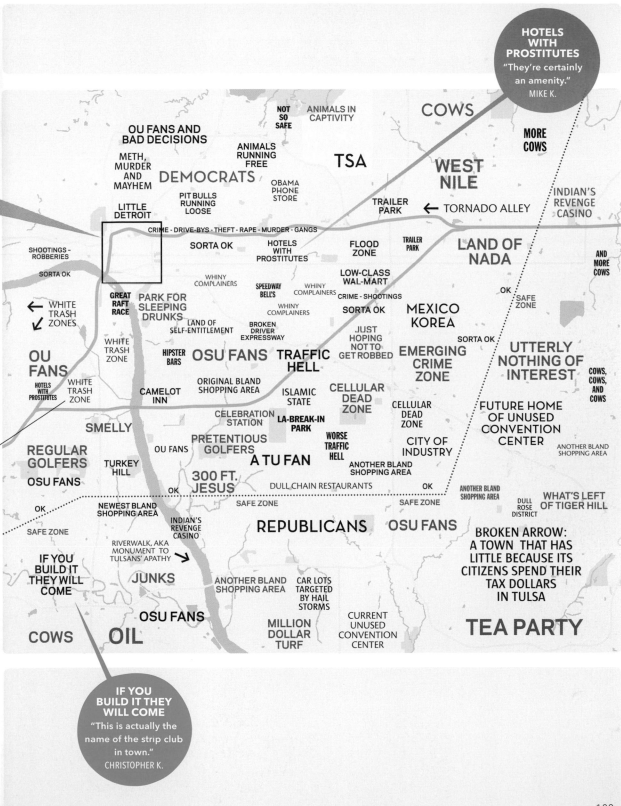

HOTELS
WITH
PROSTITUTES
"They're certainly
an amenity."
MIKE K.

COWS

MORE
COWS

NOT
SO
SAFE

ANIMALS IN
CAPTIVITY

OU FANS AND
BAD DECISIONS

ANIMALS
RUNNING
FREE

TSA

WEST
NILE

INDIAN'S
REVENGE
CASINO

METH,
MURDER
AND
MAYHEM

DEMOCRATS

OBAMA
PHONE
STORE

PIT BULLS
RUNNING
LOOSE

TRAILER
PARK

TORNADO ALLEY

LITTLE
DETROIT

CRIME - DRIVE-BYS - THEFT - RAPE - MURDER - GANGS

SHOOTINGS -
ROBBERIES

SORTA OK

HOTELS
WITH
PROSTITUTES

FLOOD
ZONE

TRAILER
PARK

LAND OF
NADA

AND
MORE
COWS

SORTA OK

WHINY
COMPLAINERS

SPEEDWAY
BELL'S

WHINY
COMPLAINERS

LOW-CLASS
WAL-MART

OK

SAFE
ZONE

WHITE
TRASH
ZONES

GREAT
RAFT
RACE

PARK FOR
SLEEPING
DRUNKS

LAND OF
SELF-ENTITLEMENT

WHINY
COMPLAINERS

BROKEN
DRIVER
EXPRESSWAY

CRIME - SHOOTINGS

SORTA OK

JUST
HOPING
NOT TO
GET ROBBED

MEXICO
KOREA

SORTA OK

UTTERLY
NOTHING OF
INTEREST

COWS,
COWS,
AND
COWS

OU
FANS

WHITE
TRASH
ZONE

HIPSTER
BARS

OSU FANS

TRAFFIC
HELL

EMERGING
CRIME
ZONE

HOTELS
WITH
PROSTITUTES

WHITE
TRASH
ZONE

CAMELOT
INN

ORIGINAL BLAND
SHOPPING AREA

ISLAMIC
STATE

CELLULAR
DEAD
ZONE

CELLULAR
DEAD
ZONE

FUTURE HOME
OF UNUSED
CONVENTION
CENTER

ANOTHER BLAND
SHOPPING AREA

SMELLY

CELEBRATION
STATION

LA-BREAK-IN
PARK

WORSE
TRAFFIC
HELL

CITY OF
INDUSTRY

REGULAR
GOLFERS

TURKEY
HILL

OU FANS

PRETENTIOUS
GOLFERS

A TU FAN

ANOTHER BLAND
SHOPPING AREA

OSU FANS

300 FT.
JESUS

OK

DULL CHAIN RESTAURANTS

OK

ANOTHER BLAND
SHOPPING AREA

DULL
ROSE
DISTRICT

WHAT'S LEFT
OF TIGER HILL

OK

NEWEST BLAND
SHOPPING AREA

SAFE ZONE

SAFE ZONE

SAFE ZONE

INDIAN'S
REVENGE
CASINO

REPUBLICANS

OSU FANS

BROKEN ARROW:
A TOWN THAT HAS
LITTLE BECAUSE ITS
CITIZENS SPEND THEIR
TAX DOLLARS
IN TULSA

IF YOU
BUILD IT
THEY WILL
COME

RIVERWALK, AKA
MONUMENT TO
TULSANS' APATHY

JUNKS

ANOTHER BLAND
SHOPPING AREA

CAR LOTS
TARGETED
BY HAIL
STORMS

CURRENT
UNUSED
CONVENTION
CENTER

TEA PARTY

COWS

OIL

OSU FANS

MILLION
DOLLAR
TURF

IF YOU
BUILD IT THEY
WILL COME
"This is actually the
name of the strip club
in town."
CHRISTOPHER K.

139

OKLAHOMA CITY

OKLAHOMA

Oklahoma City is the largest city in Oklahoma (I challenge you to name another city besides Tulsa), known for being the heart of tornado alley, which we only know about because of the American classic *Twister*. The city also features one of the largest livestock markets in the world—and that's only counting the people at Wal-Mart. Easily one of the 175 most important American cities, Oklahoma City is a diverse mix of Wal-Mart patrons and K-Mart patrons that, while never able to see eye to eye, have been able to peacefully coexist in this great, mid-size to small metropolis.

LANDSCAPERS & KITCHEN STAFF

"A good gauge of how poor you are is to measure your proximity to a Boost Mobile or a Little Caesars pizza. The closer you are to them, the poorer you are. If you are in between the two, you hit the figurative jackpot of being poor."

CAMERON U.

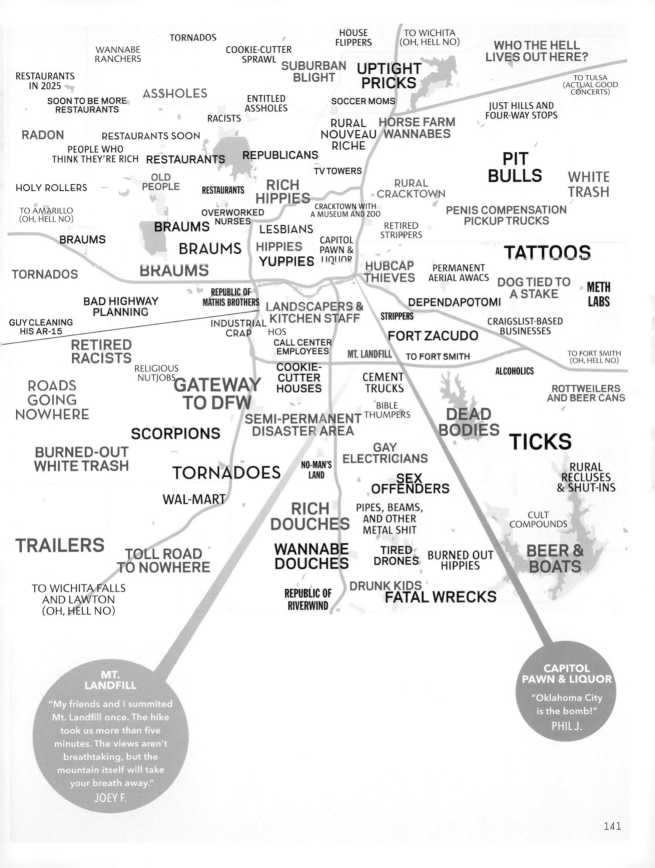

THE LEFT COAST

When American author Horace Greeley said, "Go West, young man," he was pushing our country's westward expansion to reap the benefits of the fertile farmland (and probably kill off a few Native Americans along the way). He did not say "Go left, young man" in reference to overpopulating our country's Western Seaboard with liberal weed-smoking freeloading hippies, A-list d-bag celebs, crunchy tech bros, and the entire Silicone Valley. Yes, "silicone" is spelled correctly.

The United States' West Coast is often referred to as the "best coast" because it is host to some of America's most expensive cities, greatest traffic jams, and deadliest rap scenes, as well as more Asian people than live in Asia. Whether you love spending exorbitant amounts of money for a 15-square-foot apartment, or the suicidal overcast skies of the Pacific Northwest, there is something for everyone along the Pacific Coast. LA boasts its "Botoxed Cougars in Luxury Condos," San Francisco showcases its "Once-Cool Park, Now Full of Idiot Tech Stereotypes," and Portland is close behind with its own version of "New California." But seriously, the West Coast is an amazing place to live if you have a couple million dollars lying around.

LOS ANGELES
CALIFORNIA

Crowds, mobs, tourists, people, people in cars, cars, traffic, congestion, tangled highways, mass urban sprawl: The City of Angels may sound like heaven for many people. It is a city inhabited by equal proportions of hot people and poor people, and some that fit into both categories. Those who have lived in LA for a while know it for its vibrant culture spread across over 500 square miles, its struggling actors serving grande lattes until they get their big break starring in a blockbuster film as a barista, and the smog, gangs, and Scientologists dead set on making everyone a victim. But, they don't call it La La Land for nothing. You too may be able to live the dream of making it big on the casting couch.

HIGHEST GUNSHOT RISK

"When visiting LA, just listen to 'California Love' by Tupac and Dr. Dre—and then don't go near any of the places they mention in the song. Unless it's for chicken and waffles."

LINDSAY D.

ANNOYING TOURISTS

"The people here are the type that actually buy T-shirts from Bubba Gump Shrimp Co."
CRAIG T.

DAUGHTER OR GIRLFRIEND?

"It's a game my sister and I play when shopping on Rodeo Drive. It's way harder than it sounds."
STACY S.

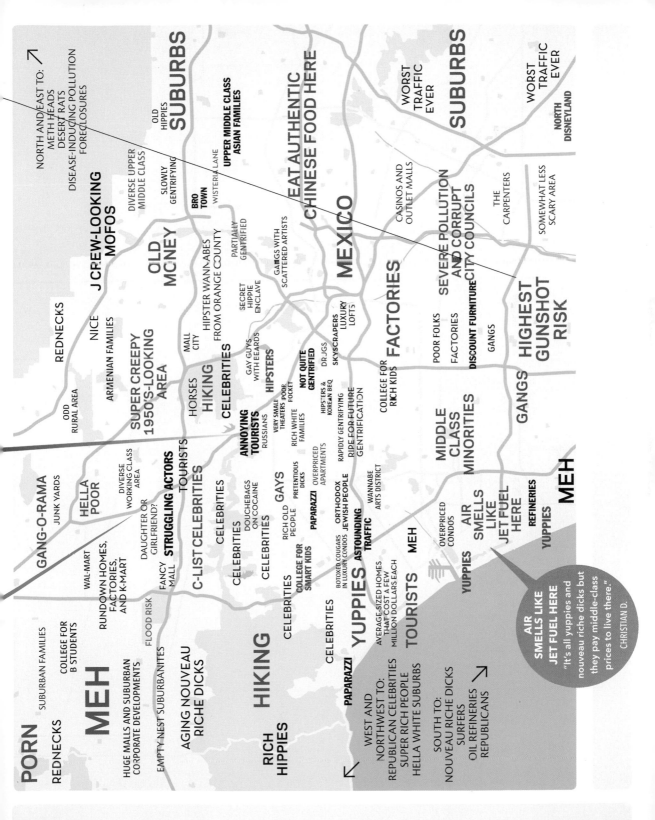

SAN FRANCISCO
CALIFORNIA

San Francisco is the only town in the United States where you can actually go to and from work uphill both ways. While many consider New York City the home of New Year's Eve, San Francisco has certainly seen its fair share of big balls drop in public— the city is ranked the gayest in the country. If the most expensive rent in America won't steer you away, the pungent aroma of street trash around every corner, never-ending fog, and Asian gangs most certainly will. But, the city is culturally diverse and claimed by many inhabitants to be The Center of the Universe. When you visit, make sure to call it "Frisco." Everybody loves that, and they will give you a personal tour of the infamous Alcatraz Island.

VENTURE CAPITALISM

"San Francisco is the type of place you can move to and history starts right when you get there. It's like those who hung out here in the '80s and '90s don't even matter."
CHRIS C.

TWITTERLAND, MINEFIELD OF HUMAN FECES

"I have personally had to throw away a pair of work shoes after an incident in 'Minefield of Human Feces.' Yay, San Francisco!"
CORDELL F.

SUTRO BATHS, CAVES,PROBABLY HOBO BJS

SUBURBIA
SURF GANGS

KARL THE FOG
NEW HIPSTERS

CHINESE DRIVEWAYS

SURF GANGS

NEW HIPSTERS

HOWLER MONKEYS

Credit: Dan Steiner, @hararuk

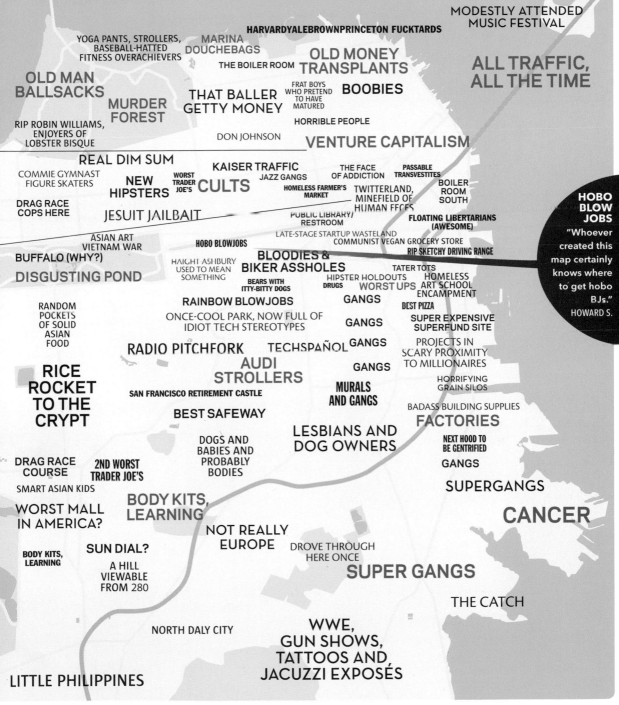

POST BOILER ROOM

MODESTLY ATTENDED MUSIC FESTIVAL

HARVARDYALEBROWNPRINCETON FUCKTARDS

YOGA PANTS, STROLLERS, BASEBALL-HATTED FITNESS OVERACHIEVERS

MARINA DOUCHEBAGS

OLD MONEY TRANSPLANTS

ALL TRAFFIC, ALL THE TIME

THE BOILER ROOM

OLD MAN BALLSACKS

MURDER FOREST

THAT BALLER GETTY MONEY

FRAT BOYS WHO PRETEND TO HAVE MATURED

BOOBIES

RIP ROBIN WILLIAMS, ENJOYERS OF LOBSTER BISQUE

DON JOHNSON

HORRIBLE PEOPLE

VENTURE CAPITALISM

REAL DIM SUM

KAISER TRAFFIC

THE FACE OF ADDICTION

PASSABLE TRANSVESTITES

COMMIE GYMNAST FIGURE SKATERS

NEW HIPSTERS

WORST TRADER JOE'S

CULTS

JAZZ GANGS

HOMELESS FARMER'S MARKET

TWITTERLAND, MINEFIELD OF HUMAN FECES

BOILER ROOM SOUTH

DRAG RACE COPS HERE

JESUIT JAILBAIT

PUBLIC LIBRARY/ RESTROOM

FLOATING LIBERTARIANS (AWESOME)

LATE-STAGE STARTUP WASTELAND

ASIAN ART VIETNAM WAR

HOBO BLOWJOBS

COMMUNIST VEGAN GROCERY STORE

RIP SKETCHY DRIVING RANGE

BUFFALO (WHY?)

HAIGHT ASHBURY USED TO MEAN SOMETHING

BLOODIES & BIKER ASSHOLES

TATER TOTS

HOMELESS ART SCHOOL ENCAMPMENT

DISGUSTING POND

BEARS WITH ITTY-BITTY DOGS

HIPSTER HOLDOUTS

WORST UPS

DRUGS

RANDOM POCKETS OF SOLID ASIAN FOOD

RAINBOW BLOWJOBS

GANGS

BEST PIZZA

ONCE-COOL PARK, NOW FULL OF IDIOT TECH STEREOTYPES

GANGS

SUPER EXPENSIVE SUPERFUND SITE

RADIO PITCHFORK

TECHSPAÑOL

GANGS

PROJECTS IN SCARY PROXIMITY TO MILLIONAIRES

RICE ROCKET TO THE CRYPT

AUDI STROLLERS

GANGS

SAN FRANCISCO RETIREMENT CASTLE

MURALS AND GANGS

HORRIFYING GRAIN SILOS

BEST SAFEWAY

BADASS BUILDING SUPPLIES

DOGS AND BABIES AND PROBABLY BODIES

LESBIANS AND DOG OWNERS

FACTORIES

DRAG RACE COURSE

2ND WORST TRADER JOE'S

NEXT HOOD TO BE GENTRIFIED

SMART ASIAN KIDS

GANGS

BODY KITS, LEARNING

SUPERGANGS

WORST MALL IN AMERICA?

CANCER

BODY KITS, LEARNING

SUN DIAL?

NOT REALLY EUROPE

A HILL VIEWABLE FROM 280

DROVE THROUGH HERE ONCE

SUPER GANGS

THE CATCH

NORTH DALY CITY

WWE, GUN SHOWS, TATTOOS AND JACUZZI EXPOSÉS

LITTLE PHILIPPINES

HOBO BLOW JOBS
"Whoever created this map certainly knows where to get hobo BJs."
HOWARD S.

SOUTH
SAN FRANCISCO BAY
CALIFORNIA

RICH, BUT ACTUALLY SMART KIDS
"Ughh, I can't even with these kids."
SUSAN H.

SLOW TRAINS BUDGET ENOUGH TIME FOR SUICIDES

BATTLE FOR WORLD DOMINATION
"How can we let billionaires come into our neighborhood and get whatever they want, simply running over poor millionaires like myself?"
STEVEN P.

LULULEMON MILFS

SCENIC ON WEEKENDS HELL ON WEEKDAYS

TECH AND VC BILLIONAIRE HOT SHOTS $$$$

SAT PREP CLASSES
"I'm taking an SAT prep class, not because I want to go to college. I'm a twenty-seven-year-old high school dropout, doing research for an SAT prep startup I'm looking to launch."
HUA L.

NATURE AND OUTDOORSY FREAKS

PLACE TO STASH A BODY

Credit: @justinmix

BRIDGE TO
PLEBIAN POORS

SELFIES WITH
THE PIPE PLANK

NAPA OF THE BAY

ZUCKBOOK

THE FUTURE

405 JUNIOR

**NAPA
OF THE BAY**
"If Freemont is the
Napa of the Bay, then
what is Napa?"
LEO S.

RICH,
BUT ACTUALLY
SMART KIDS

BATTLE FOR
WORLD
DOMINATION

SMELLS LIKE
SHIT

INDIANS AND LOUD
CHINESE PEOPLE

FREE FOOD
AND SELFIES

GENTRIFYING
TRAILER TRASH

MEDITERRANEAN EXPERIENCE
DON'T CONFUSE WITH DISH & DASH

FREE FLIGHTS
IN WHEEL WELLS

SAT PREP CLASSES OLD INDIANS
WALKING IN
EVENINGS

CLOSED AT 10PM
EXCEPT DONUTS

RICH, SNOBBY KIDS
WITH MEDIOCRE GRADES
IN SCHOOL

RATCHET NIGHTLIFE
AND ORANGE SAUCE

DELECTABLE
VIETNAMESE
COFFEE

UNDERWHELMED FOREIGN
TOURISTS TAKING SELFIES
AT APPLE

SHOOTINGS
AND STABBINGS

DAT BOILING CRAB, DOE!

GUY WHOSE
CAREER IS
WORKING AT QQQ

NERDS WITH PARENTAL
SUPPORT, ON A MISSION
TO GENTRIFY

ASIAN FAMILY
DYNASTY

CHEAP GAS
AND COMPROMISED
SAFETY

EVERWHITE

GRAVEYARD OF YOUNG TEENS'
STIS AND EVOS

LITERALLY
NOTHING

WANNABE
ROCK CLIMBERS
IN SUBARUS

TECH IPO
MILLIONAIRES

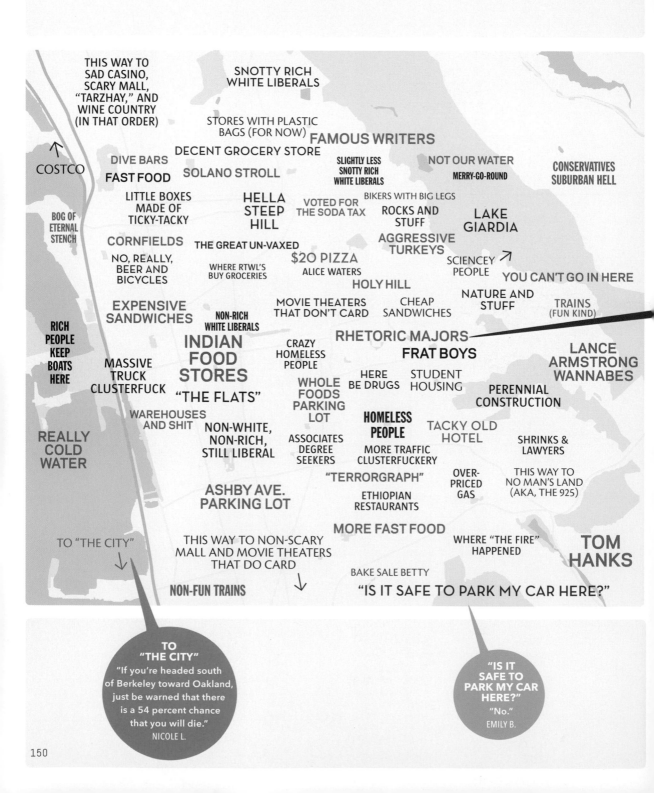

THIS WAY TO SAD CASINO, SCARY MALL, "TARZHAY," AND WINE COUNTRY (IN THAT ORDER)

SNOTTY RICH WHITE LIBERALS

STORES WITH PLASTIC BAGS (FOR NOW)

FAMOUS WRITERS

DECENT GROCERY STORE

↑ COSTCO

DIVE BARS

FAST FOOD

SOLANO STROLL

SLIGHTLY LESS SNOTTY RICH WHITE LIBERALS

NOT OUR WATER

MERRY-GO-ROUND

CONSERVATIVES SUBURBAN HELL

BOG OF ETERNAL STENCH

LITTLE BOXES MADE OF TICKY-TACKY

HELLA STEEP HILL

VOTED FOR THE SODA TAX

BIKERS WITH BIG LEGS

ROCKS AND STUFF

LAKE GIARDIA

CORNFIELDS

THE GREAT UN-VAXED

AGGRESSIVE TURKEYS

NO, REALLY, BEER AND BICYCLES

WHERE RTWL'S BUY GROCERIES

$20 PIZZA

ALICE WATERS

SCIENCEY PEOPLE ↗

YOU CAN'T GO IN HERE

HOLY HILL

EXPENSIVE SANDWICHES

NON-RICH WHITE LIBERALS

MOVIE THEATERS THAT DON'T CARD

CHEAP SANDWICHES

NATURE AND STUFF

TRAINS (FUN KIND)

RICH PEOPLE KEEP BOATS HERE

INDIAN FOOD STORES

CRAZY HOMELESS PEOPLE

RHETORIC MAJORS

FRAT BOYS

LANCE ARMSTRONG WANNABES

MASSIVE TRUCK CLUSTERFUCK

"THE FLATS"

HERE BE DRUGS

STUDENT HOUSING

PERENNIAL CONSTRUCTION

WHOLE FOODS PARKING LOT

REALLY COLD WATER

WAREHOUSES AND SHIT

NON-WHITE, NON-RICH, STILL LIBERAL

ASSOCIATES DEGREE SEEKERS

HOMELESS PEOPLE

MORE TRAFFIC CLUSTERFUCKERY

TACKY OLD HOTEL

SHRINKS & LAWYERS

"TERRORGRAPH"

OVER-PRICED GAS

THIS WAY TO NO MAN'S LAND (AKA, THE 925)

ASHBY AVE. PARKING LOT

ETHIOPIAN RESTAURANTS

TO "THE CITY"

MORE FAST FOOD

THIS WAY TO NON-SCARY MALL AND MOVIE THEATERS THAT DO CARD

WHERE "THE FIRE" HAPPENED

TOM HANKS

↓

BAKE SALE BETTY

NON-FUN TRAINS

↓

"IS IT SAFE TO PARK MY CAR HERE?"

TO "THE CITY"
"If you're headed south of Berkeley toward Oakland, just be warned that there is a 54 percent chance that you will die."
NICOLE L.

"IS IT SAFE TO PARK MY CAR HERE?"
"No."
EMILY B.

150

BERKELEY
CALIFORNIA

If you are a free-speech supporting, pro-choice, anti-war vegan with a "You Can't Hug with Nuclear Arms" bumper sticker on your Prius and a severe intolerance for gluten, you would totally love Berkeley. In recent years, the University of California's oldest campus, UC Berkeley, protested a Panda Express opening on campus, the city became the first in the country to proclaim a day recognizing bisexuals, the city now provides free medical marijuana to low-income patients, and it was the first city to approve a tax on soda. Peace, love, and happiness, right? Just don't get your head stuck too far up in the Berkeley fog.

RHETORIC MAJORS

"UC Berkeley has the best Rhetoric program in the United States. Is 'Rhetoric Majors' really the most judgmental label you have for us? Don't answer that. It was a rhetorical question."
VINCENT K.

SACRAMENTO
CALIFORNIA

The city of Sacramento built itself as a major distribution point during the Gold Rush of 1849, which likely led to it being established as the capital of California. The landmarks and historic buildings of Old Sacramento still stand on old cobbled streets, and today the city stands proud as the least memorable big city in California, famous for its proximity to San Francisco and Lake Tahoe. But, if you're not a fan of Sac Town, Davis is an easy bike ride away. Just make sure to bring your pepper spray for any UC Davis protesters.

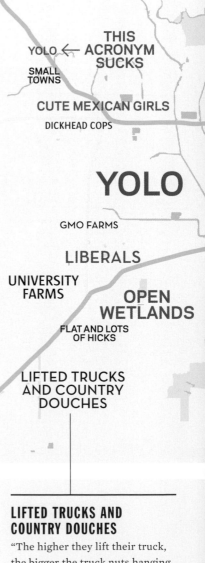

THIS ACRONYM SUCKS

YOLO ←

SMALL TOWNS

CUTE MEXICAN GIRLS

DICKHEAD COPS

YOLO

GMO FARMS

LIBERALS

UNIVERSITY FARMS

OPEN WETLANDS

FLAT AND LOTS OF HICKS

LIFTED TRUCKS AND COUNTRY DOUCHES

LIFTED TRUCKS AND COUNTRY DOUCHES

"The higher they lift their truck, the bigger the truck nuts hanging from the tow hitch."
RANDY P.

Credit: Anonymous

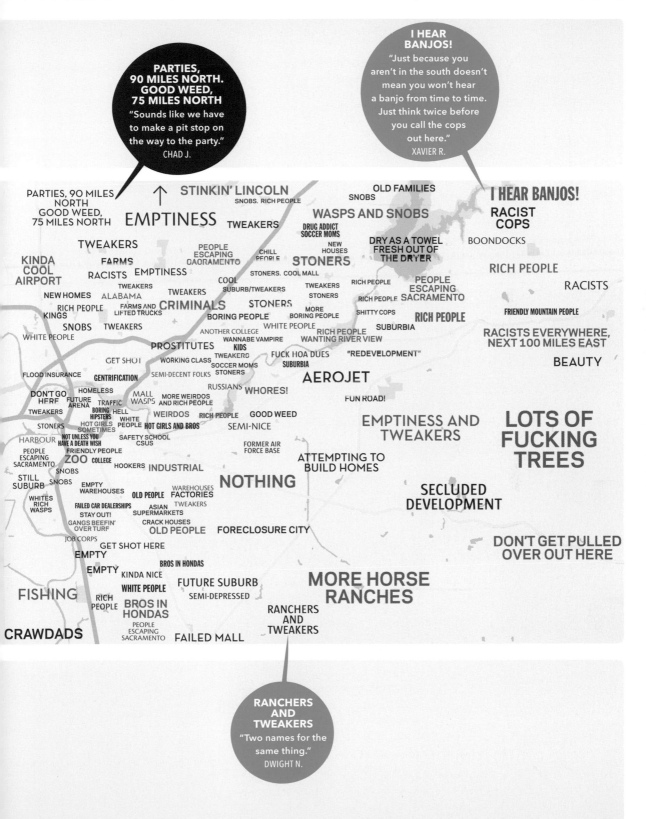

SANTA CRUZ
CALIFORNIA

Even though Huntington Beach started using the nickname "Surf City USA" in 1991, Santa Cruz served as the first home to surfing in California when it started using the moniker back in 1927. But Santa Cruz's surfers and stoners aren't ones to put up a fight because they are too busy playing disc golf and hacky sack, before they sit down in the park to play Jack Johnson covers on acoustic guitar to try and pick up chicks, dude. If you love riding surf boards as much as Beyoncé, Santa Cruz is the perfect city for you.

NUDE DUDES SACK TANNING

"Natural Bridges State Beach is one of my favorite beaches ever. Except for the fact that it is a nude beach and the only people who choose to go nude are old men who shouldn't be nude in the first place. I can't tell if it's a hacky sack, a beanbag, or an actual sack of walnuts."
TONYA K.

LESBIANS UNTIL GRADUATION
"Well, you can't say we didn't give it the old college try."
AMY S.

PEOPLE WAY TOO EXCITED ABOUT A PLANT

LESBIANS UNTIL GRADUATION

BURIED DEAD BODIES FROM THE 70'S WEED FARMS

ASIANS WHO SHAMED THEIR FAMILIES BY NOT GETTING INTO BERKELEY

FRESHLY DELIVERED MEXICAN HEROIN

UNCLE CHARLEY'S SUMMER CAMP

BUMS PUSHING SHOPPING CARTS BLOWING SNOT ROCKETS

"CAN I EMPTY MY SHITTER HERE?"

LIBERALS WHO FEAR MEXICANS

PROTESTS DURING FINALS

UNDERGRADS SLEEPING IN GARAGES & CLOSETS FOR $650/MONTH

RICH WHITE PEOPLE

ANOTHER FUCKING CALIFORNIA MISSION

SLUG SLUMS

"FREE SPIRITS" THAT OWE YOU $200

BODY WORKER FROM L.A.

HIDING COP

USED TO BE AN AWESOME VIEW

TRYING TO MOVE TO SCOTT'S VALLEY

W/S STICKERS, METH, AND DIVORCE PAPERS

HIPSTERS WITH KALE AND BLUEGRASS

SAFEWAY FORTRESS

WESTSIDE PRIDE SEWAGE

WRIGLEY'S GRAVEYARD

NEGLECTED INHERITED HOMES

DWINDLING MONARCHS

WHITE TRASH SURFERS PRETENDING TO BE FAMOUS

RUNNING OUT THE CLOCK IN A MOBILE HOME

ALWAYS FUCKING WINDY

NUDE DUDES SACK TANNING

SAN DIEGO
CALIFORNIA

San Diego's humility is quickly established through its nickname: "America's Finest City." This city that gave birth to California enjoys mild, sunny weather throughout the year, accompanied by severe costs of living and moderate incomes. The city is also a major hub for military and defense activities due to its proximity to the coast, and the probable need to defend our country from the Tijuana Cartel. If you love having sex and would love to make money for it, San Diego's flourishing prostitution scene is for you. But sex workers aren't the only people getting screwed in San Diego—just go check out a Chargers game. Stay classy.

DRUNK MILITARY
"Pacific Beach (PB) consists of three types of people: (1) college kids, (2) beach bums, and (3) adults with Peter Pan syndrome."
RYAN D.

OUR ONLY TOURIST ATTRACTION
"San Diego: come for the zoo, stay for the dreadful traffic, abundance of bros and military dudes, strange anti-intellectualism, and amazing weather we all complain about for absolutely no reason."
SANDY H.

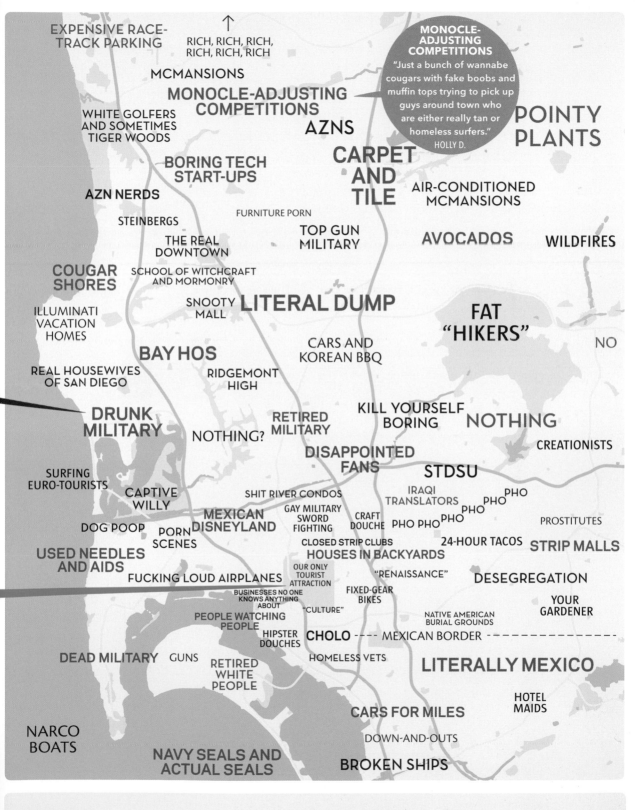

EXPENSIVE RACE-TRACK PARKING

↑
RICH, RICH, RICH, RICH, RICH, RICH

MCMANSIONS

MONOCLE-ADJUSTING COMPETITIONS

AZNS

WHITE GOLFERS AND SOMETIMES TIGER WOODS

MONOCLE-ADJUSTING COMPETITIONS
"Just a bunch of wannabe cougars with fake boobs and muffin tops trying to pick up guys around town who are either really tan or homeless surfers."
HOLLY D.

POINTY PLANTS

BORING TECH START-UPS

CARPET AND TILE

AIR-CONDITIONED MCMANSIONS

AZN NERDS

FURNITURE PORN

STEINBERGS

TOP GUN MILITARY

AVOCADOS

WILDFIRES

THE REAL DOWNTOWN

COUGAR SHORES

SCHOOL OF WITCHCRAFT AND MORMONRY

SNOOTY MALL

LITERAL DUMP

FAT "HIKERS"

ILLUMINATI VACATION HOMES

NO

BAY HOS

CARS AND KOREAN BBQ

REAL HOUSEWIVES OF SAN DIEGO

RIDGEMONT HIGH

DRUNK MILITARY

NOTHING?

RETIRED MILITARY

KILL YOURSELF BORING

NOTHING

CREATIONISTS

SURFING EURO-TOURISTS

DISAPPOINTED FANS

STDSU

CAPTIVE WILLY

SHIT RIVER CONDOS

IRAQI TRANSLATORS

PHO

PHO

DOG POOP

PORN SCENES

MEXICAN DISNEYLAND

GAY MILITARY SWORD FIGHTING

CRAFT DOUCHE

PHO PHO

PHO

PHO

PROSTITUTES

USED NEEDLES AND AIDS

CLOSED STRIP CLUBS

HOUSES IN BACKYARDS

24-HOUR TACOS

STRIP MALLS

FUCKING LOUD AIRPLANES

OUR ONLY TOURIST ATTRACTION

"RENAISSANCE"

DESEGREGATION

BUSINESSES NO ONE KNOWS ANYTHING ABOUT

FIXED-GEAR BIKES

YOUR GARDENER

PEOPLE WATCHING PEOPLE

"CULTURE"

NATIVE AMERICAN BURIAL GROUNDS

HIPSTER DOUCHES

CHOLO - - - - MEXICAN BORDER - - - - - - - - - - - - -

DEAD MILITARY

GUNS

RETIRED WHITE PEOPLE

HOMELESS VETS

LITERALLY MEXICO

HOTEL MAIDS

NARCO BOATS

CARS FOR MILES

DOWN-AND-OUTS

NAVY SEALS AND ACTUAL SEALS

BROKEN SHIPS

BOISE
IDAHO

Boise is the capital of Idaho, the potato-loving state that has a law forbidding citizens to give one another boxes of candy that weigh more than fifty pounds. But, if that isn't enough to sell you on Boise, surely the more than fifteen ways to pronounce the city's name will. The Treasure Valley area actually features an extensive urban trail system to get out and explore nature and try to forget that you're stuck in Boise. Visitors to the city will be warmly welcomed by the hundreds of thousands of Mormons that jump the Utah border just to escape to the sanity of Boise.

MORE-MONS
"Little houses made of ticky tacky and well-dressed, under-caffeinated families. It keeps property value high, so I'm not complaining."
ERIC G.

TRAFFIC AND STRIP MALLS
"Maybe it's these traffic jams that are driving all of us to meth. Gotta stay awake behind the wheel!"
SUSAN O.

HOSTILE REPUBLICANS

MERIDIAN EAST

MORE-MONS

MORMONS

MORE TRAFFIC MORE STRIP MALLS

NAMPA EAST

TRAFFIC LAND

SHITTY 2C DRIVERS

← NOTHING

STILL PISSED ABOUT ANNEXATION

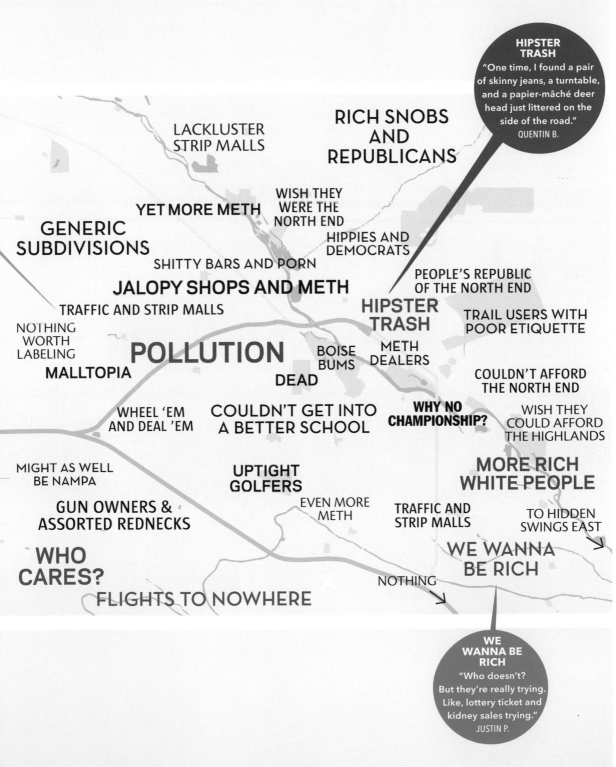

HIPSTER TRASH

"One time, I found a pair of skinny jeans, a turntable, and a papier-mâché deer head just littered on the side of the road."
QUENTIN B.

LACKLUSTER STRIP MALLS

RICH SNOBS AND REPUBLICANS

YET MORE METH

WISH THEY WERE THE NORTH END

GENERIC SUBDIVISIONS

HIPPIES AND DEMOCRATS

SHITTY BARS AND PORN

PEOPLE'S REPUBLIC OF THE NORTH END

JALOPY SHOPS AND METH

TRAFFIC AND STRIP MALLS

HIPSTER TRASH

TRAIL USERS WITH POOR ETIQUETTE

NOTHING WORTH LABELING

POLLUTION

BOISE BUMS

METH DEALERS

COULDN'T AFFORD THE NORTH END

MALLTOPIA

DEAD

WHEEL 'EM AND DEAL 'EM

COULDN'T GET INTO A BETTER SCHOOL

WHY NO CHAMPIONSHIP?

WISH THEY COULD AFFORD THE HIGHLANDS

MIGHT AS WELL BE NAMPA

UPTIGHT GOLFERS

MORE RICH WHITE PEOPLE

GUN OWNERS & ASSORTED REDNECKS

EVEN MORE METH

TRAFFIC AND STRIP MALLS

TO HIDDEN SWINGS EAST

WHO CARES?

WE WANNA BE RICH

NOTHING

FLIGHTS TO NOWHERE

WE WANNA BE RICH

"Who doesn't? But they're really trying. Like, lottery ticket and kidney sales trying."
JUSTIN P.

159

PORTLAND
OREGON

Bridgetown USA's only competition is Seattle when it comes to "Most Pretentious Hipster City in America." But, Portland may take the gluten-free cake due to its majority plaid-clad cycling douche population that is stuck in the 90s, its substantial growth trajectory in the "funemployment" industry, and enough

NAKED OLD MEN
PUMPKINS
DOCKWORKERS
TRAILER TRASH
PSEUDOEPHEDRINE

MIGHT GET SHOT

SHIPPING CONTAINERS

WHO KNOWS

NOBODY CARES
YUPSTERS
SKINNY HOUSES
KOLSCH

SUSTAINABLE LANDFILL

TRUCKER SEX
SPANDEX
HOBO CAMP

LESBIANIC ENCLAVE
12-YEAR-OLDS WITH GUNS
BRAVE SETTLERS
LUMBERJACK SHRINE
METH
VENERABLE 80'S CARPET

NOWHERE

?

COOL BRIDGE, BRO
CYCLOCROSS PRACTICE
MESOTHELIOMA KICKSTARTER
PCBS

SKINNY HOUSES
SPOILED CHILDREN
SOME NON-WHITES
FORMERLY UNREMARKABLE
DONKS
PROSTITUTES

SUPERFUND, JR
SHITTY MOTELS
14-YEAR-OLDS WITH GUNS
BORED LUTHERANS
TRAILER TRASH

INVASIVE SPECIES
GARBAGE
TOXIC SLUDGE
BLUFF MONGERS
YUPSTERS
SKINNY HOUSES
BIKE POLO
POVERTY

SPANDEX
SUPERFUND
BLUE COLLAR SLOBS
CONDOS
VEGAN TAPAS
DIVE BARS UNDER NEW OWNERSHIP
FUTSAL
MUD
ENDLESS GARAGE SAL

DEPRESSING APARTMENT COMPLEXES (PROBABLY)

OFF-LEASH DOGS
PARK EXCLUSIONS
NEW CALIFORNIA

HOBOS
HOBOS
TRAINS
TRUCKS
BIKE CONFLICTS
OLD MONEY
INSUFFERABLE BOUTIQUES
RANGE ROVERS
PORN
OLD MONEY

NIMBY'S
CYCLOCROSS PRACTICE
FUTURE CONDOS
CHEMICALS
RUST
TRAINS
CARHARTTS
FORMERLY ETHNIC
CRACK SALES
"DEEP NORTHEAST" CIRCA 2005
PHO

HUMMER DRIVERS
POOP BAGS
DECAY
INDUSTRIAL CHIC
BLAZERS
DOGGY DAYCARE
CONDOS
PRIUSI
AIRBNBS W/VIEWS

CUL DE SACS

INDUSTRIAL CHIC
CHIC
AUDI DRIVERS
USELESS STARTUPS
ELDERLY COUGARS
SPORTS
DENTISTS
14-YEAR-OLDS WITH GUNS
DIVE BARS UNDER NEW OWNERSHIP
HOSPITAL DULLARDS

SUBURBAN HELLSCAPE
OLD MONEY
TRINKETS
PARKING WOES
TECH BROS
JERSEY SHORE
HEAVY METAL
POSEURS
CONDOS
INSUFFERABLE BOUTIQUES
RUSTIC WINE BA

APPLEBEE'S
MINIVANS
HOBOS
SPORTS LAWYERS
DRUNK STUDENTS
TOURISTS
HOBOS
HEROIN
UNICYCLES
HIPSTERS
GLUTEN FREE PRESCHOOL
TOURIS

IRATE COMMUTERS
SUICIDE BUCKET DRUMMERS
STROLLERS
SPOILED CHILDREN
BOAT DRINKS
FOOD CART EVICTIONS
GUTTER PUNKS W/UKELELES
SUBARUS
YOGA
OPEN SEWERS

LANDSLIDES
WESTERN CAUCASIA
DOCTORS 'N' SHIT
CONDOS
FAUX ETHNIC FOOD
OPRAH ICE CREAM
USEL

CONGESTION
GAY DADS OLD MONEY
WET TENTS
URBAN MCMANSIONS
STRIP CLUBS
TRANSPLANTS 'N' TOURISTS
NISSAN LEAFS
SLICE O' THE BURB:
MOTELS
STRIP MALL

MUD
$500K STARTER HOMES
NEW ALBERT

"PORTLAND"
TRADER JOE'S
VERY SAD FREE BOXES
DISPLACED GOATS

FOOD CART EVICTIONS
"In Portland, we don't do breakfast. We call it the Brunch of Champions."
WILL S.
GRAVEL & HOBOS
NIMBY'S
EXTREMELY SPOILED CHILDREN
JESUS FREAKS
ARBY'S

LAND OF THE LOST
"HIP" BABY BOOMERS

NIKE EMPLOYEES?
STARBUCKS
REALLY REALLY WHITE
BIG PILE OF GRAVEL WITH PEO LIVING IN IT
LINGERIE SHOW
TOXIC VAPOR

THE ARISTOCRACY
PEOPLE WHO ONLY SEEM TO BATH WHEN THE CREEK FLOODS

"WE MOVED TO PORTLAND"
RICH ASSHOLES W/MULTIPLE BMWS
SPEED TRAPS AND SINGLE MOMS

160

farm-to-table options to choke a grass-fed cow. But, Portland wasn't even the first city to have its own name—it is named after Portland, ME. Even the city's unofficial slogan, "Keep Portland Weird," isn't an original. However, it is the hometown of both The Shins and The Decemberists, which is enough to cause anyone to jump off any one of the city's beautiful bridges.

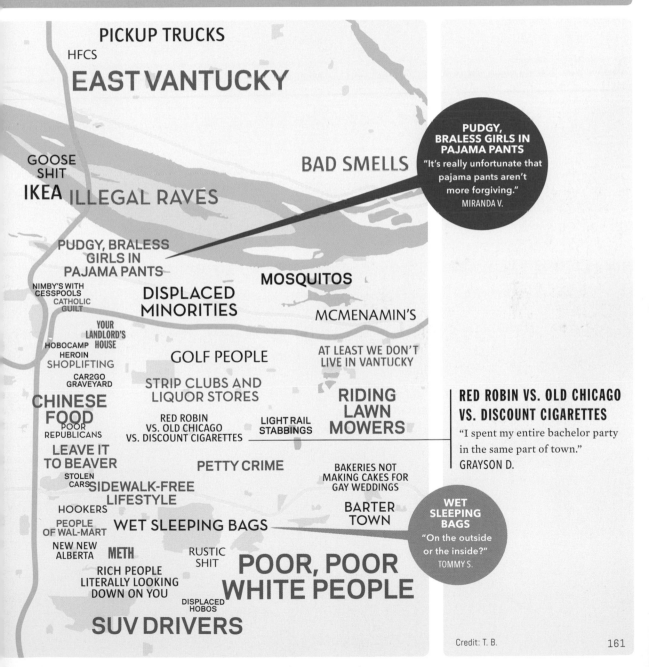

PICKUP TRUCKS

HFCS

EAST VANTUCKY

GOOSE SHIT

IKEA ILLEGAL RAVES

BAD SMELLS

PUDGY, BRALESS GIRLS IN PAJAMA PANTS
"It's really unfortunate that pajama pants aren't more forgiving."
MIRANDA V.

PUDGY, BRALESS GIRLS IN PAJAMA PANTS

MOSQUITOS

NIMBY'S WITH CESSPOOLS
CATHOLIC GUILT

DISPLACED MINORITIES

MCMENAMIN'S

YOUR LANDLORD'S HOUSE
HOBOCAMP
HEROIN
SHOPLIFTING

GOLF PEOPLE

AT LEAST WE DON'T LIVE IN VANTUCKY

CAR2GO GRAVEYARD

STRIP CLUBS AND LIQUOR STORES

CHINESE FOOD
POOR REPUBLICANS

RED ROBIN VS. OLD CHICAGO VS. DISCOUNT CIGARETTES

LIGHT RAIL STABBINGS

RIDING LAWN MOWERS

RED ROBIN VS. OLD CHICAGO VS. DISCOUNT CIGARETTES
"I spent my entire bachelor party in the same part of town."
GRAYSON D.

LEAVE IT TO BEAVER

STOLEN CARS
SIDEWALK-FREE LIFESTYLE

PETTY CRIME

BAKERIES NOT MAKING CAKES FOR GAY WEDDINGS

HOOKERS

PEOPLE OF WAL-MART

WET SLEEPING BAGS

BARTER TOWN

WET SLEEPING BAGS
"On the outside or the inside?"
TOMMY S.

NEW NEW ALBERTA
METH
RUSTIC SHIT

POOR, POOR WHITE PEOPLE

RICH PEOPLE LITERALLY LOOKING DOWN ON YOU

DISPLACED HOBOS

SUV DRIVERS

SEATTLE

WASHINGTON

The Emerald City gets its name from the lush greenery in which it is settled, but that isn't the only thing the city has going for it. Grunge, cappuccinos, heroin, jazz, and memories of the most compelling non-champion basketball team of the 90s help to fill the city with smiles in spite of the seattlecidal overcast skies. And with one coffee shop for every 4,000 people that live there, there is enough caffeine to fuel the countless brogrammers moving to the city each day, helping to make even the mild luxuries the city has to offer completely unaffordable.

SINGLE GIRLS DRINKING CHARDONNAY
"More like 'Young Moms Pushing Strollers.' Maybe it was all that wine that got these girls into this mess."
JARED G.

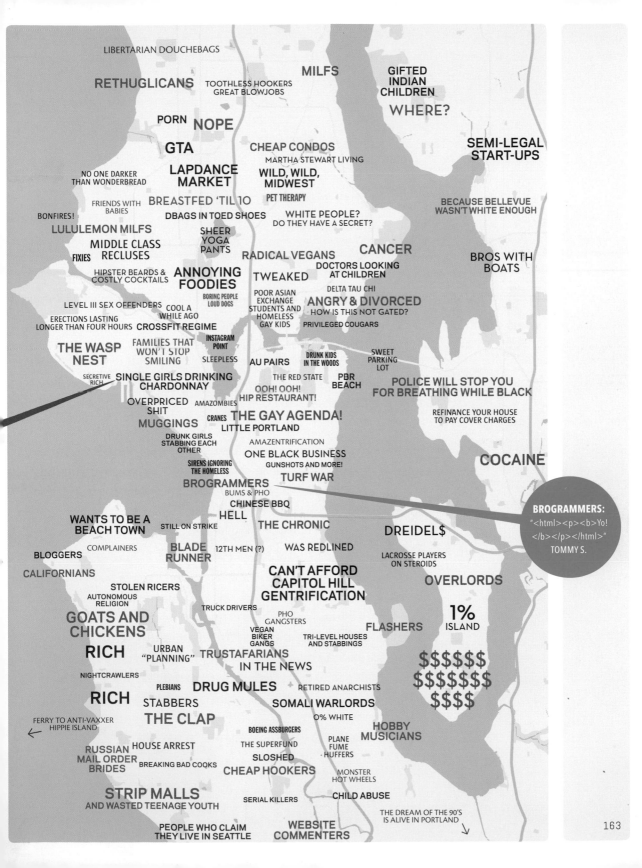

LIBERTARIAN DOUCHEBAGS

MILFS

GIFTED INDIAN CHILDREN

RETHUGLICANS

TOOTHLESS HOOKERS GREAT BLOWJOBS

WHERE?

PORN NOPE

CHEAP CONDOS

SEMI-LEGAL START-UPS

GTA

MARTHA STEWART LIVING

LAPDANCE MARKET

WILD, WILD, MIDWEST

NO ONE DARKER THAN WONDERBREAD

PET THERAPY

BECAUSE BELLEVUE WASN'T WHITE ENOUGH

BREASTFED 'TIL 10

FRIENDS WITH BABIES

BONFIRES!

DBAGS IN TOED SHOES

WHITE PEOPLE? DO THEY HAVE A SECRET?

LULULEMON MILFS

SHEER YOGA PANTS

CANCER

MIDDLE CLASS RECLUSES

RADICAL VEGANS

BROS WITH BOATS

FIXIES

DOCTORS LOOKING AT CHILDREN

HIPSTER BEARDS & COSTLY COCKTAILS

ANNOYING FOODIES

TWEAKED

DELTA TAU CHI

BORING PEOPLE LOUD DOGS

POOR ASIAN EXCHANGE STUDENTS AND HOMELESS GAY KIDS

ANGRY & DIVORCED HOW IS THIS NOT GATED?

LEVEL III SEX OFFENDERS

COOL A WHILE AGO

ERECTIONS LASTING LONGER THAN FOUR HOURS

CROSSFIT REGIME

PRIVILEGED COUGARS

INSTAGRAM POINT

THE WASP NEST

FAMILIES THAT WON'T STOP SMILING

SWEET PARKING LOT

SLEEPLESS

AU PAIRS

DRUNK KIDS IN THE WOODS

SECRETIVE RICH

SINGLE GIRLS DRINKING CHARDONNAY

THE RED STATE

PBR BEACH

POLICE WILL STOP YOU FOR BREATHING WHILE BLACK

OOH! OOH! HIP RESTAURANT!

OVERPRICED SHIT

AMAZOMBIES

REFINANCE YOUR HOUSE TO PAY COVER CHARGES

MUGGINGS

CRANES

THE GAY AGENDA!

LITTLE PORTLAND

DRUNK GIRLS STABBING EACH OTHER

AMAZENTRIFICATION

COCAINE

ONE BLACK BUSINESS

SIRENS IGNORING THE HOMELESS

GUNSHOTS AND MORE!

BROGRAMMERS

TURF WAR

BUMS & PHO

CHINESE BBQ

WANTS TO BE A BEACH TOWN

HELL

DREIDEL$

STILL ON STRIKE

THE CHRONIC

BLOGGERS

COMPLAINERS

BLADE RUNNER

12TH MEN (?)

WAS REDLINED

LACROSSE PLAYERS ON STEROIDS

CALIFORNIANS

CAN'T AFFORD CAPITOL HILL GENTRIFICATION

OVERLORDS

STOLEN RICERS

1% ISLAND

AUTONOMOUS RELIGION

TRUCK DRIVERS

PHO GANGSTERS

GOATS AND CHICKENS

FLASHERS

VEGAN BIKER GANGS

TRI-LEVEL HOUSES AND STABBINGS

RICH

URBAN "PLANNING"

TRUSTAFARIANS

IN THE NEWS

$$$$$

NIGHTCRAWLERS

$$$$$$

PLEBIANS

DRUG MULES

RETIRED ANARCHISTS

$$$$

RICH

STABBERS

SOMALI WARLORDS

THE CLAP

0% WHITE

FERRY TO ANTI-VAXXER HIPPIE ISLAND

BOEING ASSBURGERS

HOBBY MUSICIANS

RUSSIAN MAIL ORDER BRIDES

HOUSE ARREST

THE SUPERFUND

PLANE FUME HUFFERS

SLOSHED

BREAKING BAD COOKS

CHEAP HOOKERS

MONSTER HOT WHEELS

STRIP MALLS AND WASTED TEENAGE YOUTH

SERIAL KILLERS

CHILD ABUSE

THE DREAM OF THE 90'S IS ALIVE IN PORTLAND

PEOPLE WHO CLAIM THEY LIVE IN SEATTLE

WEBSITE COMMENTERS

BROGRAMMERS:
"<html> Yo!
</html>"
TOMMY S.

163

ACKNOWLEDGMENTS

I was informed that the only people who read acknowledgments are the people who are in them. That being said, I would like to thank everyone who picks up a copy of this book, and everyone in the world really. Especially Denver, Colorado, for being the most incredible city in the world—one with such a remarkable comedy scene and sense of humor for this project to spread its wings and fly.

While this book says "by Trent Gillaspie," none of this book would be possible without the fantastic Judgmental Maps online community of snarktographers judging their cities, creating maps, and sharing them with the world. The creators (when they have chosen to identify themselves) are listed below each map in the book. Thank you to everyone who has shared their maps with us, whether it is in this book or on our blog. The blog and community have been powered by Tumblr through it all. Thank you for making it so easy for us to share the maps with the world.

Thank you to my agent, Daniel Greenberg, for being a great advocate for me throughout the entire process and taking most of what I say a little bit too seriously. I also want to thank Tim Wojcik and the fine people at Levine Greenberg Rostan Literary Agency for reppin' me hard.

Thank you to my editor, James Melia, for all your humor, creative guidance, and all-around support through the project. Also, to Colin Dickerman and the team at Flatiron Books for believing that the world would be a better place with a little more judgment and humor and for really embracing the concept of the book. And a special thanks to Brian Sisco for wrapping up the book design with a nice bow and making it look like the prettiest little book of judgment, ever.

Thank you to Erin Pitts and Kristin Waddington of The Label Collective in Austin, Texas, for taking these maps from the web to beautiful print with help from Bob Boucher translating all the snark-tography into actual cartography.

A big shout-out and special thank-you to Ben Whitehair, Cody Johnson, Dustin Farivar, Jason Griffith, and Christian Dommell (per his request, his SSN is 129-30-8699), not only for their incredible friendship, but also for reading through some of the book in advance, bouncing ideas off one another, and making sure I'm not a complete asshole.

Thank you to Anthony Montoya, Joe Larson, Curt Fletcher, Rusty Rutherford, Caitlin Minton, Eric Oren, and Katey Selix for their wonderful contributions to help jump-start the blog with the creation of some the first maps featured on the site.

A big thank-you to Christina Saunders for legally covering my ass.

Thank you to Mark Meredith for having a slow-enough news day to take the blog from the web to primetime news in Denver back when this whole thing began. And thank you to all of the press for making this project a success and being on our ass through this entire journey to help make sure the world knows the good, the bad, and the ugly.

A big thank-you to my dear friend Rhea Lyons for helping someone so naive to the publishing world navigate the process and celebrating the wins with me each step of the way.

Thank you to Jenny Lawson for serving as inspiration for me to acknowledge this book.

And thank you to that guy who randomly gave me a phone call back in 2014 to ignite this entire book process.

I owe an immense debt to my mom, dad, and brother Aaron for helping make me who I am today, and for being a constant source of judgment and humor in all parts of my life. I love you all so much.

Most of all, thank you to my beautiful and incredible wife, Anne, from whom I spent many nights away while I was having an affair with this book over the past year—I cannot hide those paper cuts from you. I cannot begin to express my gratitude to you as my partner on this little journey we call life. Wherever we go, you are my home. And to our beautiful daughter, Emeryn, who I will only allow to read the dedication and acknowledgments in this book. And finally, our dog, Bowser, for providing countless hours of therapy through the writing process, even though I assume he will never be able to read this.